THE MUSCLE TRADE

The Use and Supply of Image and Performance Enhancing Drugs

Nick Gibbs

With a Foreword by
Alexandra Hall

BRISTOL
UNIVERSITY
PRESS

First published in Great Britain in 2024 by

Bristol University Press
University of Bristol
1–9 Old Park Hill
Bristol
BS2 8BB
UK
t: +44 (0)117 374 6645
e: bup-info@bristol.ac.uk

Details of international sales and distribution partners are available at bristoluniversitypress.co.uk

British Library Cataloguing in Publication Data
A catalogue record for this book is available from the British Library

ISBN 978-1-5292-2794-9 hardcover
ISBN 978-1-5292-2803-8 ePub
ISBN 978-1-5292-2804-5 ePdf

Cover design: blu inc
Front cover image: shutterstock/Improvisor
Bristol University Press uses environmentally responsible print partners.
Printed and bound in Great Britain by CPI Group (UK) Ltd, Croydon, CR0 4YY

FSC
www.fsc.org
MIX
Paper | Supporting responsible forestry
FSC® C013604

Contents

List of Figures, Tables, and Boxes

Figures

Tables

Boxes

Dramatis Personae

Aaron (46 years old) IPED harm reduction expert from the north of England. Ex-IPED user and plays a vital role in a number of large-scale research projects.

Adam (32 years old) A regular gym-goer based at Muscle Sanctuary who achieved an impressive transformation with his physique. Adam has never tried any IPEDs but is sympathetic to users and does use a number of supplements. He is good friends and training partners with Will.

Andy (32 years old) A personal trainer (PT) based at Muscle Sanctuary with whom I learned the basic compound lifts in the gym. Andy is also a recent anabolic androgenic steroid (AAS) user, starting his first cycle in the summer of 2019. He is well-researched and wants to reach out to other IPED users advocating harm reduction and disclosure of use.

Ben (33 years old) IFBB (International Fitness and Bodybuilding Federation) professional bodybuilder who trains at Muscle Sanctuary. Perhaps the heaviest IPED user of the sample, Ben sourced pharma-grade IPEDs through a contact within the bodybuilding community. He also has a large Instagram following and has cultivated a profitable sponsorship deal to supplement his income as a security professional.

Carl (46 years old) An AAS user from Wales who has been sponsored by a number of underground labs and is candid about his drug use online. Carl is active on Facebook and Instagram and is knowledgeable about the online IPED market.

David (late thirties) A former amateur bodybuilder and owner of a growing supplement company. David regularly puts on harm reduction seminars and offers a blood testing service from his shop. He is extremely knowledgeable about the supplement industry and IPEDs, and now relies on a testosterone replacement therapy (TRT) dose of testosterone due to his former heavy AAS use.

Dom (early thirties) A competitive amateur bodybuilder, PT and online coach. Dom is based at Predator Gym but also trains at Muscle Sanctuary. He is an experienced and knowledgeable IPED user and helps his clients with their drug use. Dom has connections to a national level supplier, with whom he connected with Jake and Ed. He is also sponsored by David's supplement company.

Ed (early twenties) A competitive amateur bodybuilder who turned from natural junior competitions to enhanced bodybuilding in late 2019. He also runs an online coaching company and works alongside Dom at Predator Gym. Ed is trained by Dom and has his AAS cycle run by Rob.

Harry (early forties) Owner of Muscle Sanctuary. Highly respected in Potsford's hardcore fitness community and extremely connected in the bodybuilding and powerlifting world.

Jake (25 years old) Ex-military, Jake now works doing security for a jeweller. He has only relatively recently started bodybuilding but is tipped by Sam to have a successful career given his impressive genetics. He initially sourced his IPEDs from Dom but now deals directly with a UGL (underground laboratory) owner.

Joe (early twenties) An aspiring online coach and PT who is currently studying sports nutrition at university. Joe started his online fitness account in 2019 and is hoping to grow his own fitness brand. He is knowledgeable about sport supplements and uses a number of products, although he opposes IPED use.

Johnny (31 years old) An aspiring powerlifter who, over the course of the project, went from training in Muscle Sanctuary to another local gym. Johnny dabbled in oral AAS but felt no real benefits and, as a result, does not class himself as ever having used IPEDs. Instead, he uses a few legal ergogenic aids.

Josh (31 years old) An amateur competitive bodybuilder and IPED user who trains at Muscle Sanctuary. He is an informed AAS user and employs all of the recommended post-cycle therapy (PCT) protocols. Josh sources his IPEDs from his friend, who regularly travels abroad to buy AAS over the counter.

Kyle (22 years old) An ex-services amateur bodybuilder and aspiring PT. Kyle runs classes in a local upmarket franchise gym and trains in Muscle Sanctuary. He started using a modest cycle of AAS in late 2019, which he sourced with the help of a friend. He has an awareness of harm reduction and PCT but is not knowledgeable.

Lee (43 years old) A professional bodybuilder and PT who owns a supplement brand and shop in the city. Lee is a former MC in the local rave scene who transformed his lifestyle to compete in the over-forties age class. He is an experienced IPED user who regularly gives advice to his customers. According to others, Lee sells AAS from his shop but he denies this.

Luke (45 years old) A professional natural bodybuilder turned powerlifter who works for the local police. Luke returned to bodybuilding in the early 2000s having been initially put off the sport by the widespread IPED use.

Mani (early thirties) Along with his brother, Abbas, Mani owns a small independent supplement shop in the city. Although he advocates for legal and ethical business practices, their shop openly sells selective androgen receptor modulators (SARMs) and prohormones. Other sources have indicated that Mani also sells AAS from the shop, although he explicitly denies this.

Neil (early fifities) Well-respected sports psychologist who lives near the city and used to train in Potsford's 'proper' hardcore gyms. Neil has worked with many bodybuilders in a professional capacity and has published research on physiological and psychological aspects of hardcore training.

Paul (late thirties) A sports rehabilitation professional based in Muscle Sanctuary. Paul has very conflicting views on IPED use and is extremely concerned with the ethics and malpractices of the fitness industry.

Pete (30 years old) An aspiring strongman based at Muscle Sanctuary. Pete is very anti-IPEDs and denies their existence in the strongman community, although he does use a variety of licit ergogenic aids.

Phillip (67 years old) Affectionately nicknamed 'the Doc' by other gym users at Muscle Sanctuary, Phillip is a former professor and has amassed a great deal of wealth over his career in academia and property investment. Phillip is a keen proponent of TRT and supplements himself with pharmaceutical-grade testosterone.

Rob (48 years old) An IPED harm reduction specialist and former heavy AAS user. Similar to David, Rob now relies on a TRT dose of testosterone following his abuse of anabolic steroids. He now trains police, acts as an expert witness in IPED-related cases, and runs a number of harm reduction services from his home.

Sam (24 years old) Online coach and PT based in the north, but originally from Staffordshire. He holds an MSc in Strength and Conditioning and competes in the Men's Physique category. He is also Jake's coach.

Scott (40 years old) A regular at Muscle Sanctuary who is very popular in the gym. He invited me to train alongside him following our interview and was helpful in introducing me to a number of other participants. While he is not against IPED use, he only uses legal supplements.

Tim (30 years old) A PT at P4 Fitness, a local gym that mainly runs classes and one-on-one sessions. Tim takes a range of health and sports supplements and has impressive knowledge of their effects and potency. He is friends with Andy, having competed in powerlifting competitions alongside him in the past.

Tina (late thirties) Well-respected local nutritionist and commonwealth powerlifter. She does not use IPEDs herself but works closely with Rob to design cycles for her (high-end) clients. Tina trains with Ed at Predator Gym and Muscle Sanctuary.

Will (32 years old) A regular gym-goer based at Muscle Sanctuary who has transformed his body from being overweight to extremely muscular. He holds a professional job with an engineering consultancy company. Will trains with Adam and uses some supplements but no IPEDs.

Notes on the Author

Nick Gibbs is Lecturer in Criminology at Northumbria University. Originally undertaking undergraduate and Master's degrees in Criminology at Birmingham City University, he completed his PhD at Northumbria University in 2021. Nick's research interests include image and performance enhancing drugs, gym and fitness culture, masculinity and the male body, and digital illicit markets.

Acknowledgements

Throughout my academic journey I have been extraordinarily lucky to have been guided and supported by some exceptional people. I would first like to thank my enviable PhD supervision team of Dr Alex Hall, Professor Simon Winlow, and Dr Tom Raymen. Alex, from day one of this project you have offered nothing but wholehearted support and pushed me intellectually to produce a piece of work that I remain extremely proud of. Simon, your encyclopaedic knowledge of literature and theory never fail to astound, and your insights have provided many of the tools that I have leant upon in this book. Tom, your essay-length emails were above and beyond what most second/third supervisors contribute and I feel extremely lucky to have benefitted from your support and patience. Others in the academic community worthy of mention include Craig Kelly and Dr Luke Turnock, who have been a frequent source of humour as well as an outlet for various grumbles and moans along the way!

A special thank you is owed to Harriet for being an absolute rock and putting up with me blathering on about IPEDs, UGLs, and the gym more than anyone ever should, as well as my parents, who have supported me throughout. Finally, a sincere thank you to all those who took part in the research and allowed a skinny PhD researcher into your world. The project would not have got off the ground without your openness and candour and I hope you feel represented in this book.

Foreword

Alexandra Hall
Northumbria University

Back in 2013, while in the latter stages of my PhD research, I landed a job as a researcher on a project that would go on to change my intellectual path. Never having been a student of criminology, I found myself tasked with 'finding out all I could' about the illicit market in pharmaceutical drugs. No mean feat. But it remains my most productive and encouraging period in academia to date. This is in large part due to the freedom and time I was given to immerse myself in the world of users, suppliers and officials attempting to police the trade – in other words, to do the job of a proper criminological ethnographer. I was lucky that my boss at the time was a seasoned ethnographer of illicit markets, and that he trusted me to do a good job.

Criminological ethnography is hard, even for those scholars with a great deal of experience. Some have convincingly argued that a PhD is the last period of sustained time left in today's fast academy conducive to ethnography. Yet nowadays even doctoral researchers are not immune to the growing demands of academia's specific style of managerialism and target culture. It is increasingly difficult to play the long game, something that is an essential prerequisite for any researcher attempting to gain access and build trust with hard-to-reach populations. In a bid to offer someone the space and time to experience what I had five years earlier, I advertised for a PhD student in 2018 with an idea for a project I titled 'Refitting the Self'. The aim was to delve deeper and find out more about one specific aspect of the illicit market in pharmaceuticals dedicated to performance and image enhancement. That PhD student would go on to be Nick Gibbs, the author of the book you are just about to read and whose PhD research its analysis is based upon.

As we begin to get back to life following a global pandemic, one might assume that the market in so-called lifestyle drugs is beginning to wake from a period of deep slumber. In fact, the market has only continued to build steam despite several national lockdowns. Throughout this time, news stories broke of men and women engaging in everything from steroid bulk buying to DIY Botox injections. In some ways this is a natural progression of the processes of privatization we have witnessed in the lifestyle drug trade since the late 20th century. Such processes are likely to become commonplace, as expert users, perhaps better cast as digital prosumers, find themselves stuck between a full immersion in the continual search for bodily ideals, the pressure to self-present online and a cost-of-living crisis brought on by economic stagnation. Could the shadow economy in unlicensed and unregulated enhancement products fill the gaps left for those who cannot afford the luxury of a regulated market?

These classed and gendered realities of a complex market in full swing are just some of the themes running throughout *The Muscle Trade*. Set in the context of a Midlands city where steroid users are active in both the gym scene and on social media, Gibbs finely balances online and offline lifeworlds, not only because this was demanded of him as he negotiated the research in the middle of a pandemic, but also to ensure the accurate documentation of a local market in a period of rapid cultural and technological change. What has been produced is a testament to Gibbs' ability to negotiate what is a perennially tough field, one whose difficulty was only compounded by numerous orders to stay at home preventing the type of prolonged face-to-face fieldwork associated with traditional ethnography. Instead, the flexible and connective approach Gibbs adopts is a key strength of the research. Pandemic or no pandemic, users and suppliers of lifestyle drugs exist in hybrid online-offline worlds. Gibbs unpacks this hybridity with a great deal of nuance and precision. He also presents the reader with a theoretical framework capable of capturing some of the complex realities of life for those who are embedded – or not as the case may be – in the lifestyle drug trade. Moving beyond standard public health descriptions, this theoretical excavation exposes a range of pressing themes for researchers and practitioners alike: the emergence of new forms of labour and cultural capital in England's deindustrialized locales, the lengths people will go to get ripped and stay ripped, and the complex continuum of pleasure and harm associated with the new economy of the self. *The Muscle Trade* is a study that deserves close reading by all those interested in drug markets and the crime–technology interface, or in human culture more generally in the early 2020s.

1

Introduction

Over the last two decades, the UK's health and fitness industry has experienced a meteoric rise and the physical and digital spaces of bodily modification have become prime sites of late-capitalist leisure. In line with this, interest in hardcore training – be it bodybuilding, powerlifting, or even CrossFit – has steadily increased as ever more emphasis is placed on the physical form as a site of identity formation and consumption (Kotzé and Antonopoulos, 2019; Gibbs et al, 2022a). Committed bodyworkers are now able to choose from a wide selection of licit sports supplements, from flavoured whey protein powders to potent fat-burning stimulants and pre-workout products (Mooney et al, 2017), which can even be purchased at their local supermarket.

However, the well-marketed exterior of this lucrative economy belies a darker side, and it is this illicit underbelly that this book seeks to address. This monograph sets out to uncover the use and supply of image and performance-enhancing drugs (IPEDs) – or what I have termed 'the muscle trade' – in a post-industrial Midlands city that I have called 'Potsford',[1] as well as the social media sites Facebook and Instagram. A growing body of literature documents the increase in IPED consumption domestically (McVeigh and Begley, 2017; Mullen et al, 2020) as well as globally (Sagoe et al, 2014; van de Ven et al, 2018), affording the study of these substances a relatively 'newsy' status (Wacquant, 2008) within contemporary drugs research. Although this context has generated a veritable tsunami of scholarship, most research into IPEDs falls within the schools of anti-doping (see Pineau et al, 2016; Backhouse et al, 2018; Andreasson and Johansson, 2019) or public health (see Van Hout and Kean, 2015; McVeigh and Begley, 2017) and the field can broadly be characterized by a paucity of theoretically charged critical criminological engagement (van de Ven et al, 2020). Therefore, although I acknowledge the important contributions of scholars working within both of these disciplines, this book seeks to provide a more nuanced and theoretically informed account of the muscle trade to support and challenge existing scholarship.

Over the next ten chapters, I will interrogate my participants' IPED consumption as well as the broader illicit market for gym-based enhancement drugs by drawing on sophisticated criminological theory, grounding the analysis in various layers of context, from psychoanalytic accounts of human subjectivity, through to the localized post-industrial economy and the global processes of neoliberalism. Further, this work aims to provide an account of the impact of digitization and online prosumption (Toffler, 1980), therefore simultaneously painting a picture of the hardcore gym scene in Potsford as well as the 'glocal' (Hobbs, 1998) digital platforms of social media and the surface web.

Setting the scene

First, it is worth setting out some basic definitions and context. This work is set against the spectacular rise of the health and fitness industry and bodywork as a normalized and widespread pursuit. Despite dating back to the ancient Greeks (Chaline, 2015), it was the late 20th century that precipitated the 'boom' (Millington, 2016) of gymnasia, sports supplementation, and fitness culture that we are witnessing today. The 2022 'State of the Fitness Industry' report recently found that, although the pandemic significantly dented the health and fitness market, it is in 'remarkably good shape' (Marcellin, 2022) with the number of facilities operating in the UK falling by just 2.4 per cent since 2019 (when the previous report was released). This signals that, despite the lasting effects of COVID-19, interest in health and fitness remains high. This uptake in corporeal improvement has occurred in tandem with the commodification of the body at the outset of the neoliberal project (Featherstone, 1982), and arguably began to resemble its current iteration in the 1990s as wellness became a mainstream concern (Andreasson and Johansson, 2019). Unlike early fitness institutions, the vast well-being industry has been rearranged as an individualistic duty to regulate one's health and fine-tune the body as a productive and competitive unit under the guise of 'fun' self-directed leisure (Cederström and Spicer, 2015). This has metastasized with the widespread uptake of social media, particularly the phenomena of 'fitspiration' and the various online communities that cohere around gym work and healthy living (Boepple and Thompson, 2016; Fatt et al, 2019; Gibbs and Piatkowski, 2023).

Unsurprisingly, the increased significance placed upon the body as well as the rapid growth of the health and fitness industry have been accompanied by a rise in the use of IPEDs. IPEDs can be placed within the remit of lifestyle drugs, defined as substances 'consumed through personal choice rather than illness, and often used for non-health matters or matters lying at the margins of health and wellbeing' (Hall, 2019: 1). This expansive remit of one's 'appearance and ability' (McVeigh et al, 2012: 186) includes any substances intended to enhance: the structure and function of muscle, weight loss, cosmetic appearance of skin and hair, sexual behaviour and function, cognitive function, and mood and social behaviours (Evans-Brown et al, 2012). Examples of drugs under this umbrella include substances beyond traditional understandings of IPEDs, including cognitive enhancers and sexual stimulants, which an increasingly medicalized population rely on to become 'better than well' (McVeigh et al, 2012: 186) through a process of 'intoxication by design' (Thurnell-Read and Monaghan, 2023). Evans-Brown et al (2012: 20) therefore define enhancement in this context as 'something that improves an attribute or ability beyond what is necessary to sustain or restore good health'. Conscious of this broad description of biomedical enhancement, this book specifically examines the use and supply of gym-based IPEDs, following Underwood's (2017: 78) definition as 'substances that enhance muscle growth and reduce body fat'. As such, I echo the Human Enhancement Drugs Network's (HEDN) (2020) framework, wherein I have opted to focus on the categories of 'muscle drugs' and 'weight-loss drugs'. HEDN identify the most common muscle drugs as anabolic androgenic steroids (AAS) and human growth hormone (hGH) as well as highlighting the polypharmacy undertaken by most muscle drug users with, among other types of enhancers, weight-loss drugs such as clenbuterol and human chorionic gonadotropin (HCG) consumed alongside the muscle drugs themselves.

AAS, the primary substances under study here, is a class of drugs that include the male hormone testosterone, or a synthetic derivative of it, that are commonly employed to bolster muscular performance and strength, improve athletic ability, and achieve a lean muscular appearance (Christiansen, 2020). Clinically, AAS are used to treat male reproductive dysfunction, some forms of anaemia, and breast cancer (Sagoe et al, 2014), although they are predominantly associated with performance enhancement in public discourse (Morris, 2018). The substances are the most commonly used IPEDs (Begley et al, 2017), with methandrostenolone representing the most prevalent oral steroid and testosterone enanthate being the most widely used injectable. AAS are commonly used as part of a 'cycle', whereby a course is taken in a set period (typically eight to 12 weeks) before the user is 'off-cycle', wherein they assume a period of abstinence and post-cycle therapy (PCT). PCT describes taking drugs and supplements to mitigate or reverse negative side effects of AAS and restore natural hormone levels in the body (Christiansen et al, 2017). Examples of substances employed as part of PCT include Clomiphene citrate (used to re-stimulate the production of testosterone) and Tamoxifen (which inhibits the production of excess oestrogen).

The adverse effects of steroid consumption have been well documented and can be split into serious and superficial harms. First, anabolic steroid use leads to a number of minor aesthetic ailments, including: acne; itchy skin;

hair loss; loss of sex drive; gynecomastia (the development of breast tissue in men); and fluid retention (Hanley Santos and Coomber, 2017). More severely, long-term use can lead to kidney and liver damage as well as heart conditions (Angell et al, 2012; Mullen et al, 2020). Alongside this, public health research has highlighted the dangers of HIV and other blood-borne viruses (ACMD, 2010) as well as psychological side effects such as addiction and anxiety (Evans-Brown et al, 2012).

Although Zahnow et al (2018) acknowledge that drawing a neat typology of any IPED user is virtually impossible, across the literature a consensus can be met that IPED consumption is a predominantly male activity (Svedsäter et al, 2021), as Begley et al (2017) found that 94 per cent of their National IPED Survey participants were men. Because of this, alongside my scholarly interest in masculinity and male gym culture, this book focuses on an exclusively male population. Keane (2005) notes, however, that IPED use has historically been framed as a male phenomenon and therefore the number of female users may be underreported (see also Kotzé et al, 2020). Begley et al (2017) and Pope et al (2014) suggest that the median age of the IPED-using population is 30 years old, although the use of less common substances, such as hGH, appear to be more common in those over 35 (Cohen et al, 2007; Hope et al, 2013; Chandler and McVeigh, 2013). Finally, UK studies have predominantly looked at 'white British' participants (Begley et al, 2017). Whether this is truly representative is uncertain, yet no studies exist that specifically examine race in this context. In light of this, Begley et al (2017: 14) conclude that the average UK user is 'likely to be a white British male, in their 30s; [who uses] a mixture of injectable and oral anabolic steroids and typically inject their IPEDs intramuscularly'. It is this population, broadly speaking, that this work examines.

A note on methodology

The research methodology that underpins this book can best be described as a 'connective' ethnography (Leander and McKim, 2003; Hine, 2007). This methodology accompanies a number of contemporary ethnographic approaches that aim to advance the ethnographic gaze in contemporary society (see for example, Geiger and Ribes, 2011; Postill and Pink, 2012; Horst and Miller, 2012). Put simply, the research that underpins this work was an ethnographic study conducted both online and offline and I therefore simultaneously utilized elements of classical offline observation, alongside the relatively contemporary practice of digital ethnography (Gibbs and Hall, 2021) to track the use and supply of IPEDs both in Potsford and on the surface web. The undergirding logic behind this approach was a disregard for the traditional online/offline dualism within criminological research, wherein the online and offline realms are often treated as two discrete and entirely separate spaces (Burrell, 2009; Wilson et al, 2012). Instead, taking a connective approach allowed me to acknowledge the reality that contemporary subjectivity transcends this false divide, and to observe the flows of information and interaction between the two (Prince, 2019).

The offline element of fieldwork involved an immersive ethnography of two hardcore gyms and several supplement shops in Potsford, coupled with 21 semi-structured interviews with members of the city's hardcore fitness community. Following Wacquant (2015), the offline approach I undertook can best be described as 'enactive ethnography', whereby I engaged in gym work alongside my sample, subjecting my body to the pummelling effects of regular heavy weight training. This aimed to address criminology's historical failure to incorporate the affective, bodily experience into its research practices (Wakeman, 2014) through bringing my body back onto the stage as a carnal and suffering being (Wacquant, 2015). By putting myself through the pain entailed by serious gym work I was better able to understand the sacrifices of an ascetic gym routine, making me more equipped to interrogate the powerful driving forces compelling the men under study to train and use IPEDs. Though I stopped short of using any IPEDs myself, this regimen saw me training four to five times a week over a ten-month period, adopting a strict diet, and using a personal trainer (PT), as well as working out with several participants. The accompanying interviews, which lasted between 30 minutes and two hours, took place in a variety of locations including gyms, local coffee shops, and participants' homes, as well as via telephone and video call.

The online element involved digital ethnography across various online platforms including Instagram, Facebook, and numerous IPED-related websites. I used my genuine name and image on both my Facebook and Instagram profiles, and both also identified my intent and institutional affiliation. The choice to not use a pseudonym profile was two-fold. First, I conducted the bulk of my participant recruitment through purposive sampling on social media and therefore it was important that the profile represented my authentic self. Second, throughout the research process I frequently posted gym progression updates as well as posing technical questions about the research topic to stimulate interaction. However, in order to elicit rich data during interactions with online IPED suppliers, I employed an element of covert ethnography, despite my authentic profile representation. This involved posing as a prospective customer to receive valuable data such as price lists, as well as enquire about the sellers' operations.

Initial digital ethnographic enquiry involved 'lurking' (Hall and Antonopoulos, 2016; Gibbs and Hall, 2021), whereby I passively observed users' posts, stories, and interactions without actively shaping the field. In contrast, the active phase first entailed populating my researcher accounts on both platforms to appear as genuine as possible. This included producing fitness-related content and liking other users' posts, replicating the common practices and norms of the sites under study. Having established genuine-looking accounts on Instagram and Facebook, the latter part of the active phase involved conducting online interviews with customers and sellers. Given the asynchronous nature of online messaging services, these interviews lasted between 30 minutes and three days. However, as the interviews were not subject to the vagueness that can surround post-hoc transcription (Lapadat and Lindsay, 1999), participants' voices were entirely unmediated. Reflecting the multi-sited nature of this project, these interviews frequently switched between Instagram or Facebook Messenger to encrypted mediums such as Wikr and WhatsApp. Data were generated using screenshots of relevant activity. In total, I amassed 160 pages of screenshots over the duration of the project and relied on thematic analysis to assign meaning to these as well as the interview transcripts and offline field notes.

Structure and content

This book is divided into 11 substantive chapters which aim to provide an overview of the UK muscle trade. In Chapter 2, I endeavour to ground what follows in the micro and meso contexts of the various fieldsites within which my research took place. I first offer a description of Potsford, its economic history, and its steady slump into post-industrial obscurity. I pay particular attention to the process of de-industrialization and Potsford's contemporary malaise as a city of 'permanent recession' (Hall et al, 2008), but also one of historic sporting excellence and hardcore gym work. Alongside this, the social media platforms Facebook and Instagram are introduced.

It is at this juncture that the guiding ontological and epistemic commitments that underpin the book are set out (Chapter 3).[2] Following a brief appraisal of the current criminological landscape, Hall and Winlow's school of ultra-realism is introduced, examining the transcendental materialist subject and the role of late-capitalism in contemporary personhood. Smith and Raymen's (2018) school of deviant leisure, which follows ultra-realism's ontological roots, is also laid out and its utility to the area of study is made clear. With these theoretical bases covered, the chapter explores the health and fitness industry as a site of deviant leisure. First, the tide of commercialization that has swept up the fitness arena is unpacked and the manifestation of this broader trend in my offline fieldsites is explored. Following this, the gym as a social space is critically examined in the local context, with reference to the notion of fraternity and post-industrial masculinities. Finally, I question the authenticity of these fraternal bonds in relation to harmful late-capitalist subjectivities and the notion of *amour propre*, before introducing and analysing the idea of gym-based bodily labour in this context.

The monograph then explores the 'demand-side' of the muscle trade, which spans Chapters 4 to 7. Chapter 4 provides a psychoanalytic interrogation of bodily desire and dissatisfaction in order to peer beneath the participants' draw towards IPEDs. I draw heavily on the work of McGowan (2016) to present the body as the ultimate *objet petit a* (Lacan, 1958) and IPEDs' role in prolonging bodily desire beyond one's natural capability.

In Chapter 5, the macro and meso contexts of the men's IPED use are explored in relation to the concept of instrumentality and the implications of bodily enhancement in sporting and occupational motivation. This discussion pays particular attention to Potsford's crumbling local economy and the injunction to employ IPEDs as a means of mitigating the precarity of many of my sample's employment. The question is then posed; is IPED use a manifestation of hyper-conformity to the neoliberal logic of self-branding and the free-market ethos that underpins the late-capitalist economy? In answer, I extend Backhouse et al's (2018) notion of the 'dopogenic environment' to argue that Potsford's economic insecurity has created conditions favourable to IPED consumption.

Chapter 6 addresses the pleasures of illicit ergogenic aid use with a case study of the monograph's oldest participant, Phillip. Following his journey into testosterone supplementation, I attend to Mulrooney et al's (2019) call to interrogate the lifestyle-enhancing effects of IPED use by providing an account of Phillip's self-administration of testosterone replacement therapy (TRT). The final demand-side chapter (Chapter 7) considers the role of social media sites and digital prosumption on IPED consumption. Within this, I explore my participants' 'will-to-representation' (Yar, 2012), or, as I term it, will-to-recognition, and how they perform for the Big Other online.

The book then turns to the supply-side of the muscle trade. Chapter 8 concerns the production of IPEDs. Underground laboratories (UGLs) are identified as the primary domestic manufacturers of the substances under study and the scale and nature of such operations are investigated. Alongside this, the licit pharmaceutical production of the drugs is also acknowledged and the means by which these 'pharma' products enter the UK market is unpacked. In Chapter 9, I turn my attention to Potsford's local 'closed' market (Turnock, 2021a), focusing on the centrality of peer relationships, physical space, and cultural capital for the men under study. Evidencing this, I present a case study of Dom and his relationship with the UGL Astra, to whom he informally refers his PT clients wishing to begin using IPEDs.

Challenging Chapter 9, I then track the tides of commercialization, normalization, and digitization that I encountered in the field (Chapter 10). First noting the impact of UGLs' recent tactic of direct-to-end user sales, the consequences of the increased revenue potential of the market is explored and the subsequent influx of 'market-oriented dealers' (Fincoeur et al,

2015) is critically interrogated. The work's exploration of the supply-side is then concluded with an examination of the IPED market on Facebook and Instagram (Chapter 11). This tracks both the customer and seller demographics as well as the market structure of this burgeoning space of commerce. Finally, the book is brought to a close in Chapter 12, as the main arguments and findings I have advanced are summarized and interpreted. I also provide a roadmap of future research on the topics I have explored and enjoin other researchers to build upon what I present in this work.

2

Situating the Research

In this chapter I will introduce the city of Potsford, within which this research primarily took place, before providing a vivid picture of the various fieldsites I inhabited. By offering a thoroughgoing description of Potsford, I hope to provide the context underpinning my sample's lives, before emphasizing the burgeoning health and fitness industry that has swept the area in recent years. Similarly, by furnishing the reader with a description of the sites under study, I will set up what is to come and allow for a degree of familiarity prior to my interrogation of the use and supply of IPEDs in this context.

'Myopic provincialism': the geography of Potsford

Potsford teeters between the Midlands and the North, flanked by the heavily rebranded cities of Birmingham and Manchester. The area is often misplaced as an outright northern city (see Evans, 2017) due to its heavy industrial heritage and characterization as the 'most working-class city in England' (Jayne, 2004: 199). However, in reality it lies in the upper Midlands. While Potsford is the largest city in the region with a population of just over 260,000, its industrial past is shared collectively with 'five towns', known locally as 'The Kilns'. Owing to this unique layout, Potsford lacks a conventional city centre, instead hosting various localized hubs that service residents of each town in a highly parochial manner. Discussing this, Williams notes that Potsford exhibits a sense of 'myopic provincialism' (Williams, 2006: 183), fed by locals' resounding pride in *their* town.

Potsford has been lambasted as a city devoid of any resounding contemporary identity, described as 'lacking in things for people to talk about' (Hansard, 2007: 562) besides its former industrial glory days, and, as Hart (2005) coyly notes, being the birthplace of celebrity Robbie Williams. Instead, The Kilns' five towns mostly centre around decidedly rundown highstreets (see Figure 2.1), composed mostly of shabby independent retailers, charity shops, and 'booze and fag' stores (Ancrum, 2013: 117).

Figure 2.1: A drizzly Monday afternoon on one of Potsford's somewhat dilapidated high streets (17/01/20)

A raft of scholarship has painted the city's appearance in a decidedly negative light, as is captured in local architect and illustrator Matthew Rice's lament that:

> [Potsford] looks like London in 1950, as if a world war has left huge tracts of it blasted into oblivion and reconstruction is just beginning. The shopping streets make you yearn for the much-hated uniformity of the identikit high streets of the rest of England with those dreary but reliable brands. (Rice, 2010: 12)

Though this synopsis paints a rather dismal picture, Rice acknowledges that it has 'the bones of a great city' (Rice, 2010: 13), given The Kilns' rich heritage and once-magnificent factories, halls, and public houses that have been left to stare forlornly over its numerous failed regeneration projects. This optimism was reflected by some of my interviewees, who variously characterized The Kilns as "as good a place as any other, really" (Luke) and "on the up" (Ed). Such local allegiance was best summed up by Joe, an aspiring fitness influencer, who commented, "I like [Potsford]. It's a working-class city, I'd always come back to Potsford even if I was rich and famous, I'd always want to live here". Joe's optimistic outlook taps into the provincial pride that quietly exudes from residents, who often decried the area's hopelessness, while maintaining a steadfast affection and sense of belonging.

Shaped by clay: a potted history

To suggest that Potsford is *shaped by clay* would not be an understatement. J.G. Jenkins, chronicling the city's industrial history, concludes that '[t]he story of [Potsford] is basically that of a community of potters, whose skill and business acumen have in the course of two centuries made [Potsford] the twelfth largest city in the United Kingdom and extended its reputation in the field of ceramics far beyond the shores of Britain' (Jenkins, 1963: 80). The city's football club's nickname, as well as a multitude of the conurbation's street names, pubs, and buildings, nods to Potsford's rich industrial heritage as Britain's main producer of ceramicware (Evans, 2017). However, Potsford is historically rooted in not just ceramics, but also the production of iron, steel, and coal, and the city therefore harbours a deep-rooted pride in the skilled manual labour through which it earned its moniker (Mahoney, 2015). However, Greenslade (1993: 164) notes that The Kilns is 'unique, in this country at least, in being named after its staple product', a statement that goes some way to describing the sacrosanct nature of clay to the city. Accordingly, the cityscape still bears the scars of its industrial past, even as various attempts at regeneration have sought to manoeuvre it in line with the more stylish English cities. As Figures 2.2 and 2.3 illustrate, when walking around The Kilns one is often faced with the towering bottle kilns which once fired tonnes of pottery, as well as the many ribbon-like stretches of canal, which were used to transport Potsford's exports to the docks of Liverpool.

Potsford's formalized pottery industry can be traced back to the early 18th century, when the area's natural abundance of red clay and coal was capitalized upon as part of the Industrial Revolution (Hunt, 2013; Brownsword and Mydland, 2017). A boom in Potsford's ceramics production accompanied the creation of a major canal route, which was again bolstered by the city's inclusion in the national railway system in 1848. The Kilns subsequently became Britain's principal producer of quality ceramicware, reaching an apex in the early 20th century (Squires, 2020).

By 1938, half of Potsford's working population was employed in pottery production (Buxton, 2017) and the city was home to around 2,000 bottle kilns. During this period, the ceramicware industry can be understood as an archetypal example of Fordist production, as products were standardized to produce economies of scale and labour was similarly regimented (Imrie, 1989). These conditions saw workers become highly specialized in roles such as 'bottom knocking', 'clay blunging' and 'clay wedging', labouring to produce a wide variety of ceramic products that were then shipped around the world.

Figure 2.2: One of the many graffiti-ridden stretches of canal which trickles through the city (02/05/19)

However, though the booming period of local ceramics production is often cited as The Kilns' heyday, with near full employment and high levels of productivity, I am conscious not to present Potsford's industrial heritage through 'rose-tinted spectacles' (Winlow, 2001: 60). The city harboured dangerous levels of air pollution at the height of its ceramic production (Walker Hanlon, 2015) that, despite targeted legislation in the 1950s, remains an issue to this day (Brimblecombe, 2006; Ault, 2020). Early production of ceramics in the area also exposed workers to dangerous levels of lead and, during the ascendant era of manufacture, the life expectancy of male potters was just 46 years (Posner, 1973).

Yet focusing on the ills of this era discounts the sense of stability, comprehensibility, and fixity of this period, and it is this that has shaped the area's collective memory of its industrial past (see Kotzé, 2019; Telford, 2021). This is consistent with Bauman's (2015: 188) characterization of industrial modernity as an era of 'universality, homogeneity, monotony, and clarity', where labour was clearly divided and physical institutions such as factories, shipyards, and indeed potbanks afforded workers with a stable collective identity (Winlow, 2001; Raymen, 2018; Telford, 2022). Under these 'solid' Fordist conditions, Potsford's ceramic industry, as well as its lesser documented collieries and steel mills, provided a working-class habitus (Gibbs et al, 2022a) for residents, who could feel secure in a comprehensible

Figure 2.3: Two bottle kilns, protected under Historic England's listed building legislation, at the centre of a new-build housing estate (02/05/19)

existence, often following the life trajectories of their older relations (Willis, 1977; Raymen, 2018). The notion of *structure* was central, as employees were able to accurately envisage their future, due to it being framed within the inflexible, rigid structures of clearly demarcated work and leisure.

This sense of stability and communality can be further explained with reference to Žižek (2000) and the idea of the coherent *Big Other.* According to Winlow (2019), the Big Other describes the unknown figure for whom we perform by partaking in the collectivizing structures, institutions, and laws that create meaning and order in our lives. This figure is sustained by one's belief in its existence (Kotzé, 2019, 2020) and thus the Big Other can be understood as a 'psychosocial construct without a material reality' (Winlow and Hall, 2012: 409). Therefore, provided that there is a consensus as to its validity, the Big Other acts as a means of structuring our behaviour and creating a sense of purpose, fixity, and stability, as we seek verification from it to validate our actions (Kotzé, 2019). Žižek highlights that, within industrial modernity, faith in the 'collective fib' (Kotzé, 2020: 58) of the Big Other was almost ubiquitous, as the institutions of work, community, and religion provided subjects with clear reference points through which to construct their lives. For example, the rigid structure and routine of labour, within which employees collectively toiled towards a common purpose, afforded Potsford's workers a framework through which to make sense of their lives. This is reflected in Mervyn Jones' ethnographic exploration of Potsford's pottery industry in the mid-20th century, where he discovered a 'unity and consistency of life' (Jones, 1961: 9) for workers, who often laboured at the same factory from the day they left formal education up until their retirement. Further, much of the housing in the city was built around its various potbanks and factories (Mahoney, 2015) and workers consequently tended to know their neighbours. These community bonds, forged through the collective graft and craftsmanship in the workplace (Gibbs et al, 2022a), were further strengthened by participation in the factories' brass bands, sports teams, and workers' unions (Burchill and Ross, 1977; Holman, 2020) and the industry therefore played a pivotal role in galvanizing local people and providing an essentially homogeneous lived experience.

For men labouring in Potsford's potbanks, collieries, and steel mills, orthodox understandings of masculinity could be imbued in the hard graft and bodily toil they endured (see Skeggs, 1997; McDowell, 2003; Roberts, 2018), which afforded them breadwinner status as well as a sense of collective purpose (Telford, 2021). The notion of masculinity, and particularly *working-class* masculinity, has long centred around technical mastery and pride in bodily labour (Morgan, 1992; Bourke, 1994). Therefore, the heavy toil that fuelled Potsford's productive heyday created a localized industrial form of masculinity and skilled physical culture, where men could be secure in their role and place in the strict hierarchical order (see Beck, 1992; Ancrum, 2013).

De-industrialization and the breakdown of the Big Other

However, this sense of security was shattered when the region's principal means of employment fell victim to the economic restructuring and de-industrialization ushered in by the Thatcher administration in the late 1980s (Imrie, 1989). Though it is beyond this book's remit to provide a thoroughgoing account of these seismic macroeconomic shifts, it is worth sketching out an overview of the rapid ascendance of neoliberalism and the subsequent breakdown of the Big Other in the UK. Harvey (2007: 2) understands neoliberalism as a 'theory of political economic practices that proposes that human well-being can best be advanced by liberating individual entrepreneurial freedoms and skills within an institutional framework characterized by strong private property rights, free markets, and free trade'. Put more simply, taking their lead from classical liberal economists such as Friedrich Hayek, advocates of the neoliberal agenda oppose most forms of state interventionism (besides any measures that support the flow of capital or facilitate market growth) and instead contend that the individual ought to be 'set free', resulting in economic deregulation and privatization (Plehwe, 2015). More than this, however, neoliberalism represents a realignment of life itself around the imperative of capital extraction. Crucially, the globalized nature of contemporary life is intimately tied up with the ascendance of neoliberal dogma (Slobodian, 2018) and the technological and logistical advances within post-modernity have meant that this ideology has been seared into the psyche of citizens across the world. The Thatcherite and Reaganite era of economic deregulation, which is widely credited as being the onset of the current regime of neoliberal late-capitalism (Tribe, 2015), therefore, saw the post-war Keynesian economics supplanted by a dogged commitment to the free market and the liberation of capital (Winlow and Hall, 2013; Mitchell and Fazi, 2017). Crucially, it also signalled a cessation of the Global North's economic reliance upon *production*, in line with an emergent focus upon *consumption* as the primary means of capital growth (McGowan, 2003). As a result, like myriad cities of industrial production (see Beynon et al, 1994; Lloyd, 2013; Kotzé, 2019; Telford, 2021, 2022) Potsford's ceramics industry was systematically dismantled.

Reflecting this macroeconomic shift, over 50,000 people in the region were employed in the production of pottery in 1979, compared to just 10,000 in 2008 (Tomlinson, 2015). Within this cull, 10,059 potters were made redundant between 1978 and 1981, with 765 of these resulting from the closure of a single plant (Imrie, 1989). The primary factor in this decline was the overseas outsourcing of the ceramics industry, as The Kilns' mantle as a global producer of ceramicware was rendered obsolete by the relocation of several major local employers to production sites in Malaysia and Taiwan (West, 2016; Bartolini et al, 2019). Alongside its inability to compete in the globalized export market, Potsford's producers also suffered from a slump in domestic spending and low-cost foreign importation, as British buyers increasingly sought products that undercut the local industry (Beynon et al, 1994). The final nail in the industry's proverbial coffin was the advancement in production technology, which saw many of the traditional crafts that gave the region its name rendered superfluous (Sekers, 1981). Compounding this,

Potsford's myopic pride in its three principal industries meant that 'nobody worrie[d] about diversifying [The Kilns]' (Jones, 1961: 98) and therefore very few alternative means of employment existed in the city.

What remains of Potsford's ceramic production can mostly be described as artisanal, as once mighty brands now aim to satisfy those customers in search of quaint authenticity and nostalgia. This is a far cry from the industry's heyday of mass global exportation and has left The Kilns with a lingering feel of absence and mourning (Mah, 2013). This is evident in Potsford's architecture and physical spaces, as the city is littered with commanding industrial structures that have been allowed to crumble (see Mahoney, 2015; Gillette, 2017) or, in what is perhaps the perfect metaphor for the city's post-industrial malaise, have been repurposed as large-scale cannabis farms by local drug sellers (see Cullinane, 2018; Jackson, 2020). Just a short walk from Muscle Sanctuary, the primary gym under study in this project, lies the remains of one of the city's many potbanks (see Figure 2.4), which now festers behind a large fence.

However, it is not the material impact of this period of de-industrialization that constitutes the most corrosive legacy of economic restructuring in Potsford. Instead, the collective psyche has been left as derelict as even the most decrepit potbanks and bottle kilns and it is the loss of structure and surety that has taken the heaviest toll on The Kilns' residents. This sense of ontological uprootedness is captured by Bauman and his notion of 'liquid modernity'. Bauman (2012) contends that, as the era of neoliberalism collided with the former certainties of the past, the structures that once contoured our lives have been *liquefied*, leaving the late-capitalist subject without the stability and sense of community that characterized the past. He suggests that the liquefaction process has created an altered subjectivity, steeped in reflexivity and cynicism, which is now fundamentally complicit with the innate instability of liquid modernity. This is articulated by Žižek (2009), as he describes how subjects no longer accept the meta-narratives and collectivized truth claims of the past, viewing them as 'dead weights placed on our individuality' (Winlow and Hall, 2012: 401). Žižek (2000) frames this analysis within the *breakdown of the Big Other*, arguing that the institutions and shared cultural bastions that once provided anchorage to the subject have been fatally exposed as collective fibs (Winlow and Hall, 2012; Kotzé, 2019, 2020). This led him to proclaim that the Big Other has always been dead, we just failed to recognize it. Thus, it is our collective belief in concepts like community, faith, and collective identity that sustained their existence and, following neoliberalism's fiscal and psychic restructuring of society, the Big Other has been exposed to the subject as the 'psychosocial construct' (Winlow and Hall, 2012: 409) that it is.

Žižek concludes that the contemporary subject experiences a profound sense of ontological loss and absence following the dissolution of the Big

Figure 2.4: The remains of a long-derelict potbank near Muscle Sanctuary (02/05/19)

Other, as they have become increasingly atomized without the guiding structures and coherence of modernity. Therefore, although it would appear that Potsford's principal body blow was financial, in actuality the meaninglessness, lack of surety, and deep-reaching malaise is the truly corrosive legacy of the neoliberal restructuring of the UK's economy. The demise of the pottery industry and the city's former importance in the era of 'organized' capitalism (Lash and Urry, 1987) has therefore created a psychic scar that will remain long after the final potbank site is regenerated.

"It's nowhere near what it was": the contemporary context

Rob Imrie, writing in 1989, concluded that 'the fortunes of [Potsford] are more or less dependent upon the revival of pottery production' (Imrie, 1989: 23). Regrettably, this prediction appears to have been proven true, although not in the manner Imrie had hoped. Potsford's economy is now typical of many post-industrial cities in the UK, with a proliferation of precarious low-income jobs, particularly in warehouses and logistics centres (Southwood, 2011; Lloyd, 2013; Telford and Lloyd, 2020). Indeed, David Johnson, a local author, sardonically suggests that '[i]n a few years I imagine we'll be known as the Call Centres, rather than [The Kilns]' (Johnson, 2008: 80). This dour assessment was shared by local PT Tim, who remarked:

> 'I think The Kilns things have gone. … I think it'll always be remembered for the pottery industry but now warehousing is everywhere. So many warehouses. You go [around the city] and it's warehouses, Screwfix, Amazon. … We've got Michelin up here, two Dunelm warehouses, the Sainsbury's warehouse, then you've got Well Pharmacy.'

This was echoed by casual weight trainer Scott, as he explained:

> 'There's no industry, it's just warehousing. … There's not much here anymore it's just retail and distribution. I think all Potsford's interest is dwindling away. … I grew up around here and all the old factories were open then and it was busy. It was a productive place and it was bringing people in.'

These accounts are supported by official figures, as the city's working population is made up of just 35 per cent of professionals in the upper quartile of roles,[1] compared to the Great Britain average of 49 per cent (Nomis, 2022). Relatedly, job roles in the lower quartile are overrepresented by almost a half compared to the rest of Great Britain. A similarly gloomy picture can be painted when examining rates of educational attainment, with just 29 per cent of residents achieving an NVQ4 and above, 14.5 per cent lower than the Great Britain average (Nomis, 2022). Further, Potsford was the 'debt capital of England and Wales' in 2017 (Partington, 2018), as well as having the lowest workforce productivity in the country (Corrigan, 2018). Therefore, owing to the internationally acclaimed quality of ceramic products once produced by the city's now derelict potbanks, Potsford holds a heritage not simply of industrial employment, but of highly skilled and creative jobs that Potsford's current economy has failed to replicate. Tim's account also epitomizes the drab nostalgia that many interviewees felt towards the city, as he compared his experience of working as a warehouse picker with his mother's career in the pottery industry:

> 'There's nothing, there's no skill. Anyone can warehouse pick, I did it for years, there's no skill anymore. Whereas [in Potsford's former industries] there was so many different roles, and you were paid piece work, you used to get piece work rates there. I know my mum would be on, for eight hours a day she'd be on XY rate and then for every piece she'd do she'd get a bonus. Whereas now you're lucky to even get a Christmas bonus.'

Tim decries the lack of 'skill' in Potsford's post-industrial economy compared to the accomplished craft that was central to the city's past. Therefore, in contradistinction to the pottery industry's skilled and stable employment, Potsford's current matrix of menial warehouses and retail jobs has left local men unable to imbue the same orthodox constructions of masculinity in their labour (McDowell, 2003; Roberts, 2018). The lack of hands-on 'trades' (Telford and Lloyd, 2020; Telford, 2021), which previously offered The Kilns' men a source of working-class pride and masculine respectability (Morgan, 1992; Bourke, 1994), has therefore 'displaced' labour as a form of gender-affirmation for local men (Nayak, 2006; Winlow and Hall, 2006). Potsford's men, who were traditionally tasked with the more physical and rugged aspects of pottery production (Mahoney, 2015), are therefore now trapped in a double bind, as they lack both the ontological security afforded by a coherent Big Other, as well as a stable sense of masculinity given the depleted opportunities for successful 'breadwinners' in The Kilns' job market.

Like many of my participants, Tim appeared to 'imbue the past … with particular symbolic value' (Lyon and Colquhoun, 1999: 191) as his words exposed a nostalgia for 'Fordist forms of feelings of stability and belonging' (Muehlebach and Shoshan, 2012: 318) rather than merely the favourable pay conditions. Read within the context of the breakdown of industrial modernity, this sense of nostalgia and wistfulness is almost entirely abstract in nature. Therefore, the underlying sense of collective loss can be said to be the most galvanizing social force at play in the city.

The Kilns retains an 'obsessive internal focus' (Jayne, 2004: 200) and, unlike several regenerated post-industrial cities, such as Liverpool and Glasgow, which have made the commercially successful transition to being hubs of culture and consumable 'buzz' (Hollands and Chatterton, 2002), Potsford lacks allure for outside visitors. Although efforts abound to promote creativity and entrepreneurial flair, Potsford remains fundamentally trapped in a political economy that has reduced it to near obsolescence (Edensor, 2000). West (2016: 161) characterizes Potsford as 'symbolic of a wider malaise across post-industrial communities', as it has fundamentally failed to adapt to the macroeconomic shifts and subsequent reorganization of cities as places of consumption, and instead represents a site of 'permanent recession' (Hall et al, 2008). Scott directly addressed this failure, stating:

> 'I don't know what Potsford can do now to sort of bring itself back. Like Liverpool's got the docks, it's got them areas with the posh bars. It's got the money. Nobody's round Potsford, what do you go [to] Potsford for? Sit by a canal? You know, you go [to] London you've got Canary Wharf and all the posh shops, Manchester is much the same. … Potsford just hasn't got that wow factor.'

This lack of 'wow factor' can be interpreted as Scott's disillusion with Potsford's inability to transition into being a 'creative city' (Mould, 2015), as The Kilns' many canals and former manufacturing spaces have not been transformed into locations for cultural consumption and instead remain in a state of post-industrial paralysis. Supplement shop owner Mani discussed this in relation to the local night-time economy, as he concluded that "it's nowhere near what it was". This exposes Potsford's superfluity in the late-capitalist consumer economy, as residents are not drawn to the city for the hedonistic excesses available in other larger conurbations. Instead, Mani dolefully acknowledged that 'his town' is once again a place to be remembered for its former glories rather than its present sorry state. Importantly however, I do not wish to glorify the late-capitalist post-industrial cities of buzz here, as their inherent harms have been well documented throughout the literature (see Winlow and Hall, 2006; Smith, 2014; Raymen, 2018; Ayres, 2019). Instead, Potsford's dearth of spaces of consumption merely reflects the city's failure to adjust to an economy aimed at 'sensation gatherers' (Bauman, 1997) and the 'stupid pleasures' of consumption (Žižek, 2008).

Out with the clay, in with the iron: Potsford's fitness scene

Given The Kilns' heavy industrial past, the region retains a strong physical culture that has produced a wealth of sporting figures, from world-renowned footballers, boxers, and strongmen to professional rugby players and wrestlers. Prior to the technological advances that further decimated Potsford's principal industry, many roles within ceramic production relied upon heavy physical toil and pragmatic strength. As a result, a localized industrial corporeal habitus (Mauss, 1973; Bourdieu, 1985) exists, which has long valorized working-class physicality and hard graft as a source of pride (Gibbs et al, 2022a). Potsford's long-standing physical culture, carried down the generations through the localized collective social body (Elias, 1991; Beissel et al, 2014), has laid the foundations for high levels of engagement with weight training and strength sports in the city. Consequently, according to Mani, The Kilns plays host to 47 active gyms within its 36 square mile radius,[2] and one can hardly walk around the most built-up conurbations without encountering one such establishment. This was supported by Tim, who told me over a coffee in a local supermarket café, "Especially round here [the fitness industry] has blown up. There seems to be gyms popping up left, right, and centre". Similarly, PT and online coach Dom, discussing the competition between local gym owners, stated, "I mean, within a two to three-mile radius there's four gyms around here, which are all pretty similar. But there's more than enough customers". This latter admission speaks to the substantial demand for fitness in the city. Residents are able to choose between a full complement of low-budget commercial gyms, at least four hardcore bodybuilding gyms, as well as circuit training and cross-fit spaces. Evidently, although the city's economy has suffered the descent into post-industrial wilderness, the health and fitness industry has blossomed, with myriad ex-factories and industrial sites being repurposed as spaces of bodily toil.

Therefore, it would not be unsubstantiated to suggest that it is iron, rather than pottery, that provides Potsford's men and women with the most tangible means of graft in the city's current dreary economy (see Gibbs et al, 2022a). This reality echoes numerous examples of recent scholarship into post-industrial locales (see Antonopoulos and Hall, 2016; Kotzé and Antonopoulos, 2019; Salinas et al, 2019), which have all experienced a surge in weight training and IPED consumption following the macroeconomic restructuring discussed earlier in this chapter. This correlation will be unpacked later in this book, but suffice to say that The Kilns' heritage of heavy labour, coupled with its relatively high proportion of fitness spaces, makes the city a poignant case study within which to trace the links between de-industrialization, the commodified fitness industry, and contemporary subjectivity.

Offline fieldsites

Having set out the drab backdrop to this research, it is now worth focusing on the specific sites under investigation. The next four sections will therefore shed light upon the various offline and online spaces that I inhabited alongside my participants, tracing their movements, interactions, and self-presentation.

Muscle Sanctuary

Given this project's interest in IPED use and supply, my search for an appropriate fieldsite centred on the hardcore spaces of fitness in Potsford. Demonstrative of my outsider researcher status, my initial search for an appropriate fitness space was conducted entirely through Google, where a string of keywords led me to the homepage of Muscle Sanctuary – the principal site of my offline ethnography – where I spent around ten months training upwards of five days a week.

Muscle Sanctuary is housed within a former retail unit on a non-descript sideroad not far from the city's 'cultural' quarter. The specific site was historically a heavy industrial space given its proximity to the canal – the artery for several large potbanks as they shipped their produce towards the docks of Liverpool. However, air pollution reached dangerous levels in the area in the 1970s, resulting in its near total abandonment before a half-hearted attempt at regeneration in the early 2000s. Now, Muscle Sanctuary occupies a large unit on an aging industrial park. Flanked by two of the only ceramics manufacturers left clinging onto life in Potsford, the gym would appear relatively unassuming on the trading park were it not for its imposing tarpaulin sign, which spans its grubby brick exterior. Looking out menacingly onto the newly developed houses across the road, its imposing letters are flanked by the gym's logo – a chain-adorned set of muscular arms proudly showcasing the mantra 'Strength and Honour'. This slogan, which appears to have been reappropriated from Ridley Scott's epic *Gladiator*, speaks to Muscle Sanctuary's marketing as a place of authenticity and technical repute, where strength training is the moral duty of its members and form and precision are paramount.

During my time at Muscle Sanctuary, it featured six rooms, each devoted to the cultivation of a different muscle group. Entering the bustling gym through its notoriously stiff front door, a modest set of stairs leads to the front desk, its shelves piled high with branded merchandise and sports supplements. Immediately a tsunami of noise rebounds from each white painted wall, hurtling towards you – 'I'M A MOTHERFUCKING BEAST'[3] – each ear-shattering syllable compounded by the shouts of heavy lifting and the unmistakable thud of weighty dumbbells hitting the springy black matt floor. This flooring emits a rubbery smell that consumes the entire gym and, mixed with the sweat, chalk, and potent stimulants used by most customers, gives the place an almost indescribable odour. Rounding the corner, past the socializing area, the infamous legs room becomes visible. This space features a wealth of specialist contraptions with detachable plates that aim to batter members' legs into submission. Supervised by an arresting image of bodybuilder Tom Platz' engorged quadriceps, this room plays host to a large proportion of the bellowing cries of exertion in the gym, as men succumb to the ravages of weighty iron and muscular exhaustion. A short passage then leads to Muscle Sanctuary's changing rooms. With its oak-coloured lockers and threadbare greying carpet, this space would be reminiscent of a school or leisure centre locker room, were it not for the well-built men posing and posturing in the full body mirror by the shower cubicles. Given its position tucked away from the gym's matted floors, the smell of rubber subsides somewhat in here, replaced by a concoction of stale sweat, heavy-duty cleaning chemicals, and musky deodorant. When changing before a session, this room is chillingly cold, as if Harry, the owner, has deliberately kept the tiny windows ajar to beckon in the icy air. However, this is immediately justified as bodybuilder after bodybuilder limps into the room, having laboured their exhausted bodies to the point where a halo of steam emanates from their heads as they bask in the red-hot pump brought on by their session.

Back out into the legs room and through a stooped door, a low-ceilinged room emerges that is dedicated entirely to fashioning a bulging set of arms. Widely considered the most rewarding and pump-inducing workout area, this modest room is often packed with groups of sweat-covered lads intent on blowing their arms up before a Saturday night out. Slightly further in, the strongman area is visible with its atlas stones, yokes, and logs. Here, the unmistakeable roar of the gym's resident strongmen can be felt, even from the boxing and PT area immediately above. Travelling back out through the arm worshippers' area, the main room meets the eye in all its metallic glory, with heavy-duty machines towards the back, squat racks neatly lined up against one wall, and benches positioned overlooking the large mirrors on the other. This substantially sized room which, during busy times, becomes a writhing mass of vest-wearing, grunting toilers, is the heartbeat of the gym. The racing rock and dance music that beats out in the smaller spaces is amplified five-fold in here, providing a fitting soundtrack to the remarkable feats of strength happening all around. Its movements feel systematic, with users darting purposely between machines like cogs in the highly efficient corporeal exothermic system. They stop only to spot[4] for friends or to banter with the main faces in the gym. A reinforced shelf holds most of the dumbbells, however the heavier of these (which range from 50 kg through to 100 kg) are stored on the matted floor. The air is thick with groans, snorts, and audible exertion, only broken up by the occasional groups of men bantering between sets. Well-polished mirrors stare back at straining triceps, shuddering pectorals, and weary traps, as members gaze upon their efforts, mesmerized by the ceiling-high reflections that make the gym appear almost interminable.

On a typical visit I would run into a dozen or so regulars. Perhaps the most frequent face I encountered was PT Andy, with whom I learned the basic compound lifts and was taught the foundations of form and technique. Casual trainers Adam, Joe, Pete, and Will would come in like clockwork after work, shortly followed by Scott, who routinely made the rounds joking gregariously with the burly old-school trainers in the main room. Weekday mornings saw the bodybuilders pile in, taking advantage of the casual trainers' constrictive work schedules to fiercely labour without an audience of onlookers. These stern-faced trainers included Ben, a respected IFBB

Pro and Jake, a 25-year-old aspiring bodybuilder and jewellery shop security guard. The project's only female participant also falls within this category. Tina, a well-respected nutritionist and commonwealth powerlifter, split her time between Muscle Sanctuary and Predator, taking immense joy in outcompeting her male equivalents. Another regular face was Paul, a well-qualified rehabilitation coach who prowled the gym's labyrinthine interior with a look of perpetual judgement, evaluating the shoddy technique of many of the gym's egotistic lifters.

Alongside these faces, a steady flow of more casual trainers passed through the gym, flocking in after work on a Monday or Tuesday on the promise of a week of self-improvement, only to remain absent until the following week's renewed resolve. Similarly, weekends could be described as riotous compared with the ascetic hard work of the serious mid-week trainers, as members enjoyed a catch up with their friends and exercised their jaws as much as their biceps.

Ultimately, Muscle Sanctuary was described by my participants as a hardcore, specialist gym, as the wealth and quality of the highly specified training equipment attracted many men away from the identikit commercial gyms in the city. A ubiquitous rejection of 'generic' chains was noticeable in my interviews, and the attraction of Muscle Sanctuary's status as an independent fitness space was often cited as a factor in customers' decision to sign up. The gym also regularly hosts seminars with high-end bodybuilders and strength athletes, giving the place a status as a *destination*. Tina acknowledged that "people travel from miles around to go to Muscle Sanctuary", as a simple search of the gym on YouTube illustrates. These "day passers" (Adam), who typically visit on a weekend, spending five pounds for one session, are a crucial asset to Harry's business and serve to give the gym the feel of a tourist hub at times.

Predator Gym

Having trained at Muscle Sanctuary for around seven months, I made the decision to widen my offline fieldsite to include Predator Gym early in 2020. I first came across this premises, which is situated just off the main road of one of the city's smaller towns, when arranging to meet bodybuilder and PT Dom. Having contacted him on Instagram, he agreed to speak to me while he covered Predator's front desk on a drizzly January afternoon. Once parked in the nearby retail park, I trudged down the litter-strewn high street past a forlorn Sure Start centre and a carpet shop. Scanning the street, I could make out the glossy frontage of Predator nestled just past the peeling white paint of a pub. Predator is a relatively new player in Potsford's fitness market, having opened its doors in 2019. I crossed the road, catching a glimpse of my tracksuit bottoms and sports jacket in the gym's sparkling windows. Pleased at the ease with which the main door swung open (having been fruitlessly barging through Muscle Sanctuary's doors for around seven months by then), I strolled in to be greeted by Dom, who ushered me to sit down on one of the plush chairs next to the front desk.

Commercial R&B is pumped around the spacious, mirror-lined interior of Predator, accompanied by the whir of treadmills and cross-trainers. Barking shouts are interspersed with female voices as groups of women squat, lift, and jog among the male members. Unlike Muscle Sanctuary's intricate layout, Predator is one open-plan space stretching in a U-shape around the front desk. To the left, a substantial cardio zone overlooks the grubby street outside. Behind this, the subtly patterned carpet gives way to an immaculate matted free weights area, which attracts eager groups of Gymshark-wearing young men, determined to outlift one another, capturing each dramatized lift with their state-of-the-art iPhones. Though the 100-kg dumbbells sitting proudly in Muscle Sanctuary are unavailable in Predator, the weight selection is sufficient for the gym to attract several bodybuilders and powerlifters, alongside a wider array of casual fitness consumers. Circling back around the front desk, the metallic squat racks come into view alongside a crimson hanging punching bag and strip of vibrant AstroTurf, where Dom can frequently be found bellowing at wide-eyed personal trainees as they perform weighted lunges and crab walks. Just off this, a cool faux-granite passage leads off to the minimalist changing rooms, where users often take advantage of the "anabolic lighting" (Ed) for their selfies, engulfed by a potent mixture of Lynx deodorant and mid-range aftershave.

As this description illustrates, although Predator also markets itself as a hardcore, bodybuilder-friendly gym, it lacks the grit and ferocity of Muscle Sanctuary. With its upbeat chart music, sparkling machines and smooth lighting, Predator is far more akin to a health club or leisure centre. With that said, the gym's independent status again attracted those who held commercial gyms in contempt. Predator was home to both Dom and Jack. Dom, with whom I chatted at the gym's front desk, is a six-foot-three ultra-heavyweight bodybuilder who is well known in Potsford's fitness scene. Coach to several other interviewees, his encyclopaedic knowledge of IPED compounds was vital in bolstering my cultural capital and awareness of the various nomenclature I needed to truly press participants on their substance use. Similarly, Dom's understudy, Ed, a former natural bodybuilder who started his first cycle of IPEDs around a week before I met him, worked and trained at Predator. Dom and Ed introduced me to Lee, the owner of an independent supplement shop and personal training gym on the same street. Lee, a former rave MC turned entrepreneur, provided insight not only into the IPED industry but also its licit counterpart.

Online fieldsites

As already stated, the principal platforms upon which this work's online data collection took place were the social networking sites (SNS) Instagram and Facebook. Both owned by digital tycoon Mark Zuckerburg, these are among the most used social networking platforms globally (Alhabash and Ma, 2017) with one billion and 2.7 billion monthly users, respectively (Clement, 2020a, 2020b). Importantly, far from being liminal or transitory spaces that I simply travelled through, both platforms can be firmly conceptualized as fieldsites in their own right (see Dalsgaard, 2016). Therefore, Instagram's infinitely scrollable interface, though accessed through my mobile phone, was just as tangible as Muscle Sanctuary's cacophonous main room, and Facebook's private groups and messaging service facilitated conversations that were just as real as my interviews with Dom and Ed in Predator.

Instagram

Instagram is designed exclusively for sharing images and videos (Tiggemann and Zaccardo, 2015), which are often accompanied by captions featuring hashtags that aim to increase a post's visibility and interactivity (Giannoulakis and Tsapatsoulis, 2016; Marshall et al, 2020). Therefore, an 'image first, text second' rule is imposed (Lee et al, 2015), whereby prosumers can utilize a three-in-one package of taking, editing, and posting their content within the confines of the platform. As part of the editing process, Instagram offers a variety of 'filters' which allow users to alter the colours and resolutions of images before posting, resulting in a high percentage of posts being doctored to present their creators in an aesthetically favourable light (Ridgway and Clayton, 2016; Sheldon and Bryant, 2016). Lee et al (2015: 552) note that this creates a 'strong visually-oriented culture', where text is ultimately subordinate to the aesthetic quality of the poster's visual content. Users 'follow' other accounts, whose content is then shown in their 'stream' in chronological order (Hu et al, 2014). They can then 'like' and 'comment' below photos to signal their affirmation, and track 'likes' on their own posts via notifications (Santarossa et al, 2016). In 2016, Instagram introduced 'stories', which allow users to share '24-hour ephemeral photo and video slideshows' (Constine, 2016). These act to document users' daily activities that do not warrant a post in and of themselves. Users have been able to send one another direct messages on the platform since 2013, meaning that Instagram also acts as a more conventional online space to privately chat. This effectively gives the SNS a front and backstage (Goffman, 1959), where users can post their preened images as a 'presentational front', while conversing with contacts away from public view.

Posts can be geotagged to certain locations using the 'Photo map' feature and therefore content can be assigned to specific geographies as a means of increasing visibility and signalling membership to various groups or cultures. Pertinently, this afforded me a means of observing the physical world through the digital traces shared by users. Thus, Instagram can be understood as akin to a looking glass, peering into the physical spaces under study and embellishing them with a curated gloss. Towards the end of my online data collection, I captured a typical Instagram 'session', featuring several of the most prolific posters I encountered:

> Logging into my Instagram account, I am greeted with a polished image of Ed as he poses in Predator's sparkling changing rooms, with a caption that reads '*Be yourself, fuck anyone that won't let you*' (Figure 2.5). Somewhat at odds with his genial personality, Ed stares determinedly from my screen as his text espouses the symbolically violent vocabulary of bodybuilding that most of my participants share on a daily basis. Below, around 50 commenters – ranging from experienced IFBB Pros to young gym members that are in awe of Ed's majestic physique – appraise his '*unreal*', '*massive*', and '*fucking huge*' body composition as Ed tags '*#instafit #motivation #fit #dedication #shredded*'. The homosocial support offered by Ed's followers is typical within Instagram's bodybuilding community, as the scantily clad men flatter one another's pecs, quads, and abs in a fraternal expression of affection that I can't help feeling would be admonished without the thin veil of gym work that acts to legitimize it. Each comment is accompanied by a variety of gym-based and aspirational emojis, as Ed's well-wishers exude a warmth that would validate even the most insecure bodybuilder.
>
> I then scroll down to see an image of two purposely positioned vials of 'Ultima-Tren' (a brand name for the anabolic steroid trenbolone acetate), accompanied by a caption declaring a '*DECEMBER SALE! DM FOR INFO*'. As with many of the sellers I follow, the post shows little external engagement, with a meagre five likes from unashamed IPED users. Tapping the seller, @anabolics2u's, icon however, I am transported to his profile which belies his true reach. @anabolics2u has an impressive 2,161 followers, many of whom are presumably unwilling to engage with the account on the 'frontstage' (Goffman, 1959) public post. Back on my homepage, I tap through my contacts' stories. First up, Muscle Sanctuary PT Andy's gruff Northern Irish accent discusses the intricacies of macronutrient intake. Up next, IFBB Pro Ben slides into view, his veins popping out of his mountainous biceps as he hauls two enormous dumbbells above him into the air in the unmistakable Muscle Sanctuary free weights area. Ben has embedded a heavy rock

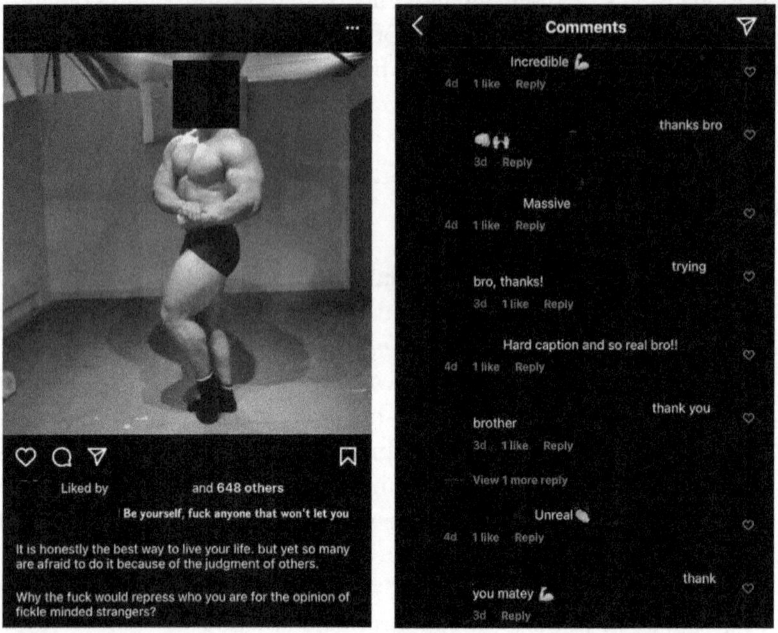

Figure 2.5: Ed's post documenting his latest corporeal progression, much to the delight of his fellow community members (02/09/20)

> song to his story, which blasts the lyrics 'Hail to the King' as his straining arms labour closer to the camera. After Ben's snippet has elapsed, IPED seller @suppspharm's content appears. This story showcases a client's 'transformation', facilitated by his product, overlaid with the text '*100% gains, message me or add on WhatsApp*'. This fleeting content is then replaced by aspiring bodybuilder Jake, who shares a meme championing the effectiveness of AAS as a sexual stimulant. Growing tired of the ceaseless flow of stories, I absent-mindedly continue scrolling down my homepage, where physique after physique slide by, only broken up by some sporadic adverts for gym wear and sports supplements or vials of IPEDs for sale. I glance up, 20 minutes have passed while I have been engrossed on Instagram. 'I was just doing research', I reassure myself, before returning to my laptop. (Fieldnote, 02/09/20)

This extract describes the typical landscape that awaited me when I tapped the enticing Instagram icon on my phone screen. As well as allowing me a glimpse into Muscle Sanctuary, Predator, and Potsford's other sites of hardcore fitness from the comfort of my sofa, the digital geography of the platform transported me to a globalized network of IPED suppliers and users as I glided seamlessly through the sleek infrastructure of the app.

Facebook

Compared with Instagram, Facebook is a more general, multi-purpose platform with a dual emphasis upon image and text content creation. In line with its self-confessed aim to create and bolster meaningful online communities (Facebook, 2020), Facebook allows users to add friends, create multi-user chats, partake in open and closed groups, and share pages with other users (Fox and Moreland, 2015). The SNS provides users with a profile, through which they can create and share content with others on the homepage. Facebook has a slightly older user base than Instagram, with proportionally more male users and those over 65 (Clement, 2020c). The following fieldnote recalls a typical visit, jotted down early in the first COVID-19 national lockdown:

> Facebook's distinctive blue colour scheme bursts into life as soon as I input my login details. Batting off the array of notifications that ambush me as I click on my homepage, I notice one of the groups I have been granted access to, 'Steroid Chat', has several new posts. Clicking on the group, which is closed to users who have not been 'approved' by its admin, I can see that a user by the name of Travis Allen has shared a question, '*Just starting out what do you suggest for test c how much per week?*'. Travis' post, which refers to the common AAS testosterone cypionate, is duly answered by nineteen group members, who suggest a range of potential beginner cycles as well as advice about appropriate post-cycle therapy options. From what I can make out, most users appear to be from the United States, alongside a smattering of British users and some Eastern European contributors. Joining this conversation thread, admin Rowdy Rob shares his email address and a link to his website which, according to him, '*has test cyp for a good price*'. The others, seemingly cognizant that Rob holds the power to expel them from the group, do not question his claim and Travis is encouraged to click on the link. This is just one of many similar groups I have been accepted into, and Rob's blatant agenda is typical across most. Directly below, another American user – Bobby – has shared his bloodwork, which shows an alarmingly elevated white blood cell count. Attaching a breakdown of his substantial IPED consumption, Bobby asks the group for possible causes for his malady. His post is met with numerous derisive comments that are quite unlike the usual good-natured, helpful exchanges on the page, as it is quickly established that Bobby must simply have an injection site infection.
>
> Manoeuvring back to my homepage, I see Luke, a natural powerlifter and local police officer based in Muscle Sanctuary, sharing an impressive

> lift in his home gym. A stream of uplifting comments append Luke's video and I drop him a like for good measure. Directly under Luke's status is a promotional post by underground laboratory EU Pharma, which highlights the supposed positive impact their products have on users' immune systems amid the current health pandemic. On any given day, my homepage is littered with similar adverts shepherding users to webpages or enjoining them to contact the seller for a discounted price. Finally, adding to the din, several posters have shared videos of them and their gym partners working out in the various open access bodybuilding groups that I am part of. These range from lads of around seventeen, who look dwarfed by their baggy designer vests and chunky trainers, through to professional bodybuilders and strongmen from across the globe, who are keen to build their following. Satisfied that I have viewed the day's new content, I log out, leaving Rowdy Rob to continue pushing his products, Bobby to lament his post, and Luke to feel gratified that his lift has been sufficiently well-received. (Fieldnote, 22/04/20)

As demonstrated, Facebook, much like Instagram, is an immersive digital world that brings Potsford's gyms and their users into contact with a global network. Its structures – most notably the closed groups I was allowed into – were crucial in shaping users' behaviours and providing a front and backstage view that reflects the offline environment. Similarly, users like Luke, who I knew both in person and online, illustrate the need to incorporate an online element, as they flitted between the physical spaces of the gym and the online platforms, providing a bridge between the two.

Chapter summary

This chapter has served to contextualize this project within the post-industrial city of Potsford, as well as introducing the various micro fieldsites that I operated within during the research. Potsford can be seen as emblematic of myriad post-industrial towns and cities across the UK, governed by a forlorn wistfulness and a nagging discontent with the endless low-paid precarious labour and pervasive sense of loss. The decline of The Kilns' principal industry has decimated the region's sense of surety and ontological stability and, as a result, Potsford can be characterized as a place of profound nostalgia. However, despite its contemporary malaise, data from interviewees and ethnographic observations point to a myopic pride in the city, whose formerly collectivized working-class communities still harbour a warmth when identifying themselves as locals. It is atop this post-industrial context that the city's burgeoning health and fitness economy should be viewed, as I have laid the foundations in this chapter for a full understanding of localized hardcore gym use and IPED use and supply in The Kilns. The latter part of the chapter has endeavoured to introduce the reader to the specific sites under study, from the hardcore physical spaces of Muscle Sanctuary and Predator, to the preened digital platforms of Instagram and Facebook. With this groundwork complete, analysis of these spaces and their inhabitants can commence.

3

Reimagining the Health and Fitness Industry as a Site of Deviant Leisure

Introduction

Having established the context underlying the work, it is now time to introduce the ontological and epistemic commitments underpinning this monograph. The following chapter will first introduce the schools of ultra-realism and deviant leisure before embarking on a critical exploration of the health and fitness industry. Drawing on these frameworks, the tide of commercialization that has swept up the world of fitness will be unpacked and the manifestation of this broader trend in my offline fieldsites will be explored. The gym as a social arena will then be examined in the local context before the authenticity of these fraternal bonds will be questioned. Finally, the idea of gym-based bodily labour will be introduced and analysed.

Deaptation, theoretical stagnation, and the need for revitalization

Before shedding light on the ontological underpinnings of this monograph, it is important to present the abject philosophical landscape which precipitated the conception of ultra-realism, the theoretical lens through which this book is framed. Critiquing the discipline of criminology, Hall and Winlow (2015) propose that the subject's theoretical canon is not simply deficient at the level of analysis, but instead the discipline is fundamentally premised upon several problematic conceptions of human nature, which fail to capture the essence of the subject in contemporary society (Kotzé, 2019; Hall, 2020). This is important to note, given this book's aim of exploring the use and supply of IPEDs in a fundamentally innovative manner.

Hall and Winlow evoke Johnston's (2008) concept of deaptation to describe how the same paradigms are continuously lent upon by criminological scholars, despite the dramatically altered socio-political backdrop of contemporary crime and harm. Many of the theoretical bastions of criminology were conceived in the 1960s or earlier, and therefore continuing to rely upon such explanations in the contemporary world has created something of a slow puncture, whereby a constant repurposing of the 'tried and tested' theories is deflating the discipline's analytical potential.

Hall and Winlow (2015) contend that current criminological theory can be characterized as a dualism of classical liberalism (currently manifested as right realism) versus left liberalism. The former of these paints the subject as always capable of deviance and in need of control (see for example, Clarke and Cornish, 1985; Hirschi, 1998), while the latter understands them as oppressed but innately good, valorizing the concept of resistance and transgressive agency (see Ferrell, 1999). This duality is situated within the hegemonic liberal paradigm, whereby agency and rational choice are positioned as sacrosanct, and any acknowledgement of the unconscious, underlying drives shaping human behaviour are dismissed out of hand (Hall and Winlow, 2015; Kotzé, 2019; Raymen, 2022). Instead, current criminological theory privileges 'controlology' (Ditton, 1979) over any meaningful interrogation of the aetiology of crime, and therefore Hall and Winlow (2015) call for a 'return to motivation' within the discipline (Hall et al, 2008), a mantle that this book dutifully aims to take up.

Transcendental materialism and ultra-realist criminology

Set against this landscape, ultra-realism has emerged as a means of overcoming the current stagnation of criminological theory (Kotzé and Lloyd, 2022). Though the perspective has roots in the schools of Left Realism, victimology, and feminist criminology, Roy Bhaskar's (1997) critical realist framework is widely credited as the principal criminological influence on the approach (see Kotzé, 2019). Importantly, in line with its 'realist' roots, ultra-realism accepts that the harms resulting from criminal and deviant practices are extremely real for victims. Therefore, going beyond the tired debates around the socially constructed nature of the law, the approach dovetails with the growing zemiological turn within criminology (Kotzé, 2018; Canning and Tombs, 2021), aiming to cut to the heart of harmful subjectivities. To this end, the essence of ultra-realism is captured in its central question: '*why do some individuals and groups risk harm to others in pursuit of their own instrumental and expressive interests?*' (Kotzé and Lloyd, 2022: 7, italics in original). In pursuit of this, the perspective advocates for the use of in-depth qualitative research that goes beneath the easily manipulated crime statistics, and instead interrogates the lived reality of crime and harm (Treadwell et al, 2013; Hall and Winlow, 2018). Unlike the swell of ascendant criminological theory, ultra-realism acknowledges that human beings are not merely reducible to a biological or neurological essence, and nor should we be viewed as 'free-floating' social subjects divorced from natural drives or impulses. Rather, we are 'hardwired for plasticity' (Winlow, 2019: 59) and therefore our subjectivity inevitably reflects the socio-economic environment in which we live. This crucial insight stems from the perspective's engagement with transcendental materialism, a Žižekian repurposing of Lacanian psychoanalysis reappropriated by Adrian Johnston (2008), which allows for a more nuanced account of contemporary subjectivity and our relationship with the political economy.

Transcendental materialism, which interrogates the subject in the 'intransitive realm' (Hall and Winlow, 2015: 110), aims to explore subjectivity in a far more basal manner than the aforementioned liberal-pluralist perspectives. At the heart of this ontological position lies Lacan's triad of the Real, the Imaginary, and the Symbolic, psychic realms, or orders, which interconnect to make up human subjectivity (Lacan, 1974). Crucially, for Žižek (2000), at the core of human subjectivity lies a pre-symbolic void, a nothingness that must be 'filled up' through the solicitation of coherence and meaning (Ellis et al, 2018). This lack is conceptualized as the Real, a traumatizing state of primal needs and disorienting drives that resist comprehension (Eagleton, 2008; Hall et al, 2008; Winlow and Hall, 2012). Due to the phantasmagoric terror of this realm, the subject seeks a coherent symbolic order, a realm of anchoring symbols, customs, and laws through which to make sense of the world. As such, subjectivity can be viewed as a process of active solicitation (Hall, 2012b), whereby the underlying void at the heart of the subject generates the perpetual desire for order and a sense of fixity. However, it must pass through the Imaginary realm to reach this satiation. The Imaginary realm sees the ego rupture and misidentify with spectral objects in the external world in the mirror phase (Raymen, 2018; Ayres, 2022), yet it cannot obtain a coherent and stable self through these objects. It is at this stage that Žižek's (1997) reappropriation of the transcendental materialist framework offers its unique insight into the neoliberal consumer capitalist epoch and its effects on human subjectivity.

In the current political economy, characterized by a breakdown of the Big Other and a transition into post-Fordist consumption, the trappings of the Imaginary are thrust upon the subject through consumerism's barrage of unattainable lifestyles and the cultivation of desire for consumer goods (McGowan, 2016). Enabled by the system's sophisticated advertising industry, ephemeral goods and images manipulate the underlying lack at the heart of the subject with a promise of fulfilment that can never be fulfilled, thus leaving them to perpetually solicit the Imaginary order of consumer capitalism and the never-ending supply of 'trendy' products (Hall, 2012b). Put more simply, desperate to attach themself to some structure of meaning, and unable to see beyond the ubiquity of neoliberalism (Fisher, 2009), the subject reaches for the Imaginary order of consumer capitalism and commodity fetishization. However, the transient, fleeting nature of material consumption is ultimately unable to satiate their thirst for coherence and anchorage, given the fundamentally dissatisfying nature of consumer capitalism (Ayres, 2022). This inevitably leaves them with a cloying 'objectless anxiety' and sense of misdirection (Hall, 2012a), as no real point of fixity can be reached. Though never quite making the leap into psychoanalysis, Zygmunt Bauman captures this reality through his metaphor of the consumer race, wherein 'the finishing line [or the satisfaction of consumer desire] always moves faster than the fastest runners' (Bauman, 2012: 72), and therefore it is staying in the race of perpetual dissatisfaction that constitutes the true motivation for the subject. Understood this way, commodity consumption is premised more upon the symbolic process or 'promise' of acquisition (McGowan, 2016: 11), rather than the product itself, which is divested of its value once purchased. Therefore, our constant desire sustains neoliberalism's insatiable thirst for perpetual growth, while offering us an unstable meaning system upon which to hinge our identity. Though this macroeconomic theorization of the subject's relationship to the political economy may seem far removed from the world of the muscle trade, this conceptualization of subjective lack and desire will be leant upon heavily when unpacking my participants' motivation to consume their IPEDs.

Deviant leisure

Though fundamentally underpinned by ultra-realism, this work can most accurately be situated within the school of deviant leisure. Sharing ultra-realism's ontological roots, deviant leisure follows the growing zemiological turn in the discipline of criminology (Pemberton, 2015) by setting out to uncover the inherent harms within normalized commodified leisure practices in the late-capitalist epoch. The approach, therefore, constitutes the cornerstone to this book's engagement with the commercialized health and fitness industry.

Deviant leisure is premised upon a fundamental reimagining of the concept of leisure away from its traditional conception as simply time spent away from work (Kelly, 1990; Roberts, 1978) or as a politically emancipatory space, within which the subject can forgo the repression and tedium of an overbearing political economy (Lyng, 1990; Riley et al, 2013). Instead, the perspective illuminates contemporary leisure's role in both generating and perpetuating the demise of what Bauman (2009) describes as the 'duty to the other', as it functions to promote the sacrosanct nature of individual freedom in the wake of any coherent symbols through which the subject can understand their lives (Hall et al, 2008). As a result, Raymen (2018) notes that our identities are increasingly constructed through our leisure pursuits in post-Fordist, 'liquefied' society (Bauman, 2012) and therefore leisure has been constructed as an inalienable right in the Global North (Raymen and Smith, 2019a). As a result, deviant leisure scholars argue that the inherent harms within normalized leisure practices have been overlooked and criminology, and the social sciences more generally, have tended to neglect this arena, with the exception of a handful of studies into 'extreme' forms of edgework that romanticize deviance as a means of political resistance and radical identity construction (see Ferrell, 1996; Vaaranen, 2004).

However, following Smith and Raymen's (2018) seminal article, criminological understandings of the function of leisure have advanced, and a growing body of literature has been drawn together under the auspices of deviant leisure to interrogate the relationship between consumer capitalism, normalized leisure practices, and harmful subjectivities.

Central to understanding the role of leisure in late-capitalism is Žižek's (2008) identification of the cultural 'injunction to enjoy', which describes a reorientation of the superego whereby the subject is compelled to seek maximal enjoyment, even at the cost of the collective good. This concept is situated in a shift from a society oriented around prohibition, to one centred on unrestrained individual enjoyment and consumption (Bauman, 1997; McGowan, 2003). Winlow (2019) contends that this command is duly stimulated by the leisure economy in the form of commodified, pseudo-transgressive activities characterized by hedonism and excess. Importantly however, Žižek stresses the inherent irony of the injunction to enjoy, which 'sabotages enjoyment, so that, paradoxically, the more one obeys the superego command, the more one feels guilty' (Žižek, 2008: 30). Therefore, this reimagination of enjoyment, driven by a profound fear of missing out (Raymen, 2018), fails to deliver true satisfaction and instead can lead to a state of jouissance – a Lacanian term describing the excessive, painful pleasure derived from an overexposure to the barrage of 'enjoyment' (Žižek, 2006) generated by the economy of commodified leisure (Ayres, 2022). Acknowledging this, deviant leisure drives at the heart of the late-capitalist subject, for whom identity is premised upon an ever-mutating set of consumer products and trends, having been untethered from a stable Big Other following the West's immersion into wholesale neoliberalism and the attendant culture of the individual (Lasch, 1979). As a result, far from utilizing leisure as a space for transgression and resistance, the subject actively solicits its consumerist trappings (Hall, 2012b), be it through hedonistic alcohol consumption, displays of conspicuous spending, or blind adherence to 'expressive' fashion or bodily trends. In light of this, deviance in this context is understood as 'steadfastly conformist' (Raymen and Smith, 2019a: 19) as the subject's energies are channelled into the desire and acquisition of commodities that are essential to perpetual capital growth, rather than offering any true form of resistance to the system.

This can be contextualized within the historical process of pseudo-pacification (Hall, 2012a) wherein arbitrary interpersonal violence has steadily declined from the late 14th century to be replaced by a symbolic violence that is harnessed by the economy to promote intersubjective competition and inflate capital growth (Hall and Winlow, 2015; Hall, 2020). This symbolic violence is manifested as 'special liberty' (Hall, 2012a), wherein subjects transcend ethical and moral codes in adherence with the underlying value of competitive individualism as the subject's energy is repackaged into the constant desire for consumer goods and experiences (McGowan, 2016). Read in light of this, previously overlooked harms within normalized leisure practices such as gambling (Raymen and Smith, 2017), the night-time economy (Smith, 2014), and tourism (Large, 2019) can be understood in relation to contemporary subjectivity and the all-encompassing grip of consumer capitalism. This framework therefore allows a thorough analysis of hardcore gym use and IPED consumption and supply in relation to the incumbent political economy.

Consuming health and fitness

In line with the wider economic shift in the Global North from production to consumption (Amin, 1994), my sample can best be described as health and fitness *consumers* (Nettleton, 2013). However, echoing Andreasson and Johansson (2019), the older interviewees made it clear that the commercialization of the fitness arenas under study is a relatively recent occurrence that has, in the space of a generation, swept the community. This perspective was sentimentally shared by 45-year-old professional natural bodybuilder and police officer Luke, as he sat across from me shouting over the pulsating rock music at Muscle Sanctuary, remonstrating animatedly as he described his first experiences of "learning the trade":

> 'When I first started training in the nineties, people didn't have coaches and there were very few personal trainers about. If you wanted to get into bodybuilding, you just spoke to a bloke in your gym who'd already done it and they would take you under their wing and help you out. That's just what I was used to, and so this idea of paying somebody a load of money to do a diet for you or put you on a training programme – I've never paid anyone for a diet in my life, I learned from other people, and I've retained it and used it.'

This old-school mentality was shared by IFBB Pro Ben who, although over a decade younger than Luke, fondly recalled his formative experiences of the gym as recently as the early 2000s, where he was unofficially mentored by a local gym owner:

> 'The way that I describe it is that when I started there was no fitness industry, it wasn't an industry it was just what people did, it was a hobby. There never used to be any PTs, I had no idea what a PT was and there were certainly no online coaches. I had some good guidance starting off though. The guy [the owner of a gym in nearby Cheshire] he worked with me every day, gave me my diet, looked at me, gave me my adjustments – I had really good advice right from the word go. He did it because he loved it, he wasn't like those guys who do online coaching now and PTs, where it's important to them only as long as they're getting paid for it. This guy was training me for free and I wasn't even paying a gym membership. There's just not people like that now.'

These accounts reflect a lament for the more genuine, authentic fitness spaces that, according to Luke and Ben, existed free from the myriad professionals that I encountered during my time training. Situating this within the macroeconomic shifts that have swept Potsford, whereby service sector and customer-facing roles have metastasized in the wake of traditional skilled industry, the professionalization and monetization of fitness need hardly come as a surprise. Locals working within post-industrial economies like Potsford's now increasingly rely upon precarious, leisure sector employment given the dearth of meaningful and stable occupations in the city (West, 2016). As a result, given the health and fitness industry's ascendence within the leisure economy, many of my sample opted to work as PTs, online coaches, and gym staff rather than labour in the city's various warehouses and distribution centres. Thus, to older gym users like Luke and Ben, a degree of authenticity and community has been lost due to many relationships in the health and fitness industry being wholly premised upon financial exchange, rather than true mutual support and kinship. This is demonstrative of the wider marketization of health and wellness (Smith Maguire, 2008), wherein the contemporary injunction to look after the physical self has been manipulated to generate highly profitable enterprises, which rely upon numerous fitness professionals in order to function. Following legislative changes under the New Labour government, the number of PTs and fitness instructors grew exponentially in the early 2000s (Lloyd, 2007), resulting in a wealth of consumer opportunities within the gym environment. Paul, a sports rehabilitation practitioner, spoke scornfully about this development, diagnosing the marketization of fitness as a result of what he termed "the *Heat* generation", but which can better be described as the infiltration of consumer capitalism into the leisure arena:

> 'I think it links to the whole *Heat* generation thing. *Heat* magazine, the only magazine to be about celebrity for celebrity's sake. Now all of a sudden nobody drives a Ford anymore, they drive some German car on PCP, nobody does their own eyebrows anymore, girls go and pay someone else to do them. All this stuff's new. PT is part of that, the teeth whitening, all that.'

Read within the context of consumer capitalism's injunction for the subject to define themselves through a perpetual stream of transient consumer goods and experiences, Paul's positioning of the personal training market within a move towards beauty treatments and credit-financed luxury cars is salient. In light of this, the gyms under study can best be described as *commodified leisure destinations* which, unlike Luke and Ben's formative experiences, fundamentally exist as sites of consumption and capital generation.

Commodified authenticity and gym gentrification

It is at this juncture that both Muscle Sanctuary and Predator's status as hardcore, authentic gyms ought to be re-examined. As was laid out in Chapter 2, both fitness premises market themselves as places of serious leisure (Stebbins, 2007), in contrast to the low-end budget gym chains that constitute a large part of the UK's fitness landscape. However, there exists a fundamental tension between my sample's experiences of the gyms as sites of commodified consumption and the gyms' self-identification as spaces of gritty authenticity. To unpack this incongruence, it is vital to understand both gyms' place in the health and fitness industry and the undergirding processes of commercialization at play.

While Predator was described by my sample as a "modernized gym" (Dom), newly refurbished and immaculately laid out, my initial impression of Muscle Sanctuary rather echoed Brighton et al's (2020) description of a 'spit and sawdust' venue given its highly masculine aesthetic and initially intimidating atmosphere. However, over my months of attendance, parallels between Muscle Sanctuary and Predator began to emerge, and the former's initially foreboding atmosphere faded somewhat. This is evident in a brief fieldnote I wrote in August 2019, having been training regularly at the gym since early June:

> Muscle Sanctuary is starting to feel more like home now that I'm going most days. My first impression of the place may have been wrong and, since becoming a card-carrying member, I'm starting to appreciate how well-kept and professional the set-up is. Harry's staff are constantly cleaning and updating the equipment and, if I am ever struggling to structure my sessions, they are happy to give me some

> pointers. Having gone in focussing on the 'meatheads', I seem to have overlooked the ordinariness of many of the customers like Adam and Will. Maybe Muscle Sanctuary is not as hardcore as it first seemed. … (Fieldnote, 22/08/20)

Here, I reflected upon Muscle Sanctuary's fundamental adherence to the health and fitness industry's marketization of exercise and the focus on *customer experience*. This sentiment was echoed by Andy, the PT with whom I learned the basics of gym work, during our initial 'client consultation', where he breezily informed me that "there's plenty of people in here who aren't strongmen, aren't bodybuilders, aren't powerlifters … it's a gym for everyone really". This was reinforced by Ben, who acknowledged that "it's not quite as hardcore as it used to be in here". Ben's confession hints at what Brighton et al (2020: 71) term the 'gentrification' of hardcore gyms, whereby former 'spit and sawdust' spaces have been repackaged as consumer-friendly venues in line with the industry's increased commercialization. Crucially however, Brighton et al note that, despite their new-found customer focus, these gentrified gyms attempt to retain a veneer of their authenticity for users to consume. Their description perfectly describes Muscle Sanctuary as, beneath its lurid music and gruff aesthetic, the gym provides a high standard of hygiene, as well as hosting a lucrative sales area where members can buy sports supplements and branded clothing. Pertinently, users like Pete, an aspiring strongman, are attracted to the gym's faux spit and sawdust image due to Muscle Sanctuary having "a bit more Potsford to it" than the generic chains and leisure centres. Muscle Sanctuary's 'commodified authenticity' (Outka, 2009: 13), therefore, created a *hyper-real* environment within which members could consume fitness, feeling assured in the knowledge that they were not part of the generic mainstream. This was put into perspective by local sports psychologist Neil, as he regaled me with his experiences of training in Warrior, one of Potsford's former spit and sawdust venues, as we sat in his generous garden drinking Earl Grey tea early in my data collection:

> 'I mean when Warrior was at its peak you ought to have seen it, the facilities were good, nice heavy weights and some real heavy-duty machines, but the toilet was really grotty. At one point it didn't even have any running water, which I'm sure was completely illegal [laughs] apparently someone had left the tap on all night, and [the manager] had a strop and said, "That's it", and shut the water off. People wouldn't put up with that to the same extent now. I think [real spit and sawdust gyms are] on the decline, a lot of people are gonna say why should I go somewhere with a manky toilet, no running water, nothing nice, when I can pay a little more and I can go to this nice plush health club?'

Neil's recollection, which dated back to the 1980s, sheds light upon Muscle Sanctuary's comparative adherence to the values of the late-capitalist health and fitness industry as, according to him, consumers "wouldn't put up with" the truly hardcore facilities of his youth. Again, this speaks to the gym's role as a site of commodified consumption, where the 'authentic' aesthetic is enjoyed within the consumer-friendly parameters of comfort and hygiene. Therefore, far from rejecting the sweeping commercialization of the health and fitness industry, both Muscle Sanctuary and Predator fundamentally adhere to this ascendant culture of commodification.

"My main social life is in here": the gym as a social arena

In line with their status as sites of commodified consumption, both gyms represented spaces within which to socialize and conspicuously consume for my sample (Veblen, 2005). As a result, the vast majority of my participants acknowledged that the gym was their primary means of building friendships and participating in the leisure economy. Sam, a well-respected bodybuilding coach and amateur Men's Physique competitor, noted that he has met around "90 per cent of [his] friends" through the gym. This was summed up by Scott:

N: So how much of a role does the gym play in your life? Is it your social time as well or is it like work?

S: Massive. It has become that, it's become my social time. I've gained a lot of friends in the gym now over a couple of years, talked to a lot of people, there's always someone you know and say hiya to. … [On] weekends I'll go in and spend a couple of hours in there. I'll have a coffee, a bit of something to eat and there'll be someone there to chat to.

Scott describes the gym in line with Sassatelli's (2010) notion of the 'health club', whereby one's overall well-being and a sense of enjoyment are valued alongside physical fitness. Scott's assessment hints at Muscle Sanctuary's gentrified nature, as his acknowledgement that the gym is a social destination nods to the burgeoning role of the health and fitness industry as a mainstream form of leisure and identity formation, not simply just a place to exercise. Similarly, Pete conceded that, "My main social life is coming here. … I don't drink anymore, I don't smoke, so yeah this is going to the pub on a Friday night for me". This admission is particularly striking, as Pete places Muscle Sanctuary as tantamount to a night-time economy venue, as it facilitates his social life and constitutes his primary arena of consumption. Adam supported this sentiment, likening the gym to a "social event" where, "it's like going out on the town [and] having a few beers". Further, during my time in the field I was constantly surrounded by men sporting high-end gym clothing, as well as the gyms' own clothing lines. For these customers, the gym was a space to forge an identity of cool individualism by exhibiting one's fluency in mass consumer trends (Raymen, 2018) just like a trendy bar or club. Crucially however, their consumption of such fashion items sits comfortably alongside their health-focused lifestyle, allowing the gym to become a site of consumption divorced from what they see as the ills of hedonistic drinking culture (see Smith, 2014). This perfectly captures the commodified nature of the health and fitness industry and how the gym has been constructed as a consumption destination where the subject can practise self-maintenance, echo bodily and material trends, and share the experience of fitness with their peers (Andreasson and Johansson, 2019). This idea was furthered by IFBB Pro Ben, as he discussed his female friend's experiences of fielding advances from male gym users after training:

> 'I think for a lot of people that go now it's a social thing. There's a girl that I train with and she trains harder than most lads. She's not a regular there, so people only see her there on like a Saturday or a Sunday, and the amount of lads who've seen her training and they've found her on Insta[gram] and added her and like tried to speak to her. It's absolutely nuts. But then everyone's lifting weights and they're all on testosterone, they're all horny, it's bound to happen.'

Muscle Sanctuary's likeness to the night-time economy is strengthened as Ben contends that the commodified space of the gym can also act as a means of seeking romantic opportunities. While Ben simply attributes this behaviour to the virile effects of the men's enhanced testosterone levels (discussed in Chapter 6), read in the context of the gym's burgeoning role as a commodified leisure space, this sexual element supports the view that Muscle Sanctuary and Predator are arenas of competitive consumption, which ultimately do not present as largely different to the sites of the night-time economy.

Furthermore, Ben's admission that the 'lads' located his friend on Instagram following her session sheds light upon the entanglement of the physical gym space and the virtual social media platforms under study. Though Instagram's role in shaping gym and IPED motivation will be discussed at length in Chapter 7, it is worth emphasizing how the platform impacts upon the gym as a site of consumption here. This was discussed in rather derogatory terms by 39-year-old sports supplement company owner and former competitive bodybuilder David, as he critiqued young gym users' infatuation with social media:

> 'I first went to a gym in Lincolnshire, I used to push weight there every night. I was 15 but I lied and said I was 18 to get in. … But you didn't

have camera phones and all that. I realize I sound old as fuck, but you would get mates to come to the gym and they'd come once and they'd never come back. Whereas now everyone in that age group goes to the gym because they need to check in on Facebook and Instagram and post photos. If you made it so you couldn't post about what you were doing in the gym, you would probably have a third or less of the people who go, still going. You see people setting up tripods and stuff to film their sets, it all becomes very self-indulgent, and ultimately nobody cares.'

According to David, younger gym users' attraction to the gym is almost entirely premised on seeking the rewards attached to conspicuously prosuming fitness online (Millington, 2016), rather than using the gym to improve their *inner* health (Featherstone, 1982). Therefore, social media sites simply extend the gym's reach as a commodified site of consumption and, just as night-time economy venues and tourist spots become immortalized in the Instagram posts of digital prosumers, the gym can be consumed twice over: once by the user and then again by their following.

Muscle Sanctuary and Predator's online presence also impacts the friendships that are cultivated in the spaces of fitness, as both gyms' social networks spill over onto social media. I encountered this with Will, an affable casual Muscle Sanctuary member, who complimented me after I posted an update on my gym progress to my research Instagram account (Figure 3.1). Having posted a self-deprecating Instagram 'story' making light of myself being the 'smallest guy in the gym', Will praised my physique whilst playing down his own worked-on body. This altruistic gesture paints the online fitness space as one of socializing and mutual consumption, as members of Muscle Sanctuary and Predator frequently engaged with each other's social media content, providing similar encouragement to that shown in the physical spaces of the gyms themselves. Will particularly noted how his supportive relationship with Adam (another casual weight trainer) played out on Instagram, where "he'll share my pictures and give me a confidence boost". Clearly, the online and offline spaces under study are inherently connected as social arenas and the communal element of fitness consumption reaches beyond the mirrored walls of Muscle Sanctuary and Predator (see Marshall et al, 2020).

Will's complimentary message speaks to a more profound aspect of gym culture that I encountered during my time in the field. Opposing the transient, individualistic friendships typical of late-capitalist sites of commodified leisure (see Hall et al, 2008; Smith, 2014), the gyms, and to an extent the SNS, frequented by the men provided a network of mutual support and kinship. This is reminiscent of Hammarén and Johansson's (2014) notion of horizontal homosociality, which they understand as a nonprofitable form of friendship between members of the same sex, allowing bounded intimacy and emotional support. Read in the context of Potsford's post-industrial economic decline

Figure 3.1: Will sharing some words of encouragement in response to my Instagram 'story' update (22/10/10)

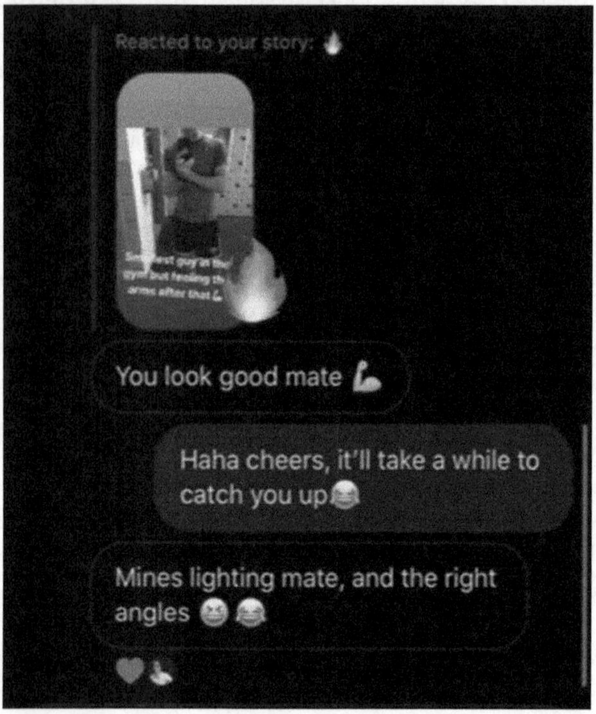

and the dearth of collectivizing toil in the city, the gym appears to offer a sense of shared purpose and fraternity that is otherwise absent in The Kilns (see Gibbs et al, 2022a). Male friendships are traditionally premised upon shared experiences and activities (Sprangler, 1992; Hanna et al, 2020), and therefore the demise of Potsford's homogenized industry, which facilitated thousands of fraternal relationships centred around the region's principal export, has left a lacuna that the gyms partially redress. The comradeship and fraternal warmth of the gym was reflected in the numerous times that strangers approached me with advice or offered to spot me, altruistically extending their cultural and bodily capital through an offer of what Rothmann (2022: 133) terms the 'bromantic touch'. This was echoed in Scott's experience of seeking help in Muscle Sanctuary from retired bodybuilder, Alan:

> 'I'll even ask people [for advice] in the gym. There's people in the gym like Alan who used to be a professional bodybuilder. So I'll be working next to Alan and I'll ask him, "have you got anything to do for rear delts?". Anything like that, and he'll show you, he'll show you what he does, and so will the next person and the person after that.'

As demonstrated in Scott's willingness to seek help from Alan, Muscle Sanctuary offered him a means of collaborating with other like-minded men and building fraternal relationships based upon shared endeavour. Therefore, by aiding one another towards the mutual goal of muscular hypertrophy and enhanced fitness, members replicated the labour-based friendships that existed in the era of industrial modernity.

Importantly however, as The Kilns' transition into post-industrial late-capitalism signalled not only the loss of employment, but also the sense of community and fixity that my sample spoke so fondly of, the men in both gyms provided one another with a supportive space where a genuine sense of community and anchorage could be found. Will's compliment (Figure 3.1) was typical of the affirming acknowledgements of size, definition, and form shared between members in the gym and across social media platforms. These commendations represent a means for men to support one another and is evocative of Greif's (2008) concept of 'shoulder-to-shoulder' friendships, whereby men tend to premise their homosocial relationships around participation in an activity rather than the traditionally female 'face-to-face' communication. Thus, bodywork can be seen as a proxy in some sense, presenting as a medium through which men can act out their friendships.

Further, Kimmel's (1996: 7) declaration that 'men define their masculinity, not as much in relation to women, but in relation to each other' is salient here, as a consensus emerged across my sample that, despite their initial motivations frequently involving a desire to become sexually attractive, as their physique progressed it was their fellow male gym members from whom they sought validation (see Rothmann, 2022). I broached this topic with Sam:

S: [What got me into the gym was] one of my best mates, he was into weight training and was really big, and if I'm being honest, he seemed to do quite well with the girls. So I thought 'I'm going to go into that'. … So I just started training with him and ever since then I just continued from there. Then quite soon it became less and less about girls and more about getting on stage [at bodybuilding competitions].

N: In a weird way, does it go from impressing women to impressing guys?

S: That's it, you don't do it to impress women because really they don't like really big muscly guys, generally. Then you get a lot of attention from lads, especially when you're around show day and building up to a show. So when you're in the gym you'll be chatting to lads all the time about your [preparation] and stuff. It's definitely that, don't think that if you're gonna get massive it will get you girls [laughs].

Here, what is sometimes referred to as the homoerotic aspect of male weight training and bodybuilding (see Klein, 1993; Denham, 2008) is evident, as Sam concedes that the initial pull of bolstering his erotic capital was surpassed by a desire for fraternal validation (Rothman, 2022). Similarly, Ben, who was first drawn towards the idea of "get[ting] loads of girls", was resolute that his physique did not function to "impress women anymore, I'm more bothered about what the lads think". Clearly, unlike the ephemeral friendships that typify many sites of late-capitalist leisure, the gyms and their digital counterparts function on some level to create meaningful fraternal bonds between members in the absence of a collectivizing industry in the city. An acknowledgement of this nuance is vital given the deviant leisure framework's natural proclivity to focus upon the pejorative and harmful aspects of such spaces of consumption. Indeed, having experienced numerous acts of genuine altruism, fraternal kinship, and meaningful friendship, it would be misleading not to portray these layers. However, a recognition of the genuine bonds formed within the fitness arena need not contradict the ontological basis of this monograph. Arguably, aspects of fraternity exist *in spite of* the commodified nature of the fitness industry, and sites of consumption such as the gym are simply the only remaining space for men to bond over common practices and shared endeavour.

False sociality, competition, and *amour propre*

Despite some of the genuine friendships and fraternal elements that I encountered during my time at the two gyms, however, an undertone of instrumentality always seemed to bubble away below the enthusiastic handshakes, profane shouts of encouragement, and laddish banter. The nature of such leisure-based friendships is discussed by Winlow and Hall in relation to the night-time economy, as they assert that, in place of the meaningful altruistic relationships described earlier in this chapter, the current epoch of transient leisure-based identities produces 'superficial, temporary and fragile alliances' (Winlow and Hall, 2006: 91). This should be understood in line with Hall's (2012a) identification of the pseudo-pacification process, as the self-serving relationships simply facilitate the symbolically violent spirit of competitive individualism promoted within the leisure market. Though few of my sample candidly spoke about this, a narrative of competitive individualism was rife in both gyms. This was reflected by Ben, who acknowledged that the gym is an "outlet for me to be competitive. I can scratch that itch, that competitive side of me". Similarly, Dom proudly declared, "I have an athlete's mindset, a competitive mindset and that's why I do everything really". The effects of this combative ethos were felt across both gyms, as users were constantly comparing their physiques and performance with others. Recounting his experience of a significant injury as we sat in Muscle Sanctuary's socializing area late on a Tuesday evening, aspiring bodybuilder Josh agonizingly recalled his first session back with his training partners:

> 'Normally when you walk in people are like, "Yeah you're looking big", but when I broke my elbow when I first got back in the gym again, because I thought "I've got to get back training", the first four or five people who I hadn't seen for a while were like, "What's happened to you? You look so skinny" and I was like, "Wow, cheers". Not exactly what you want to hear. You're always conscious of [how you look compared to others].'

This recollection, delivered with a grimace, drives at the heart of many of the sample's relationships with their training partners and gym acquaintances. Following a pressure to return to the gym, Josh's declined bodily capital was judged harshly by his peers, whose valuation of him seemingly relied upon him 'looking big' and competently consuming fitness alongside them. It can therefore be deduced that those with whom Josh formed a fragile alliance rely upon what Hall et al (2008) term '*amour propre*', wherein they elevate themselves through the denigration of others. This concept explains their readiness to admonish Josh's new-found 'skinny' frame, which suddenly paled in comparison to their own. This precarious, contingent set of social relations speaks to late-capitalism's effect on the subject, as Josh hinged his identity on the fleeting appraisal of others in the wake of a symbolically efficient point of anchorage. Therefore, while Adam, Scott, and Will's accounts present the gym as a fundamentally pro-social environment, this undertow of insecure self-centredness paints a decidedly more cynical picture of intra-member competition, alongside the fraternal aspects of the gym. This underlying tension was brought starkly into focus during one PT session, where a fracas broke out after Andy supposedly pushed into an aggressive customer behind us:

> I was just finishing up my last set on the lat pulldown machine when a wave of raised voices and jostling bodies engulfed me. Swiftly returning the handle to its stand, I turned to see a vest-wearing gym-goer, no older than 20, swearing furiously at Andy for apparently nudging him mid-set. The altercation soon calmed down when the user's friends, presumably aware of Andy's influence in the gym, pulled him away towards the legs room as he branded Andy an 'Irish c★★t' from the free weights area. Bizarrely, as quickly as it happened, the gym fell back into its usual clinking and clanging rhythm, seemingly having forgotten the incident already. (Fieldnote, 06/02/20)

This altercation, to which Andy steadfastly proclaimed his innocence, was one of the few times that the civilized, pseudo-pacified symbolic violence (Hall, 2012a) of the gym was ruptured, laying bare the undercurrent of competitive individualism and aggression. Despite the gentrified polish of Muscle Sanctuary (Brighton et al, 2020), the libidinal forces pulsating below the commercialized skin of the gym were momentarily exposed, and the violence usually masked by the symbolic practices of lifting and posing were revealed. This was, on reflection, perhaps the most telling and authentic insight I gained during the entirety of my fieldwork and represented a glimpse of the forces that are repressed and repackaged within the hyper-real spaces of Muscle Sanctuary and Predator.

"It's like a full-time job": the gym as a site of labour

Ascetic hedonism and individualized graft

Despite the fundamentally communal nature of both gyms and the men's consumption of fitness as a site of leisure and sociability, commitment to the gym and a lifestyle premised on fitness seemingly challenges the Žižekian injunction to enjoy, given the inevitable need for deferred gratification and corporeal labour. The hedonism inherent within commodified practices such as excessive drinking or Black Friday shopping (see Smith, 2014; Raymen and Smith, 2016) is, on some level, absent in the asceticism and routine of the gym. However, Žižek (2006) proposes the concept of 'hedonistic asceticism' to address such a paradox. Premised on the inevitable feelings of guilt experienced by the subject following the injunction to enjoy, he describes a dualism whereby hedonism is simultaneously counteracted by a guilt-induced restraint. Examples of this include alcohol-free beer and de-caffeinated coffee, where the indulgent ingredient is stripped from the product, rendering it both a 'treat' and a means of assuaging the guilt of such enjoyment. Žižek applies this concept to the jogger who combines a life of narcissistic self-fulfilment with the punishing routine of exercise and healthy eating. Accordingly, several of my participants conceptualized the gym as a means of "working off the weekend" (Scott) and counteracting other health-damaging activities. Will explained:

> '[The] busiest [time] is Monday at five o'clock, you can't get in the car park. I think it's because everyone binges on the weekend and feels guilty on a Monday, so the rest of the week isn't so bad. Like most of the people I've spoken to they go out on a Friday so, on Monday, they feel bad and can't get in the car park. Then [on] Tuesday they don't come in again [laughs].'

I experienced this Monday post-work stampede myself on numerous occasions, where I frequently performed several loops around Muscle

Sanctuary's poorly tarmacked car park, before pouncing on a vacant spot. The guilt experienced by the hordes of Monday evening customers speaks to the narratives of personal responsibility and autonomy within Cederström and Spicer's (2015) notion of the wellness syndrome, and late-capitalism's hollow emphasis on personal well-being (see Davies, 2015). Here, members' weekends of jouissance and 'stupid pleasures' (Žižek, 2008), driven by the guilt-inducing injunction to enjoy, are effectively cancelled out within the parallel consumptive process of corporeal repair and improvement. As such, far from contradicting the injunction, the gym, on some level facilitates the hedonistic excesses of the leisure market, while also serving as a form of consumption in and of itself. As much as Muscle Sanctuary and Predator are spaces of commodified leisure, representing destinations to socialize and even flirt, for my sample they were also places of graft and labour (Gibbs et al, 2022a). This is perhaps the underlying paradox of the gym as a site of consumption, as Paul explained:

> 'People who like sport don't like the gym, because people who like team sports like to turn up at a place, have some camaraderie with their mates, do something together and bugger off again. People who don't like that like to turn up on their own, put their earphones in and do it on their own. So the gym doesn't actually appeal generally to people who like organized sports – that's my opinion.'

Paul touches upon a common thread within my participants' reporting of their gym routines: working out as an individualized form of discipline or labour (see Rothmann, 2022). Muscle Sanctuary and Predator's status as 'hardcore' gyms inevitably made them places of 'serious leisure' (Stebbins, 2007) and an ethic of discipline and individualism underlay even my least committed participants' workouts. Although he was perhaps the most sociable gym-goer I met, to my surprise Adam summed this mindset up, stating:

> 'I just see it as a job really, if you don't come here, you don't get paid, if I don't come, I'm gonna end up losing what I've got so it's always fixated in my head. I'm not here to look pretty or anything, I'm just here to get it done and go home'.

A far cry from his previous assertions, Adam captures the gym's instrumental nature, where bodily capital is topped up through hard graft. Similarly, Pete conceded that for him gym work felt like "a full-time job", due to the ascetic routine and accompanying injunction to eat and live well.

This introspective attitude was most prevalent within the more serious trainers and competitive athletes whom I met, as aspiring bodybuilder Josh attested to with his matter-of-fact conclusion that, "you go to the gym to train, at the end of the day". For these men, whose training went beyond recreational leisure, their experience of the gym was certainly not one of hedonism, as Jake, a promising amateur bodybuilder and security guard, summed up when discussing his experiences of preparing for bodybuilding competitions:

> 'When I'm on prep I'm in there with minimal chat. If I'm training, I want to focus on me and not be side-tracked or whatever. Also, I've got a time limit about how long I can be in the gym for because I have to get home, get washed, changed and I've got to eat another two meals and prep meals for the next day. Any chatting I'm doing is just adding to that, and I've already got up at 5am to do cardio. So any chatting is just an extension of my already long day that I don't need. So you just have to become very selfish for those weeks.'

Here, the regimented nature of the extreme end of the health and fitness industry is laid bare, as the run up to Jake's competition was almost mechanistic in structure and rejected all unnecessary social interaction. This is clearly a departure from the conventionally enjoyable forms of leisure discussed within Smith and Raymen's (2018) school of thought, and instead reflects a deep-reaching desire for bodily attainment (discussed in Chapter 4). This idea of leisure as labour was supported by Ben, who told me:

> 'When I'm training, I'm pretty switched off from everything else. I'll train with the usual guy I train with and we kind of just keep ourselves to ourselves. There's not a lot of chit-chat between us while we're training, a bit of banter maybe but nothing massively sociable. … There is definitely a social side to it, but a lot of the people [who] know me at the gym know not to come over to me while I'm training.'

Although Ben hints at there being a sociable aspect to his gym work, he ultimately trains in the individualistic manner described by Paul. This is at odds with his gregarious and highly likeable personality, and it is clear that this earphone-wearing persona is simply an instrumental necessity employed in order to work on his physique most effectively. Similarly, during a follow up interview with Dom, who was able to access the gym during the national COVID-19 lockdown under the guise of being an 'elite athlete', he spoke glowingly about his altered training environment:

N: What do you miss about a busy gym?

D: Now this is where you'll get the difference between someone who trains at a higher level and an amateur. The answer is nothing, for

> me. I am happy to go in there and just train on my own or just with a spotter or whatever. Just get it done and get out. Whereas your guys who don't compete, you'll tend to find that they go for a social, so they'll miss their mate, or for example they might even miss looking at the hottest girl in the gym. Guys on a lower level would miss things like that, the community aspect of it, whereas me, I'm just happy I get to train and use the kit. I don't have to wait for kit, I can use what I want, when I want. Then get out and get home, eat, sleep, repeat.

Ironically, for Dom, the unique opportunity to train in an isolated, community-free environment satisfied his desire to simply "get out and get home, eat, sleep, repeat", avoiding all unnecessary social contact and the distractions which, for him, afflict less committed trainers (See Gibbs, 2021). Dom demonstrates an almost snobbish attitude to his bodywork, drawing distinction between "someone who trains at a higher level" versus "an amateur" and insinuating that the gym as a site of graft is exclusively the reserve of competitors and professionals, rather than the "[g]uys on a lower level". However, despite his aspersions, these "guys who don't compete" in fact shared the same myopic focus upon the self, despite their sociability in the gym. Again, Adam's voice articulated this most accurately:

> 'I'm here for myself, nobody in here or anybody you interview can say they're not in here for vanity or they're not here for social acceptance, because they are. If people are in here standing by the mirror, it's because they want to look good and that's why mirrors are there, you walk in and it's there for a reason.'

In line with the ascendent culture of medicalization and health as an individual duty (see Orbach, 2009), Adam cuts through the narratives of camaraderie and kinship, and drives at the heart of the health and fitness industry. This obsessive internal focus reflects the inherent narcissism that is so celebrated in contemporary leisure (Lasch, 1979; Davies, 2011) and again speaks to Cederström and Spicer's (2015) concept of the wellness syndrome. Adam's acknowledgement that 'vanity' plays an epicentral role in gym work was echoed by Ben who, discussing my initial concerns about being judged for not being muscular enough to enter Muscle Sanctuary, counselled that "everyone's so wrapped up in themselves and so bothered about what they look like that no one will even notice you". Thus, while the men in my sample trained alongside me for the duration of my fieldwork, they presumably would not have even noticed my relatively lean frame. However, according to David, this has not always been the case: "I remember growing up, people who worked out being almost looked down on like they were vein and self-obsessed. Well they are [laughs] we all still are, but it's more socially acceptable now and why that is I don't know."

Again, David illustrates the centrality of the self in the contemporary health and fitness industry and how this culture of individualism has become mainstream, having been the subject of derision during his bodybuilding career in the 1990s. Though he was at a loss to explain this development, this rise of individualism can be contoured perfectly alongside the growth of the health and fitness industry, the commodification of leisure, and the neoliberal promotion of self-interest. As a result, through their competitive individualistic focus on self-improvement and exhibits of *amour propre*, my sample's gym use hyper-conformed (Raymen and Smith, 2016) to the edicts of neoliberalism and ultimately reflected the contemporary rejection of the 'duty to the other' (Bauman, 2009). Importantly, this conclusion does not invalidate the genuine displays of fraternal affection that occurred in spite of the commodification of health and fitness. Rather, it highlights the effects of the neoliberal leisure environment on the subject and how this new ethic has extended into the world of fitness.

Chapter summary

This chapter first served to introduce the key ontological and epistemological framing of this book. After critically evaluating the current landscape of criminological theory, the intimately connected schools of ultra-realism and deviant leisure have been presented and a case for their utility in this work has been made. The latter part of the chapter has sought to discuss the health and fitness industry through this lens. First, my online and offline fieldsites were located within the commodified leisure sector. The gyms under study, alongside the wider health and fitness industry, can best be described as commodified sites of consumption that present as 'steadfastly conformist' to the edicts of neoliberalism (Raymen and Smith, 2019a). This was first reflected in the increasing professionalization and commercialization of the gym environment, wherein the former sense of community and kinship has become somewhat overshadowed by the influx of fitness professionals soliciting their services. Second, while an aspect of communality and fraternity was identified in both gyms, the genuine bonds I observed in the field were shown to have been impinged upon by the late-capitalist subjectivity of competitive individualism and *amour propre* (Hall et al, 2008). Finally, the gym has been shown to be a site of labour and should therefore be viewed as fundamentally different from other forms of commodified leisure on account of the aspects of graft demonstrated by committed trainers. This discussion has illustrated the solipsistic nature of labour in the gym, and the inevitable focus upon the self promoted by the health and fitness industry.

Ultimately, through this chapter's engagement with the school of deviant leisure, my fieldsites have been situated not only within the burgeoning health and fitness industry, but also within the wider commodified leisure spaces of late-capitalism. This positioning allows this book's exploration of IPED use and supply to be contextualized within the theoretical frameworks of ultra-realism and deviant leisure, and therefore builds a platform upon which a thorough analysis of IPED consumption can take place.

PART I

Consumption

4

Desire and Dissatisfaction in the Gym

Having explored my fieldsites through the lens of deviant leisure, attention can now be turned to my participants' motivation to consume IPEDs. This exploration is divided into four interconnected chapters, spanning several levels; from a psychoanalytic account of lack and bodily dissatisfaction, through to a broader recognition of the meso and macro cultural contexts that shape my participants' world.

The first of these aims to address the current lacuna of deep theoretical engagement with the motivation to consume IPEDs and build the body that exists within the academy (van de Ven et al, 2020). This therefore answers Kotzé et al's (2020) call for psychoanalytic engagement with the concept of lack within spaces of hardcore bodywork, alongside an acknowledgement of the politico-economic backdrop to IPED use and gym culture in the Global North. The central questions that this collection of chapters sets out to answer are *why* the sample of men to whom I spoke risked long-term health issues and myriad aches, pains, and strains, to build their physiques, and what compelled them to haul their engorged bodies to the gym when most of us would prioritize rest, ease, and comfort. In pursuit of an answer, this initial consumption chapter draws on psychoanalytic theory to interrogate the role of deficit and desire in driving compulsive bodywork and explaining the allure of IPEDs.

Lack, desire and the *objet petit a*

As set out in the previous chapter, the starting point of the ultra-realist conception of personhood is Lacan's contention that the subject is governed by a sense of lack and deficit (Žižek, 2000; Hall and Winlow, 2015; Ayres, 2022). Lacan contends that all human behaviour can be understood to be motivated by an attempt to overcome this innate lack and reach a state of satisfaction that never, *and can never*, truly exist (Gammon and Palan,

2006; Flisfeder, 2014; Raymen and Smith, 2017). This imagined sense of satiation is understood by Lacan as the *objet petit a*, or the lost object, and describes an intangible *thing* that 'orients the subject's desire even though the subject has never had it' (McGowan, 2016: 26). This perpetually out-of-reach object, therefore, represents a means of overcoming the lack at the heart of human subjectivity, and thus exerts a force that can ultimately be understood to drive all human action (Raymen and Smith, 2017; Hall, 2019).

Crucially, however, the subject does not wish to ever truly locate the *objet petit a*, and instead derives satisfaction from their continual, unsuccessful search (Raymen and Smith, 2019b; Hall, 2019) like a boisterous hound chasing its own tail. This is articulated by McGowan – a thinker on whom I will lean a great deal in this chapter – who contends that 'the subject finds satisfaction in repeating loss' (McGowan, 2016: 28). Therefore, what we desire most is *desire itself*. To this end, needing to preserve a state of continuous desire, we deliberately sabotage the satiation of our dissatisfaction by erecting barriers to its accomplishment (McGowan, 2016). This understanding of the true nature of desire forms the bedrock of McGowan's account of consumer capitalism's stranglehold over the contemporary subject. He argues that capitalism's enduring ascendance hinges upon its successful capture – and subsequent suspension – of human desire as, aware that there can be no ultimate resolution to the subject's dissatisfaction, the system provides us with a limitless supply of commodities that we gladly substitute as the *objet petit a*. Thus, we articulate our desire of the lost object by coveting the plethora of novel commodities that are advertised to us each day (Ayres, 2019). However, following the acquisition of these longed-for commodities, these stand-ins – be it the latest fashion trend, the newest model of luxury car or technological gadget – are ultimately revealed to be devoid of the significance formerly bestowed upon them by the consumer and are drained of their psychic value (McGowan, 2003; McGowan, 2016; Raymen and Smith, 2017).

This explains, for example, why the apex of Christmas day is the anticipation of receiving the enticingly wrapped gifts under the tree as, crucially, their desirability drastically reduces upon being opened. Similarly, the reason that the vast industry of product packaging, which is responsible for much of the immeasurable non-degradable waste populating our landfill sites and oceans, has such a hold over us is that the flimsy plastic casing or colourful cartons represent a symbolic barrier to the attainment of their contents. The myriad consumable commodities and aesthetics that the late-capitalist system sells us therefore act as a proxy to the *objet petit a*, as consumerism preys upon our psychic make-up, keeping us suspended in the race for consumption where there exists no actual finishing line (Bauman, 2012). If this dissatisfaction were to ever cease, neoliberalism would be unable to sustain the insatiable growth that underpins it and the very fabric of our economy would crumble (Hall, 2019).

The body as the object of desire

But what relevance does this analysis bear to the study of bodywork and IPED consumption? And how can an understanding of desire illuminate my sample's relationship with their corporeal development? To answer these questions, it is first worth engaging with the existing literature around the commodification of the body under consumer capitalism. Featherstone (1991: 177) contends that, 'within consumer culture, the body is proclaimed as a vehicle for pleasure … and the closer the actual body approximates to the idealized images of youth, health, fitness and beauty, the higher its exchange value'. Accordingly, the body has increasingly become a site of *consumption* rather than *production*, and a toned physique is now endowed with a symbolic significance beyond its functional capacity (Lasch, 1979; Kotzé and Antonopoulos, 2019). This contemporary role of the 'worked-on' body is described by Smith Maguire (2008: 3) as becoming 'fit for consumption', as she contends that productivity no longer lies in the output of the physical form. Instead, Smith Maguire argues that the body itself has become a site of investment for the late-capitalist subject as a means of promoting the best version of oneself for 'competitive circulation' (Wernick, 1991: 193). Similarly, Featherstone (1982) describes the altering relationship between the inner (health-related) and outer (image-related) body under consumer capitalism. Featherstone contends that consumer-driven bodily commodification relegates the inner body's importance, and therefore its extrinsic value outweighs its intrinsic health-related worth. In line with this, the aesthetic body has become a positional good that subjects strive to attain, and the physique can be viewed akin to the commodities described by McGowan earlier in this chapter. Given the symbolic value attached to a worked-on body as a site of consumption (Rosenmann et al, 2018) then, this corporeal commodity has become just another object of desire mobilized as a means of generating capital within gym users' struggle to navigate the ascendant economic system (Hall, 2012b; Raymen, 2018).

This is where existing scholarship on the body, dissatisfaction, and beauty ideals can benefit. Current literature concerning the unattainability of hegemonic bodily ideals and the subsequent harms around bodily dissatisfaction fundamentally misunderstands the nature of the subject's relationship with desire and dissatisfaction. While these accounts correctly identify the ever-changing nature of bodily 'perfection' for committed gym users, they labour under the impression that the subject is driven by the *realization* of these ideals. These scholars therefore document the sense of lack and deficit as a harmful imposition upon gym users and suggest that, if they could somehow feel entirely contented and secure in their body, their issues would be resolved. This cultural analysis, of course, ties into the public health axiom to provide 'solutions' in the form of policy or safeguards, which somewhat explains why psychoanalytic approaches of bodily dissatisfaction are few and far between. Instead, if we accept Lacan's account of desire and McGowan's subsequent interpretation, it is not displeasure that we derive from our failure to attain the prevailing body ideals, but psychic *pleasure*.

Therefore, the ever smoother, harder, more defined bodily features that goad the committed gym user to persist in their training represent the self-erected barriers that suspend the subject in a state of permanent desire. Understood this way, the body becomes a stand-in for the *objet petit a*, feeding upon the lack at the heart of the subject to keep us striving to achieve increasingly minuscule enhancement. Conscious not to stray too deeply into this murky theoretical undertow without hearing my sample's voices, the theme of lack was rife in the interviews, as there was an acknowledgement that, for them, bodywork had become something of a rabbit hole and their corporeal goals and ideals had steadily shifted as their physiques developed. This was summed up by Ben:

N: Was there a point where what you wanted to look like became a bodybuilder rather than just someone in decent shape?

B: For me, I never really saw it. I obviously saw that I looked better, I had a bit of a chest and arms and a bit of a six pack, but I'd never have thought that I had the potential to go and do something with it. But my goals just kept getting bigger and bigger and now [gestures to his physique] here we are.

Similarly, Andy acknowledged that, "a lot of people say, 'Oh I don't want to get too big', but I think that changes as you get bigger", while Scott, discussing his evolving bodily aims, remarked:

> 'I didn't care [about chasing bodily ideals] before but now I do, and I think that's just got worse and worse. Like the better I started looking, the worse I got. I think you start off like 18 stone like I was, then I've been sub-14 stone and think, "Oh I look really good". It gets in your head, and you want to look better.'

More broadly, during my time in the field, I became well-versed in the rhetoric of goals and the *journey* of bodywork as I logged my progression, scrutinized the drawn-out changes in my body and identified how best to advance my physique. As such, my mind was constantly envisioning what I *could* look like or how many plates I *might* be able to lift given more hours under the bar, rather than the material changes that I had already achieved.

The perpetuity of this mindset was echoed in amateur strongman Pete's admission that, "I've always got something to aim for ... there's always something in my head that I'm trying to work for". Pete's statement epitomizes McGowan's (2016) claim that it is dissatisfaction that drives action as, with the proverbial goalposts continually moving further away, the gym user is placed in a state of unending desire. In this sense, bodywork becomes a hamster wheel, with the trainer's exertion ultimately driving the process onwards ad infinitum to ensure that their desire does not 'meet its object and die' (Hall, 2019: 170).

Suffering and bodily jouissance

Ultimately, the production of an engorged body is the result of the subject desiring too intensely and finding not only pleasure in their dissatisfaction, but also jouissance. As was explored in Chapter 3, Žižek (2008) highlights the nature of enjoyment under late-capitalism, describing how the subject's overexposure to pleasure can drive them towards the excessive, painful form of enjoyment that Lacan termed jouissance (Lacan, 2013). This concept is particularly apt when interrogating the compulsive gym work undertaken by my sample and their consumption of IPEDs.

My foray into the world of hardcore fitness saw me wake up each morning with a different ache or pain, and frequently sporting a limp after a heavy legs session. My previously soft hands were mutated by welts and toughened skin after a few months of training, caused by repeated leverage of barbells, exercise machines, and dumbbells. However, my discomforts, which were soon reversed, paled in comparison to my sample's. Gym users frequently spoke light-heartedly of the "twisted mind" (Tina) of the bodybuilder and their experiences of near-constant pain. On this, Ben admitted:

> 'My knees and my elbows are excruciating. ... I saw a meme the other day, it was a doctor saying to a bodybuilder, "Are you in any pain?", and he says, "Just the normal amount". Then he says, "The normal amount is nothing", you know? That's how it is, constantly something's aching or hurting when you train like I do.'

However, far from decrying this state of perpetual suffering, Ben delivered the revelation with a broad smile, coyly cursing himself for his affliction. I probed further:

N: So, do you enjoy the whole being tired at the end of [working out]? Is there some pleasure to be had in aching and suffering?

B: Yeah definitely. It's a bit weird and not everyone gets it, it's almost a bit sadistic when you get the enjoyment of walking out and

> it hurts or waking up the next morning and you've got DOMS [delayed-onset muscle soreness] in your legs or your arms hurt, because you know that you've been in there and you've given it everything. There's definitely a sense of satisfaction with it all.

Ben's contention that there exists a "sense of satisfaction" in the aching muscles and inability to walk after a laborious gym session (see Nash, 2018) speaks to his fetishization of his body as an object of desire, and how this frequently leads him into a state of jouissance. This was reflected in aspiring bodybuilder Jake's assertion that:

> 'If you ask people whether pain the day after a big session feels good, I reckon 99 per cent would say yes because you know you have actually worked and you have actually achieved something. Like if your legs or shoulders are hurting, it's like, "Yeah, that feels good" because you know you've actually done something. Then if you're not hurting the day after, it's like "Maybe I didn't work that hard then". The burn definitely can drive you sometimes, you can have a bit of a second wind if you're doing something and it's burning and you're just in that zone like, "Right, I'm just going to get through this now".'

Though Jake predominantly views the feeling of exertion as evidence of his hard work, he also describes 'the burn' as a means of motivation in and of itself. The pain brought on by hardcore, excessive bodywork is therefore the inevitable result of trainers like Jake's over-identification of the physique as a stand-in for the *objet petit a*. Transfixed by the perpetually self-sabotaged quest for bodily progression, pain and suffering are simply viewed as a necessary evil or, more poignantly, a tangible manifestation of the men's constant, pleasurable state of dissatisfaction. Accordingly, my sample frequently admitted that their training directly flouted their friends' and families' concerns and even medical advice. This was epitomized by Adam:

> 'I'll be honest with you, the gym's that fixated in my mind that in the middle of August last year I woke up in the middle of the night and did my lower back, so I probably shouldn't even be training, but it hasn't stopped me. So I now have a bulge in my lower back that presses against my spinal cord, which even now affects my legs. … It took me three hours [to] get to work once because I couldn't walk. I had people telling me [to] rest but I was that fixated that if I rest, I'm gonna lose what I've done. So I was still coming in [to the gym], and now obviously I can squat 120[kg] again and train legs again. … There was a day, I was walking bad for about four months, and there was one time … I was nearly in tears like, "Am I ever gonna fucking

> walk properly again?" But then I carried on going [to] the gym and I was like "I don't give a shit". Why should I stop going?'

Adam's training took ultimate precedence despite numerous suggestions that he seek medical consultation and rest. His fixation on fruitlessly striving for an idealized physique was such that he risked his long-term health for the continuation of his desire and, even as he neared tears through the pain, it was not enough to dissuade his lack-fuelled drive. Adam's extreme example also alludes to bodywork's status as what Derrida (1998) calls 'pharmakon', a term describing a 'drug' that simultaneously acts as a remedy and a poison. Wiens and MacDonald (2020: 2) explain that pharmakon 'encapsulates both cure and toxin, positive and negative, possibility and constraint' and is therefore a phenomenon that sustains an affliction while masquerading as a solution. Gym work can be read as a form of pharmakon, as Adam further contended, "I think it's like when you stop [training] I think your body knows it. I genuinely think your body knows when your time is up and it starts degrading". Therefore, according to Adam, if he were to submit to injury and cease his bodywork, he would simply 'degrade' and therefore the only option he has is to persist despite potentially causing himself more harm.

Why the body? Fitness as a never-ending journey

It is at this juncture that a vital question emerges: why the body? Why, of the myriad leisure activities, commodities, religions, and political ideologies available to them, does my sample's desire centre around the cultivation of their physiques? The partial answer to these critical questions is the innate suitability of the concept of fitness to our unending pursuit of desire. To unpack this, it is first worth considering the paradox that lies at the heart of the *health* and *fitness* industry. According to Bauman (2012), though commonly cited as symbiotic, the terms health and fitness belong to two paradoxical discourses. Health, on one hand, describes the 'proper and desirable state of human body and spirit' (Bauman, 2012: 77), measurable by both medical apparatus and one's ability to function. Alternatively, fitness lacks any tenure to the present and instead is defined by a constant state of readiness for an unclear future task. Fitness provides no natural end or sense of completion for the subject, who may reach milestones or targets, yet these only represent a respite on the journey towards an ultimately unattainable state. We can forever be stronger, faster, lighter, more balanced, more powerful, and more agile, regardless of the training we complete or the state of optimal *health* we achieve. Bauman sums this up:

> The pursuit of fitness is a chase after a quarry which one cannot describe until it is reached; however, one has no means to decide that

> the quarry has indeed been reached, but every reason to suspect that it has not. Life organized around the pursuit of fitness promises a lot of victorious skirmishes, but *never the final triumph*. (Bauman, 2012: 78, italics added)

Bauman identifies the never-ending nature of fitness and how, even through an existence devoted to optimizing one's body, a state of completeness can never be achieved. As such, the corporeal form can be conceptualized as an 'unfinished entity' (Shilling, 2003: 138), which constitutes extremely fertile ground into which the seeds of desire can be sown. Regrettably however, Bauman's account of fitness ultimately falls foul of the misapprehension that gym users are duped into following a damaging life of fitness and wish to reach a level of bodily satisfaction. Instead, it is the multitude of barriers, constantly evolving ideals and out-of-reach goals that represent the true psychic appeal of bodywork. Therefore, while Boer (2007: 42) concludes that the 'ideal built body is ultimately unattainable', it is this unattainability that makes the physique such a potent stand-in for the *objet petit a*. This was echoed by veteran bodybuilder Phillip, as he recounted his initial attraction to the sport of bodybuilding:

> 'What I liked about bodybuilding was [that] to be successful it's 100% training, 100% nutrition, 100% mental focus, so it sets you on this path of compliance which is absolute. When I was a runner there came a point where I couldn't do any more, I couldn't run any faster and nothing I could do would allow me to beat my fastest time. Whereas with bodybuilding, because there's the potential to improve in so many different ways – you can improve your technique, or your diet, or your consistency, or your sleep, or your mental focus stepping into the gym. It's a sport you can do and not get bored after a few years and go, "Well I've done bodybuilding, I've completed it".'

The allure of building the body therefore lies in its incompleteness and the multitude of potential barriers by which gym users can shield themselves from a state of satisfaction. Whether it is one's diet, exercise regime, technique, or sleep that can be improved, a state of absolute accomplishment is inevitably elusive. Luke, discussing the uniqueness of bodybuilding as a sport, also alluded to his drive for bodily dissatisfaction through an admission that it was the training, rather than the actual competitions, that held the appeal:

> 'Bodybuilding is more like a beauty contest than a sport when you think about it. But the training and the nutrition and the gym work, all that stuff that goes into it, there's where the sport is for me. The

preparation that's required to look like that in the first place, that's my favourite part of it.'

Again, this demonstrates the psychic appeal of building the body, as for Luke it is the process of continual striving, rather than the accolades, that constitutes the pleasure of the sport. Further, Scott epitomized the lack-fuelled energy that propelled him to train, admitting, "I do look in the mirror and think, 'bloody hell I look crap today', then I'll go [to] the gym and get the pump and think 'Yeah, I look good'. Then the next morning it's the same again because you haven't got the pump, everything settles back down". The illusory role of the pump – a term for the immediate aftermath of vigorous exercise where the muscles look and feel 'pumped' up – was also discussed by Will, as he complained, "In [the gym] I just feel pumped up, I feel good and happy … but when I leave, I just deflate". Here, the emptiness experienced by the consumer upon acquiring their desired commodity that McGowan (2016) describes is played out in the body as, no sooner than Scott and Will attain a level of bodily *satisfaction*, they subconsciously erect further barriers in the form of bodily *dissatisfaction*. Despite Will's superficial dejection at his enduring bodily lack, he possessed no inclination to disturb the cycle, stating "I don't think I could ever quit; I'll just have to carry on". This resignation captures my sample's inability to cease the excruciating state of jouissance brought on by their carnal manifestation of desire and how, long after their fleeting conversations with me have dissolved from their memories, their bodies will remain a necessarily unfinished project.

The role of IPEDs

Given the body's potency as an object of desire, what role do IPEDs play in my sample's pursuit of bodily goals? These questions are addressed by Hall (2019) as she invokes McGowan's (2016) understanding of desire under consumer capitalism to conceptualize IPEDs as chemical products that stimulate dissatisfaction in the user. She contends that:

> Lifestyle drugs promise to enhance the subject's body and mind in its continuous search for satisfaction through dissatisfaction but can never fully satisfy the underlying sense of lack. This process reproduces the need to continuously search for newer and better products that promise faster and longer-lasting effects. (Hall, 2019: 170)

Hall makes clear that the same energies of continuous desire and dissatisfaction that perpetuate late-capitalism's insatiable appetite for economic growth also drive the consumption of IPEDs. Therefore, following the earlier identification of the body as a stand-in for the lost object, the attraction of

IPEDs lies in their ultimately false *promise* of satiation. Just as McGowan describes the emptiness of the latest consumer objects of desire once they are acquired, the desired corporeal changes brought about by the consumption of AAS, fat burners, or hGH inevitably fail to satisfy the subject's underlying lack once they are reached (Kotzé et al, 2020). Therefore, IPED consumption can be conceptualized as a means of intensifying the state of bodily desire, pushing the physique beyond its natural limits to sustain its status as the substituted *objet petit a*. In short, IPED consumption is the result of the subject desiring too strongly and becoming consumed in the never-ending building of the body as a means of addressing the lack at the heart of their subjectivity.

Phillip explained this to me when I enquired about his decision to start using AAS, stating "I reached a ceiling where I felt that I knew everything that I needed to know about my training and my diet, my mental state and my ability to sleep. … I felt having accumulated all that, now was the time to put in a supplement". Similar narratives of reaching a natural limit or 'ceiling' were common, as aspiring powerlifter Johnny, when asked about the likelihood of IPED consumption in the future, concluded "I think long-term definitely, but naturally I haven't exhausted a good diet and good training protocols yet". This again speaks to my sample's compulsion to continually erect barriers to their satisfaction as, when the natural 'limit' is attained, its hollowness as a means of addressing lack is revealed and IPEDs must be introduced.

Hall (2019: 170) also explains the potent psychic appeal of IPEDs, arguing that, 'when this commodity has a corporeal effect—such as that provided by lifestyle drugs—its function of bringing about a sense of growth, of enhancement, of accumulation, is … further intensified'. This differentiation is crucial in addressing the potency and widespread appeal of IPEDs and was expressed by my sample within their numerous acknowledgements that consumption constitutes "a treadmill" (Neil) that ultimately results in long-term medicalization and negative health implications. Leaning again upon the concept of jouissance, though careful to distance themselves from notions of drug misuse (see Monaghan, 2002), most users were keen to regale an anecdote of a friend or acquaintance whose IPED consumption embodied the damagingly perpetual nature of enhancement. Exemplifying this, David spoke gravely about his client, John:

> 'John's coming down later, he's had a kidney transplant, cancer, heart issues, he's now diabetic. He used to be one of the UK's strongest men, he used to take 500 mg of Anadrol [brand name for the AAS oxymetholone], he used to use 5 mg barrels – normal people use two. He used to use a lot. The reality is that he has spent a good year in hospital, he's had a kidney transplant, he's now diabetic and is extremely depressed because his whole identity was around being a strongman.

> Now he's probably got another three or four years to live and he's in his mid-forties.'

David's account of John, whose unending quest to enhance his strength had left him with life-threatening health issues, speaks to the potency of IPEDs as a means of perpetuating dissatisfaction and the resultant state of corporeal jouissance. Similarly, Ben told me:

> 'I don't just want to have a house full of trophies and nothing else. I know guys who've had good competitive careers but got nothing and their bodies are all used up from all the gear. They've got a shitty little flat with a load of trophies, no wife, no kids – nothing to show for it other than when they go in the gym people say, "He used to be massive".'

Ben's description captures the inevitable long-term effects of constant bodily desire and how a misrepresentation of the *objet petit a*, fuelled by IPED consumption, can ultimately result in a life devoid of any true substance. Though less extreme than David's client or Ben's dour example, within my IPED-using sample the normalization of significantly harmful side effects of consumption was commonplace. Just as easily as the men could list the various compounds and quantities of drugs they consumed, they could also recall the catalogue of physical and mental ailments they experienced as a result. Dom, for example, spoke candidly about his experience of AAS compound trenbolone during our lengthy interview in Predator:

> 'The insomnia that comes with trenbolone, that can be a real fucking battle. That really grinds you, and that's from personal experience as well. Paranoia comes with trenbolone, mixed with insomnia and high levels of test[osterone], that's not something to be [underestimated] for mental health. That's, for example, what pushes people to suicide.'

However, despite this troubling admission, Dom expressed no inclination to cease his consumption, instead viewing the extreme impact of the drug upon his mental health as a necessary evil given its efficaciousness (see Underwood, 2022). This was reflected in David's experiences of the compound, which had left him with enduring psychological impairments. Speaking at his supplement company's headquarters on a drab industrial estate, he told me, "I don't get anxiety attacks, I get – I believe the medical term is manic spells – where I become very erratic and I have to be busy doing things. So it kinda looks like an anxiety attack but it's not. … I never had that before I used trenbolone". Both of these serious repercussions, alongside a multitude of physical impacts ranging from "acne and bad spots" (Sam) through to David being "convinced that [he] was gonna die" from excessive DNP[1] use, illustrate the extreme levels of jouissance that result from the perpetuity of bodily dissatisfaction and the ceaseless reproduction of IPED-fuelled desire. While previous scholarship has documented the serious financial and psychological harms caused by the suspension of desire in practices such as gambling and excessive retail consumption (see Hall et al, 2008; Smith and Raymen, 2018), the lasting bodily damage caused by the physical manifestation of this lack in the enhanced body takes a more noticeable and, arguably, more dangerous form. Thus, by directing the subject's desire to the carnal being itself, IPEDs provide an endless cycle of dissatisfaction and, ultimately, irreversible health implications.

Addiction and desire

Given the role of IPEDs in fuelling the subject's desire for bodily progression, it is also worth addressing addiction and dependence. Although calls for IPEDs, particularly anabolic steroids, to be conceptualized as addictive substances date back to the late 1980s (see Kashkin and Kleber, 1989; Brower et al, 1991), users' dependence has only relatively recently received any robust academic scrutiny (see Quaglio et al, 2009; Tan and Scally, 2009; Kanayama et al, 2009).

Both the IPED-using and non-using populations within my sample acknowledged the psychologically addictive nature of the substances, in line with the orthodox view that they ultimately exacerbate users' underlying bodily insecurity and create a cycle of dependence (see Greenway and Price, 2018). The narrative of psychological addiction provides an important frame within which to highlight the unending nature of bodily enhancement. IPED harm reduction specialist Rob, speaking in relation to his own long-term AAS use, addressed this:

> 'There is a huge psychological dependency [to IPED use] where people feel that they're not a man anymore and there's a paranoia of losing size if they don't take the gear. … The physical becomes so important to you that any damage to that is much more damaging to you as an individual, so you feel like you're losing who you are. So there's a big driver right there to stay on chemicals, because if I don't then I can't retain this physique and I'm no longer anybody. It's something I've been through, going from benching 220 kg for reps and being an absolute monster and every time you walk into a room everyone going, "What the fuck has just walked in here?", to now just being a fat middle-aged bloke who's as weak as a kitten.'

Rob's candid admission is telling, as having substituted the body as the *objet petit a*, his desire was entirely bound up within its perpetual dissatisfaction, to the detriment of "other aspects of [his] personality". However, his distress at having transitioned from being a formidable member of the hardcore fitness community to being "as weak as a kitten" appears to contradict my contention that the subject is wilfully drawn towards bodily dissatisfaction. While, on the face of it, this is a valid critique, the apparent paradox actually illustrates the wretched nature of subjective lack and the need to differentiate between *happiness* and *desire*. Hall (2012a) describes how the constant state of dissatisfaction leaves the subject with an insecure feeling of objectless anxiety. From this, it is clear that a life of perpetual dissatisfaction and suspended desire, while psychically appealing, inevitably leaves the true *objet petit a* unresolved and therefore the subject must continue to live with a gnawing anxiety. Thus, although Rob's significantly decreased bodily capital represents a further source of desire, it simultaneously characterizes a loss of identity that he struggles to grapple with. Rob's experience of corporeal *loss* captures the long-term emptiness of the physique as a stand-in for the lost object and the inherent issue of attaching such meaning to a biological, fallible entity. The inevitable decay of age and wear that it is subject to means that, unlike other objects of desire, it is forever moving away from the subject's efforts of enhancement. However, as was made clear earlier, it is this incomplete nature that endears the body so effectively to the subject's innate sense of lack, and therefore Rob's nostalgia for the period where he was an "absolute monster" reflects his enduring misidentification of the physique as the *objet petit a*.

Atop this psychological dependence, a chemical element of addiction acts to increase IPEDs' potency in accelerating bodily desire. An awareness of this was evident in many of my sample's acknowledgement that their bodies had ceased the natural production of testosterone[2] and therefore, even if their inclination to enhance their physiques were to subside, they would remain reliant upon synthetic hormones. Lee explained:

> 'I don't think I'd ever be able to drop gear completely, at my age and the amount of time I've been using it I'll probably have to stay on a low dose just to maintain libido and keep clarity in my day-to-day functions. I'd need TRT [testosterone replacement therapy]. I think if I dropped it out, I would probably end up being not in the best shape and possibly mental state as well. If my test levels are low that's going to lead to all sorts of issues.'

This acknowledgement was common across my IPED-using sample and the necessity of self-administered TRT is consistent with the existing literature on this population (see Underwood et al, 2020; Christiansen, 2020; Turnock, 2022). Sam conceded, "You'll rarely get a retired bodybuilder who's competed over a number of years that won't have to use TRT. Especially if they're using at an older age. … Me at the age of 60, I'll definitely be on a TRT dosage". Though presented as an easily remedied inconvenience by users like Sam and Lee, the severity of the IPED-consuming population's chemical dependence was emphasized by Rob, as he compared users' reliance upon synthetic hormones to other recreational drugs:

N: You mentioned earlier about an addictive quality to steroids – is that more chemical or psychological?

R: It's both, but I'd say more of a chemical dependency. If you're not producing hormones anymore you haven't got a choice – you need gear otherwise you feel like shit. So if you think about that when it comes to describing addiction, like when I take heroin I don't want to stop because I feel like shit when I don't. If I've got no test[osterone] production then I'm gonna feel like shit, and I'm gonna feel ill and I'm not gonna sleep and feel depressed and emotional – so here's a drug that chemically fixes me.

The severity of users' reliance upon AAS from a chemical, as well as psychological, perspective is striking as, unlike the objects of desire described by McGowan, long-term IPED use also adds a biological component. It is here again that Derrida's (1998) understanding of pharmakon can be applied as the synthetic testosterone in AAS, given its exogenous nature, acts to 'cure' the users' lack of natural testosterone, while simultaneously being the cause of the hormonal deficit in the first instance. This demonstrates the unique nature of IPEDs compared to traditional recreational drugs and how the long-term harms play out. Ultimately, this illustrates the suffering that users are willing to endure to perpetuate their bodily desire and how, given IPEDs' role in perpetuating a state of bodily dissatisfaction, human enhancement so successfully captures the lack at the heart of the subject.

Chapter summary

This initial consumption chapter has served to provide the theoretical underpinning of my exploration into why the men under study engage in hardcore bodywork and use IPEDs. I opted to undertake a bottom-up approach whereby analysis has been undergirded by an investigation of the lack that lies at the heart of the subject. From this foundation, I have argued that a thorough understanding of IPED consumption ought to be grounded in the Lacanian notion of desire, wherein the subject is drawn towards dissatisfaction and consequently erects barriers to its satiation. The body is therefore employed as a substitute for the *objet petit a*, allowing my sample to perpetually strive to improve their physiques in place of addressing the lack that underlies their subjectivity. Therefore, they continually erect new barriers to their bodily satisfaction – in the form of ever-mutating ideals or increasingly challenging goals – as a means of suspending themselves in a constant cycle. In line with this, IPEDs can be understood as a means of perpetuating bodily dissatisfaction, as users are able to desire the increasingly minuscule corporeal improvements promised by chemical enhancement, only to be left seeking further growth when these gains are achieved. This explains the ever-growing cocktail of substances they sought, as well as the jouissance that they underwent because of their suspended desire. Chapter 5 will move on to examine the contextual and environmental motivations that surround my sample, but the reader ought to understand this through the lens of lack and desire described in this chapter, as the foundation set here fundamentally runs beneath the men's contextualized narratives.

5

Instrumentality, Competitiveness, and Hyper-conformity

Building out from Chapter 4's psychoanalytic foundation, we can now turn to the more instrumental motivations as well as the immediate environmental influences that drive my sample's drug use. While I have argued that the need for perpetual dissatisfaction is universal, this chapter looks at the specific contexts in which the motivation to enhance the physique is played out.

Sporting success and the need to win

The most common instrumental motivation behind IPED consumption cited by my sample was a will to win in their sporting endeavours, coupled with the acknowledgement that "everybody else is going to be [using IPEDs]" (Ben). Involvement in competitive sport increases the likelihood of IPED consumption by 91 per cent (Sagoe et al, 2014) and therefore the instrumental use of drugs for athletic success constitutes a mainstay in the existing literature. A typical example of this can be found in my interview with amateur bodybuilder and online coach Sam, when I asked him about his decision to initiate drug use:

N: So when was the moment that you chose to go on cycle for the first time? What drove you to that?

S: Basically, I wanted to win. I wanted to become a pro, but with my genetic make-up if I didn't push onto that next level then it would have taken me a very long time to get there. In competitive bodybuilding it's not illegal, it's not like you're a professional footballer where you'll fail a doping test. So for me it wasn't a decision that I'll cheat, it was just part of the sport.

This excerpt epitomizes the dual themes discussed within this section. First, Sam's privileging of his comparative performance over his long-term health illustrates his deep commitment to the competitive individualistic values of the bodybuilding community (see Kotzé et al, 2020). This dogma was echoed by Dom, who told me "I have an athlete's mindset, a competitive mindset and that's why I do everything that I do". This "athlete's mindset" works in concert with a resignation that "everyone you're up against will be taking gear" (Kyle) to create a perfect storm for competitors, who feel a pressure to use IPEDs to avoid being cut adrift from their fellow contenders (see Grogan et al, 2006). Therefore, driven by hardcore gym culture's injunction to excel and avoid the dishonour of defeat, IPEDs become a mandatory part of "hold[ing] your own on stage" (Josh) (see also Fussell, 1992). Competitive bodybuilder Josh spoke of his consumption in strictly instrumental terms, expressing his disdain for non-competitive users when he argued:

> 'It's pointless screwing your body when you're not competing. … If it was a level playing field, if [IPED consumption] was all completely taken out, then I don't think there'd be anyone using it. But it's not a level playing field so you're going to have to [use IPEDs] really.'

Were it not for the instrumental gain that results from "screwing your body", Josh would prefer not to use enhancement drugs. However, he feels that the burden of sporting performance outweighs his long-term health. Thus, as the proverbial genie has been out of the bottle within competitive bodybuilding and other strength sports for over six decades (Toohey and Veal, 2000; Kremenik et al, 2006), the competitive athletes in my sample unanimously conceded that "you'd be stupid not to [use IPEDs]" (Tim) within untested events, where consumption is fundamentally "part of the sport" (Sam). This was echoed by David, who described the moment he first discovered the ubiquity of IPED use in competitive strongman events:

> 'I started in strongman at 21. I did my first competition and turned up and everyone was like, "What have you had?". I was like, "I had two coffees and like four flapjacks". And they were like, "What are you talking about? We meant gear". That was 2009 and they were all talking about what steroids they were taking, and I remember being annoyed that I believed all the bullshit [about natural athletes] and within four weeks I was on my first ever cycle.'

David's recollection captures the reality that, far from perceiving themselves as deviant, the use of IPEDs in the context of competitive strength sports in fact echoes the prevailing values of individual attainment and *amour propre* (Hall et al, 2008) within the hardcore fitness community. For this reason, users like Dom, Sam, and Josh's consumption ought not to be castigated as inherently deviant, transgressive behaviour, but instead understood to reflect the values of their peers and the commercial interests of competition organizers (Hughes and Coakley, 1991; Waddington and Smith, 2009; Matthews and Jordan, 2020). This speaks to the normalization of IPED consumption within the bodybuilding community (see Parker et al, 1998; Turnock, 2018) and how this cultural context is crucial to consider in relation to my sample's use (van de Ven and Mulrooney, 2017; Turnock, 2021a).

This somewhat throws into question the actual *enhancement* offered by the substances themselves. Drug use in this context more closely echoes Conrad and Potter's (2004) notion of biomedically enhanced normalization. Conrad and Potter assert that normalization, in this sense, refers to users bringing the body in line with prevailing norms or standards, and therefore, as Josh's consumption functions to level the playing field, it creates a measure of fairness rather than advantage (see also Hoberman, 2005). Therefore, sporting arenas such as bodybuilding shows and powerlifting competitions can be described as 'dopogenic environments' (Backhouse et al, 2018), as they foster a sense of legitimacy and acceptance of use as well as connecting competitors with like-minded bodyworkers to whom they can assimilate their drug use. However, looking beyond this basic definition, the events can also be described as dopogenic due to their efficiency in perpetuating athletes' bodily desire. My sporting participants' constant concern for their fellow competitors' physiques – under the guise of "checking out the opposition" (Luke) – illustrates the impact of the physical environment on the stimulation of desire, as the multitude of built bodies provides the men with a means of erecting yet more barriers to their satisfaction.

"My physique ... is my advertisement for my business": the importance of enhanced bodily capital for health and fitness professionals

Throughout my time in the field, it became evident that a range of employment opportunities availed themselves to those with 'boosted' bodily capital (Kotzé and Antonopoulos, 2019). These roles often centred on the precarious health and fitness industry, which many of my IPED-using sample worked in as PTs, online coaches, and gym staff. As was noted in Chapter 2, the health and fitness industry has "blown up" (Tim) in Potsford and, given the collapse of the city's hubs of production, constitutes a seductive avenue of employment for the city's many bodyworkers. Within this context, and particularly given the ocular nature of the sector, my sample continually stressed the importance of their bolstered bodily capital as a means of attracting and retaining clients. On this, aspiring bodybuilder Josh conceded, "When it comes down to it, you need the look". According to Ed, this 'look', which is broadly in line with the prevailing masculine body ideals (see Wagner, 2017), has grown increasingly important in marketing online coaching and PT services, as "potential clients will look to people who are in good shape to help them, because it shows that they know what they're talking about". Ed's chemically enhanced bodily capital therefore functions as proof that he is capable of enacting similar corporeal development in his clients, despite the fact that a layperson, even with the aid of IPEDs, could not realistically achieve his physique without years of sustained bodywork and ascetic dieting. Therefore, according to Sam, "My physique, in effect, is my advertisement for my business". This striking statement echoes Hutson's (2013) finding that health and fitness professionals' bodies constitute their 'business card', fostering trust and respect from their clients and offering a physical depiction of their qualification.

Delving deeper, however, Sam's corporeal 'advertisement' arguably functions as the object of desire for his customers, as they purchase his expertise on the promise of similar bodily growth. The coach–client relationship is therefore, to some extent, premised on what Girard (1979) terms 'mimetic desire', the suggestion that desire is stimulated not from within but instead is best understood as coveting others' looks or possessions. As such, the PTs and online coaches I encountered marketed themselves as manifestations of the desirable and largely unattainable ideals discussed earlier and their services therefore fed upon their clients' underlying lack. They described the cyclical nature of their relationship with their clients, whose motivation inevitably waxed and waned throughout the year, rendering their long-term progress minimal. However, if the clients ultimately did not desire the attainment of their bodily goals, working under a coach with an idealized physique was perhaps more of an attraction than bodily progression itself. Therefore, the professionals whose physiques most closely echo these bodily ideals are more attractive to prospective customers. Bemoaning this, Paul told me, "It used to be your client's change in appearance that led to them coming to see you, so they wouldn't necessarily give a shit how you looked. But now it's your body that attracts the clients, you can't separate the two". Paul's resentment was mirrored by Dom, who admitted:

> 'I've had people come up to me and say "I wouldn't go to so and so for PT because they look like this" or they're not in shape. By all means you don't have to be in shape to know what you're talking about, and anybody in shape doesn't necessarily know what they're talking about, but that's the perception. … But it's a complete assumption that they come to me rather than the overweight or the skinny guy in the corner, who might have a PhD in sports science or mobility or whatever. But because they don't look the part not everybody will go to them. That puts a lot of pressure on you, so you have to train and stay in shape yourself. Even as small a pressure as that might be, it's

still a pressure in the back of your mind thinking, "If I get fat or out of shape am I gonna get as many clients?"'

Dom's acknowledgement epitomizes the sacrosanct role of the body as a means of attracting business, as well as the superficiality of the health and fitness market. In this context, the worked-on body can be read as a means of self-branding (Lair et al, 2005; Khamis et al, 2017), wherein the PTs and online coaches treat their physiques as products that can be sold to their customer base (Marwick, 2015). As such, they are in a constant state of bodily self-promotion, as Sam explained:

> 'That's my bugbear about the industry. You get a lot of guys who might not know a lot, but they'll be in awesome shape and get a load of clients because of that, but they're rubbish coaches. Then on the other hand I've worked with world-class strength and conditioning coaches and if they were on social media they just wouldn't get the clients because they don't come across as marketable. So it's having to play that game of marketing yourself and doing what you think is right to draw people in.'

For my sample, this "game of marketing" was largely played out on SNS, as Ed explained that to be successful in the industry, one has to have a "nice physique and be good at marketing [oneself] on social media". Echoing this, Sam continued:

> 'It frustrates a lot of people who are qualified and have gone through degrees and all that, who can't get a good following because they don't look the part. Then someone who's got one hundred thousand followers and posts photos of themselves looking ripped, they can create a client base in a day.'

This again demonstrates the privileging of image over ability. But how does the importance of a self-branded physique relate to my sample's IPED consumption? And why is marketing the corporeal self such a pressing concern?

The answer to both of these questions concerns the precarity of many roles within the health and fitness industry and the subsequent anxiety experienced by this predominantly self-employed population. In his earlier admission, Dom describes the "pressure" brought about by a reliance upon the biological form as a basis for one's branding and how, if he were to become "fat or out of shape", his income may be negatively affected. By nature, the body is a highly unstable entity through which to market oneself, as the unenhanced physique fluctuates depending on the season, whether one is bulking or cutting, and even what time of the day it is presented. As a result, for men whose branded identity is premised on 'the look', a constant, cloying anxiety underpins their marketing strategy. This pressure is compounded by the precarious nature of many roles within the health and fitness industry, particularly within post-industrial locales like Potsford. On this, Ed acknowledged, "It can be terrifying if the work isn't there. Especially in the winter months when everything fitness takes a dip". Ed's words speak to the seasonal nature of the market and the reality that, during the dreaded pre-Christmas period, attracting and retaining clients is particularly challenging. Interestingly, in their work on doping in professional cycling, Aubel and Ohl (2014) describe a similar pressure on athletes given the precarious careers of competitors and the economic security that illicit enhancement can bring. Most notably in this study, the series of national and local COVID-19 lockdowns during the latter part of my fieldwork exposed the true job instability and precarity in the lives of men like Ed and Dom. Discussing this in our follow up interview in November 2020, Ed admitted:

> 'The first lockdown was tricky, and I did take a bullet where I lost a few clients. The focus became trying to survive and just retain the clients I had. Then after that, because I haven't really had access to anything in regard to self-employment support from the government, I knew I just had to try and get as many clients as possible. I think where some coaches have gone wrong has been that they've treated it as a time to slack off, when in fact it's a time where you have to be as on it as ever.'

Ed's unenviable predicament demonstrates the lack of financial support available to this cohort throughout the pandemic. Indeed, he temporarily took up a job at his local supermarket during the second national lockdown. However, he retained an upbeat, self-justifying positivity while discussing this instability, particularly as he emphasized the importance of not "slack[ing] off". In line with his self-branded persona, it appeared that the injunction to perpetually sell himself even bled into our interview, as he enthusiastically repeated the symbolically violent language of neoliberalism, wilfully ignorant of the structural factors that had left him in a position of occupational precarity. Set against this, the use of IPEDs represents a means of bolstering job security and successfully competing in a highly saturated market. Therefore, to some extent, the drugs counteract the inherent instability of the body as a basis for a brand, and give the men heightened control over their commodified image.

It is here that we must address another fundamental question; what exactly is *performance enhancement* within this context? Unlike conventional conceptualizations of increased capability in the sporting arena and 'doping', for health and fitness professionals, their enhancement was predominantly carried out to stay afloat and compete within the health and fitness market. As such, IPED consumption in this context can be seen as fundamentally in line with the prevailing values of neoliberal capital accumulation. This is discussed by Kotzé and Antonopoulos (2019) in terms of *hyper-conformity*, as they extend the notion of instrumental use to encompass the advantages of an enhanced physique as a means of competing in the late-capitalist system. Therefore, users like Ed, Dom, and Sam illustrate a deep commitment to the values of neoliberal capitalism and, quite literally, embody this in their marketable frames (Marshall et al, 2020; Rothmann, 2022). However, while Kotzé and Antonopoulos (2019) present this hyper-conformity entirely through the lens of *consumption*, within my sample, the enhanced physique operated as a means of *production*, or more accurately prosumption, enabling them to instrumentally market their services like a curriculum vitae (see Turnock, 2018). Therefore, their hyper-conformity can best be understood as reflecting the 'entrepreneurial ethic' (Kotzé and Antonopoulos, 2019: 9) of late-capitalism, and their IPED consumption can be read as a means of adding value to their corporeal asset.

This is supported by Hall (2019), as she critiques the suggestion that IPED consumption is a subcultural activity. Hall argues that, on the level of values, users are essentially aligned with the dominant edicts of late-capitalism. This is not to say that the hardcore fitness community do not constitute a group with their own norms and cultural practices. Rather, the core ethos of perpetual self-promotion and the monetization of the self precludes any suggestion that IPED consumption contradicts the values of the system. Digging deeper, if men like Ed feel a reliance upon their enhanced bodies to solicit business, could the cut-throat health and fitness industry, and the broader local economy of Potsford, be considered a dopogenic environment itself? If one must rely upon one's bodily capital to stay afloat and remain at all times "on it" (Ed), does this economic backdrop not encourage IPED use? For some of my sample, the precarity of their employment was an important factor in their consumption and therefore any advantage which allowed them to better build their brand was potentially the difference between relative prosperity and struggling to stay afloat. This illuminates the relationship between performance enhancement and late-capitalism as, it can be concluded, the enhanced self is better equipped to compete in the 24/7 show of self-promotion and rugged individualism that is demanded (Crary, 2014). Ultimately, this speaks to the instrumentality of human enhancement in a far broader sense than simply the professions under study in this section, a thread that is picked up by Mann (2021, 2022) in relation to cognitive enhancement. Mann argues that enhancement drug use can be viewed as a 'functional' response to the underlying neoliberal context, much like my sample's employment of IPEDs as a means of economic advancement and job precarity mitigation. This represents a fruitful avenue for future research on human enhancement drugs and their relationship with the political economy.

Chapter summary

Building out from the foundation set in Chapter 4, this chapter has examined the importance of place and context in my sample's IPED consumption. It is clear that involvement in competitive strength sports directly drives consumption and that, as Backhouse et al (2018) conclude, spaces of hardcore fitness constitute 'dopogenic environments'. Beyond this however, a number of my sample used IPEDs to gain enhanced bodily capital that worked instrumentally to increase their occupational marketability. Focusing specifically on PTs and online coaches, I have demonstrated the sacrosanct nature of the self-branded body within this highly ocular market, and the subsequent draw of illicit enhancement. Ultimately, IPED consumption as a means of better marketing the self and competing in the health and fitness industry demonstrates a hyper-conformity to the values of competitive individualism, and maximal capital accumulation that characterize neoliberalism and can be viewed as a functional response to the hegemonic neoliberal context of use.

6

The Pleasures of Consumption: The Curious Case of Phillip

Following on from the investigation of instrumentality, competitiveness, and hyper-conformity, this chapter turns to Mulrooney et al's (2019: 3) contention that an acknowledgement of pleasure constitutes 'an essential part of a coherent and reasoned response to steroid consumption'. As such, the following analysis will examine the chemical, symbolic, and psychic pleasures of IPED consumption through the case study of Phillip, the project's oldest participant and ardent 'lifestyle' user.

Introducing Phillip

Arriving uncharacteristically early to the retail park which housed the Costa Coffee I was to meet Phillip at, I turned off the car engine and instinctively checked my phone. As the drone of BBC Radio Potsford's daily phone-in was cut short, I messaged Phillip on Facebook to let him know of my arrival. No sooner had I sent the message, Phillip had replied to say that he was sat inside by the window, having still managed to beat me there. At this, I picked up my Dictaphone and other essentials and rushed through the icy air into the refuge of the coffee shop.

Phillip waved me down immediately, his dyed black hair shimmering under the glow of a nearby lamp as he sipped his coffee. Broad-shouldered and immaculately dressed, he clasped my hand in a firm handshake and, once I'd ordered and received my drink, broke energetically into a sweeping monologue about his enthusiasm for my area of research, before grilling me on my methodological approach and academic career plans. Initially taken aback by this beguiling start, we soon settled into the well-versed debate around the relative worth of qualitative and quantitative research and my rather messy approach to data collection.

> Dictaphone set to record and settled into my flimsy metallic chair, it was time to interview this man whom Paul had assured me would add something 'different' to my data. (Extract from fieldnotes, 11/03/20)

The first point to mention about Phillip was his choice of career, which immediately explains his fascination with the minutiae of my methodology. Nicknamed 'The Doc' in Muscle Sanctuary, Phillip is a retired biology professor whose illustrious academic career has seen him employed by several prestigious universities in the UK. During his preamble to our interview, he ran me through his career trajectory:

> 'I have a BSc in [redacted],[1] I did my PhD in [redacted] and I was working in [redacted] and I then had an academic career with the research council. I worked with them for about 21 years in different research institutions. … I became Head of Department and managed a large team of people and then moved to [a well-respected red brick university]. … I retired last summer. I published a lot of papers in my thirties and forties and I travelled the world, and that was one of the most enjoyable times of my life. Then later on in my career I managed people and taught hundreds and hundreds of students.'

However, it was not Phillip's enviable academic career that had motivated me to reach out to him, but his decision to enter the world of competitive bodybuilding in his early sixties. It was here that our interview began in earnest, as I asked him, brow furrowed, what had led a successful scientist into the typically anti-intellectual pursuit of building the body:

> 'I've always been interested in sport. I've been a surfer and a kite surfer all my life and when I was a teenager I was a rock climber and climbed many places in the world. Then in my late thirties and forties I became a fell runner and I was an over-40 and over-50 world champion. But I got to a point where I had run enough, I ran a million miles and I thought, "That's it, I'm gonna give up running". I remember I was competing in an ultra-distance event and we'd been racing against these guys from North Wales who were old but were very hard to beat. But they were like a bag of bones, like wiry old guys and I remember saying, "I don't want to look like that".'

Following this glimpse of the long-term aesthetics of ultra-distance running, Phillip subsequently changed tack:

> 'After that I used to train in gyms just to keep up my fitness and people would come up to me and go, "Excuse me sir, do you mind me asking

> how old you are?", and they'd make a comment about how good my body was for an old guy. Eventually, a couple of guys came up to me and said, "Have you ever thought of competing as a bodybuilder?" I looked online, went and did my first competition and won it. … I felt like at that stage in my life I was living a very healthy lifestyle, I was a WADA[2]-compliant natural and felt like the lifestyle I decided to lead for a guy in his early sixties was a sensible way of approaching those years. I was retaining lean muscle at a time where I should have been losing it, I felt like I could either drink and not do much like a lot of old guys do and become miserable like a grumpy old man, or I could achieve something. When I won that first title it was such a fantastic feeling and I just felt like this is the right thing to do. It gives you a huge emotional boost as an over-60 male who's approaching retirement. I followed that path religiously as a natural athlete for that time and I was very successful.'

Phillip's initial forays into competitive bodybuilding stemmed from several chance encounters in the gym where he received praise for his age-defying appearance and was encouraged to enter a local contest. His meteoric rise as a natural competitor, motivated by his determination to "achieve something" as an older man, can be interpreted in line with his long-standing aspiration for excellence, and illustrates his focus on personal attainment. Beyond this instrumentality however, during this period Phillip took great pleasure in feeling "healthy and strong" alongside the psychological benefits that accompanied this as an older man, and this appeared to be his principal motivation to compete. However, this rather idyllic picture was ultimately unable to satisfy his bodily desire and, from this straightforward narrative of bodybuilding as a "sensible" form of leisure, Phillip's exposure to the hardcore fitness community, coupled with his long-standing competitive individualist world view, soon led him, in his rather coy words, to "taking gear just like all the other meatheads are".

"I saw what happens when you compete in your seventies": enhancing the aging body on stage and 'responsible' consumption

At first glance, Phillip's reasons for chemical enhancement appear misplaced in this chapter, as the same steely, ultra-competitive instrumentality that dominated Ben, Dom, and Ed's motivations were evident in his initial decision to use:

> 'What happened was, I got to know all of the over-seventies athletes who compete in the natural federations, the best of them in the world. I had been on stage with most of them and I saw what happens

> when you compete in your seventies. An over-seventies athlete who's trying to strike a pose would do that [half-heartedly lifts arms above head] and would struggle to get their arm all the way up. I saw, in the over-seventy athletes, that they couldn't do it any longer. … Anyway, I looked at my genetics and my physiology and had medical tests done, and … after my final [drugs-tested competition] in 2016, I decided to start self-administering testosterone, which I have now been doing since then. But I did it from a very informed basis, I did it with sports scientists at the university and my personal goal was to get into my seventies but still be able to have that mobility.'

Phillip placed his initial decision to consume testosterone firmly within the realm of enhanced performance, as his repudiation of the idea that he may be unable to perform basic bodybuilding poses was motivation enough to seek chemical assistance. His formative use in 2016 can be seen to be essentially goal-oriented (William and Taylor, 2002), allowing him to maintain the suppleness that his comparatively younger physique afforded him, and achieve the "personal goal" of "get[ting] into my seventies but still be[ing] able to have that mobility". In this regard, Phillip instrumentally set his sights on beating "the best of them in the world" and viewed chemical enhancement as a means to an end in this pursuit.

Opposing the other sporting motivations discussed earlier however, Phillip concertedly framed his use within a narrative of expertise and academic rigour, taking great care to emphasize the medical tests that ensured that he consumed IPEDs from a "very informed basis" under the supervision of qualified sports scientists. Phillip conceptualized himself as an 'expert' user (Christiansen et al, 2017; Macho et al, 2021), which was demonstrable in his eagerness to inform me, "I'm doing it for a very different reason to all of the other people who you've spoken to". This self-identification as a fundamentally 'different' IPED consumer was evident too in his linguistic choices, as he opted to describe his drug taking as "self-administering testosterone" in order to overplay the medicalization of the consumption process, portraying the act not as one of "taking gear" (Ben), but as a clinical procedure. Phillip made clear that his consumption was "informed through reading all the scientific literature" as, unlike swathes of the bodybuilding community (see Underwood, 2017; Mulrooney et al, 2019; Gibbs et al, 2022b), he held faith in medical and scientific institutions and advocated for a controlled, low-risk approach to use. He furthered his self-identification with the expert type through a continual denigration of other less responsible users, as he put himself in contradistinction from many nameless ill-informed drug takers:

> 'I've had many conversations with men who've taken drugs in gyms, and I've often said to them, "What was your testosterone level before

> you started?" They look at me blankly and I say to them, "So you won't ever know if you come off the gear whether you're going back to how you were before you started then?"... They're so clueless about it that they didn't even think to measure everything before they made that first injection.'

Phillip's assessment of other users as 'clueless' compared to his regimented consumption is reminiscent of Monaghan's (2002) finding that IPED users develop a specific vocabulary to play down the harm or severity of their actions. In keeping with this, Phillip painted himself as a responsible and informed user compared to the unidentified reckless other. Admittedly, considering Phillip's elite academic background and understanding of human physiology, the risk attached to his enhancement was limited, as was confirmed in a later interview by IPED harm reduction specialist Aaron, who conceded, "If you're just doing relatively small doses, it's not going to do a great deal of harm and the long-term effects don't really matter at that age". This was reflected in Phillip's offhand remark that, "If it ultimately means that I pick up an issue in my eighties, who cares?" as, following his typically scientific mindset, he had calculated that the relative risk of harm was offset by the pleasurable benefits.

"I am my own living experiment": the medicalization of old age and mastery of nature

Although Phillip's initial motivation to enhance his testosterone levels can be understood as a form of sports performance, the subsequent effects he experienced led his consumption away from the instrumentality of bodybuilding and into the realm of medicalization and pleasurable lifestyle enhancement. Central to Phillip's thesis was his argument that, for healthy older men, enhancing one's testosterone levels can not only boost mobility and muscle mass, but also reverse the decline of libido and energy levels brought about by waning natural testosterone:

> 'We all reach this point when we go downhill, and the downward graph is strength, speed, intelligence, fitness, power, muscle mass – we're on a slippery slope. Some years ago, when I was married to my wife, who was a consultant, a gynaecologist, she used to talk about getting her HRT [hormone replacement therapy] when she was 55. I talked with my fellow scientists at [redacted] and we discussed why it is that our wives are on HRT when they reach the menopause, and yet men who are post-menopausal and are beginning this slippery slope can't access TRT because it's not recommended by the NICE guidelines. The reason they don't is because many of them have got cardiovascular

disease and diabetes, so the recommendation for the population as a whole is no TRT. Yes, if you've had testicular cancer you get TRT, but we recognize that in the UK there is a group of over 30/40/50 men, and I was an over-60 example, who've looked after themselves all their lives – who've never been overweight or smoked or drunk excessively – but can't get TRT. I knew when I won my title there was only one way I was going to go, and it wasn't to go and join the over-70 old guys. So we decided that we would kind of use me as a case study and then try and present an argument that if you are a fit and healthy over-50 or 60-year-old male and your wife is getting HRT, and she says, "Let's go to the Caribbean for three weeks and do a windsurfing holiday", and you say, "No no, why don't we just stay at home and potter round the garden?" because your testosterone levels are bottoming out – why shouldn't you get some testosterone as well and say, "Yeah, and we'll do some motocross as well or we'll get some mountain bikes"? Why shouldn't you be able to live your life to the full as an older man if you're fit and healthy?'

It is first worth stressing that the current scientific literature supports Phillip's contention that men experience a natural reduction in their testosterone levels as they age (Hoberman, 2005; Andersson et al, 2007; Travison et al, 2009) and a growing body of work now exists to examine this relatively new-found phenomenon of self-medicated TRT (see Underwood et al, 2020; Dunn et al, 2022; Harvey et al, 2021; Turnock, 2022). Begley et al's (2017) UK National IPED Survey found that 7.8 per cent of male users employed drugs as a means of hormone replacement. Although it is important to acknowledge that a diversity of motivations may lie behind this use, these data suggest that Phillip is not alone in employing IPEDs as a means of remedying declining testosterone levels or 'low-T' (Dunn et al, 2022: 2). However, unlike Underwood et al's (2020) sample of online forum and SNS users, who sought AAS to remedy their self-diagnosed low-T as young men, Phillip situated his advocacy for self-administered TRT firmly within the discourse of anti-aging. This is discussed by Kimergård (2015: 289), as he notes that one of his AAS-using sample's auxiliary motivations for consumption was 'maintain[ing] appearance when getting older', given the potency of substances like testosterone and hGH in combatting the natural degradation of users' muscle mass and restoring energy and drive (Perls, 2009; Sattler, 2013).

Phillip highlighted what he perceived as the gendered hormonal health inequality between aging men and women (see Hoberman, 2005). This discord led him to advance an argument for the *medicalization* of the male aging process, as he volunteered his body as "a case study" through which to combat the natural degradation of the corporeal self and set a scientific precedent for other fit and healthy older men. While Gruman (2003) notes that anti-aging is far from a contemporary phenomenon, Dunn et al (2022) contend that contemporary society somewhat conflates the natural physiological decline of the body with the discourses of disease and infirmity (see also Fleming, 2019; McGee, 2020). Within the medical community, de Grey (2005: S49) pejoratively conceptualizes the aging process as 'the lifelong accumulation of various intrinsic side effects of normal metabolic processes, which ultimately … disrupts metabolism and causes severe dysfunction of tissues and the whole organism'. Viewed this way, *natural* aging is seen as something of a contradiction in terms and thus becomes a malady to be overcome and mitigated against, particularly through a chemically driven 'discourse of healing' (Askew and Williams, 2021). It is this perspective that Phillip can be seen to be adhering to in his central argument for regenerative TRT. This is evident throughout his account, as he painted the natural process of bodily aging as a "slippery slope", where one's "strength, speed, intelligence, fitness, power [and] muscle mass" are steadily eroded and replaced by the symbolic death of withdrawing from public life and "potter[ing] round the garden". Before unpacking this however, it should be stressed that this analysis does not set out to deride Phillip's displeasure at the realities of aging. Instead, it is his refusal to accept this natural decline and subsequent motivation to prolong a youthful, efficient physique through medicalized means that is of interest here.

Phillip acknowledged that his natural testosterone levels for a man of his age "were not low or anything" prior to his IPED consumption and therefore, he told me, there was "no doubt whatsoever in my mind, it is performance enhancement". This statement, as well as reflecting his fixation with competitive attainment, placed Phillip's use within the realm of medicalization as he problematized his natural, ostensibly healthy, bodily decline and instead sought to feel 'better than well' (McVeigh et al, 2012: 186). This mindset was reflected in his earlier question, "Why shouldn't you be able to live your life to the full as an older man if you're fit and healthy?" Phillip therefore viewed enhancement as a means of corporeal 'repair' (Conrad and Potter, 2004), as it enabled him to stave off the 'slippery slope' of old age and maximize the pleasures and prestige attached to his physique. This is reflective of Christiansen et al's (2017) 'well-being' type IPED user as, although he demonstrates 'expert' type qualities, Phillip's motivations are fundamentally in line with an ethic of enhanced lifestyle. This medicalized ethos extended to other, licit means of anti-aging:

> 'Do I look 67? There's a good reason for that, I go to a cosmetic surgeon and he takes the clock back 20 years by treating my face. … In all honesty if you were to say to me, do you bother with moisturizer? Nah, Botox works mate. Also, things like general sports supplements,

> I take a few of them. But stuff like BCAAs [branched-chain amino acids[3]]? No. Dianabol, because that actually does something.'

Here, Phillip's conviction to medicalized anti-aging was particularly evident as, reflecting Kraska et al's (2010: 181) contention that biomedical enhancement reflects an ethic of 'immediate gratification', he jettisoned what he perceived as ineffective substances in favour of more potent alternatives. This, again, speaks to Phillip's medicalized *lifestyle* enhancement, as he sought out a 'pill for every ill' (McVeigh et al, 2012: 186), extending his concern beyond his muscles to encompass his skin, hair, and teeth.

Within my sample, this mindset was certainly not unique to Phillip. Ben told me that, following his competing years, his "priority will be trying to de-age" using a combination of AAS and hGH. Phillip was, however, unique in his self-perception as a medicalized specimen or, in his words, "my own living experiment" (see Bloor et al, 2005). This approach to biomedical enhancement was captured in his candid self-analysis at the close of our interview:

> 'I'm doing it because I can, and I can't help myself … that's my personality. I'm a scientist, I'm doing an experiment on myself like I have been doing for years and this is definitely an extension of that. When I was a kid, I had two laboratories in my attic, I was either going to be an electronic engineer or a biologist. So from a very early age I was a scientist and I was doing experiments in my own little way, I don't see this as much different.'

Phillip therefore placed his penchant for enhancement within his wider identity as a scientist and conceptualized his IPED consumption as an extension of his academic career. Beyond the immediate conclusion that his latest project simply represented a means of combatting the perceived obsolescence of retirement however, Phillip's experimentation with the natural aging process speaks to a far more deep-rooted discourse of human mastery over nature that is fundamental to this epoch of liberalism. Deneen (2018: 35, italics added) notes that a cornerstone of the current hegemonic ideology of liberalism is the injunction that 'man should employ natural science and a transformed economic system to seek *mastery over nature*'. This is in line with the contemporary privileging of selfhood over all other aspects of life (Milbank and Pabst, 2016), wherein individual sovereignty is understood as epicentral and inalienable. Phillip, therefore, adhered to thinkers like Buchanan's (2011) deeply liberal notion that scientifically led intervention in natural processes is a human inevitability. His substantial efforts to reverse the aging process and subvert his body's natural degradation represented his concerted attempt to declare 'war on nature' (Deneen, 2018: 26). Thus,

Phillip's steadfast refusal to 'go grey, retire, and mow the grass' speaks to an underlying liberal hubris that humans singlehandedly have agency over their existence (Sandel, 2007). Therefore, Phillip's statement, "I don't want to get old just yet because I've had a great life so far and I want to keep going while I can" fundamentally illustrates a disregard for everything but his personal well-being because, after all, why should a minor inconvenience like aging get in the way of his enjoyment?

Testosterone as a gateway to the good life of 'perma-adolescence'

Having unpacked Phillip's antagonistic relationship to his body's natural decline, it is crucial to answer some pivotal questions about his relationship to the drugs he injected. Before exploring this pivotal question, however, it is worth painting a fuller picture of Phillip's lifestyle and, more importantly, the image he liked to broadcast to his 416 Instagram followers. Following his retirement, Phillip's attentions were myopically focused upon the upkeep of his chiselled physique and his even more chiselled sports car, and it was these two objects that constituted the main themes of his SNS posts. Devoid of any close family and long-since divorced, he wholeheartedly carried his professional focus upon attainment and perpetual betterment into these pursuits and, drawing on a seemingly endless reserve of capital, lived his life in transit between gyms, airports, and his towering rural home. Phillip summed himself up most accurately when he told me, "To put me into context, it was my 67th birthday recently and I spent the morning driving an E-type Jaguar around the Warwickshire countryside and then in the evening I went to a lecture about George Mallory and the Everest expedition of 1920". This recollection of his 'perfect day', as he described it, illustrates Phillip's yearning to feel his experiences intensely (see Greif, 2017) and, to draw upon popular Instagram parlance, to *live his best life*.

Given this context, Phillip's motivation to chemically enhance his body can be understood as the epitome of lifestyle drug use (Hall and Antonopoulos, 2016). His consumption, therefore, represented an enhancement of *existence itself*. This sentiment was captured perfectly in his earlier fictitious example of a holiday in the Caribbean, where he placed his testosterone level as the fundamental difference between "potter[ing] around the garden" and engaging in extreme sports. This is reminiscent of Macho et al's (2021) conceptualization of IPEDs as a means of unlocking the 'extraordinary self', wherein, to borrow John Hoberman's (2005) phraseology, Phillip played out his 'testosterone dreams' through this drug consumption. Throughout Phillip's account, enhanced testosterone was bestowed with the status of an elixir of youth, providing him with the lust for life that he perceived the aging process to be gradually stealing away:

> 'I'm [taking AAS] partly because I'm interested in competing again, but to a greater extent I'm more interested in the quality of my life and being able to do things. I live on my own, if I do something, I'm doing it on my own. If you're on your own and you are going to go on holiday, it's very easy to talk yourself out of it and not do it, and you can just get very down in the dumps. But one of the benefits of having elevated testosterone is having more get up and go. I think when I started out doing it, I was thinking about bodybuilding, but the result for me has been that it has improved my ability to just go and do stuff.'

Phillip's description of AAS' significance in encouraging him "to just go and do stuff" speaks to his conceptualization of IPEDs as broader lifestyle-enhancing substances. Considering his esteemed career and the attendant opportunities to travel and impact the world he was privy to as a younger man, Phillip viewed his enhanced testosterone as a means of reclaiming these past victories and constructing (or extending) the good life in spite of his old age. Phillip appeared to imbue his youthful past with an intense desire, as it sat (dis)satisfyingly out of his reach despite his efforts to chemically recreate it. The pleasure he derived from his, quite literally, testosterone-fuelled lifestyle was captured in his recollection of his most recent trip abroad, as he told me:

> 'If you look back through my Instagram, you'll see that I went to Miami for a month and had a fantastic time. If it weren't for coronavirus, I would be shipping my [sports car] out to the States in June, driving across America in it and then going to Pebble Beach. Then I'd go and have a coaching session with my driving coach. … I am certain that if I had let my testosterone levels be normal … I would probably not bother to do that. It makes me more likely to do something rather than not do something, it livens you up.'

This excerpt perfectly captures the status that Phillip afforded his elevated testosterone in his self-constructed good life. It is immediately clear that his ego ideal (Lacan, 1997), that is to say Phillip's idealized conception of himself in society's eyes, revolves around this description of taking in the vistas of Miami through his high-performance sports car's windscreen, evoking the culturally ascendent ideals of liberty and wanderlust. Crucially, Phillip positioned his chemical assistance as the object through which his ego ideal could be realized, imbuing the synthetic testosterone he injected into his body with a great significance. In his eyes therefore, without the "get up and go" that lay within the vial of testosterone he consumed each week, his ego ideal would remain an abstraction, or a fleeting, soon-dismissed thought that flittered dimly through his mind as he "clean[ed] the garage then [had] a sit down". Instead, with the aid of his enhanced testosterone (and despite governmental advice), Phillip spent the Christmas of 2020 in a luxury apartment in Dubai, triumphantly posting photo and video content of his lifestyle of conspicuous consumption (Veblen, 2005) for his followers. Thus, his enhanced testosterone levels, as he saw it, set him in distinction from the "miserable … grumpy old" men sheltering from the virus in their prison-like sheds and garages, and instead delivered him to a life of unencumbered sensation gathering (Bauman, 1997) and high-end commodified leisure (Raymen and Smith, 2019b).

This fantasy state was also intimately tied to his sensuality, whereby Phillip's heightened testosterone levels further recreated the experiential aspects of his youth through an adolescent-like libido:

> 'I remember when I first started using testosterone, sex was all I was thinking about all the time- I was like, "Switch this off" [laughs]. There was a significant sexual improvement when I took testosterone, to the extent that I honestly could have done with a couple of nice 20-year-old girls who would pop round and see me every night.'

Phillip sought to transcend the natural decline in sex drive that accompanies the aging process and instead positioned his lifestyle as more akin to the hedonistic exploits of younger men. This further example of Phillip's 'testosterone dreams' paints his sexual activity as something of a performance, echoing Hoberman's (2005: 8) description of '[d]rug-induced sexual fitness' whereby Phillip's libido and virility are enhanced in preparation for the 'intimate competitive sport' of love making. As well as signalling his absolute commitment to medicalized lifestyle enhancement, this further illustrates Phillip's valorization of youth and the indulgent, excessive physicality that he found lacking without the aid of IPEDs. Ultimately, the object that lay between the decrepit, sexless wastefulness of old age and the prolongation of the good life of youth and virility for Phillip was the testosterone that he used, and it was this commodity that in effect protected his ego ideal from irretrievable obscurity.

However, Phillip's consumption not only allowed him to enact his version of the good life, but also afforded him an enhanced experiential viscerality in the form of heightened confidence and assertiveness. Existing literature suggests that AAS consumption can provide users with a 'confidence boost' (Hanley Santos and Coomber, 2017: 37) wherein users experience a fundamental shift in their outlook and self-concept. This experience of heightened self-confidence and forthrightness was present across my sample, as Dom asserted, "Testosterone will give you the … confidence to do things you never thought you'd be able to do", while Sam noted, "You feel better when you're on cycle … there's definitely that psychological boost". More pertinently, Phillip enthused, "My view of the world changes when I take testosterone. … Take, for example, this conversation that I'm having with you now, [enhanced testosterone] makes me more assertive and full of ideas … it makes me want to go and make the most of life". This again emphasizes testosterone's role in facilitating Phillip's concept of the good life, as the pleasurable effects of increased assertiveness and confidence underpinned his drive to reject the passivity expected of him as an older man and instead, as he told me with a flash of his whitened teeth, inspired him to behave like he did when he "was in [his] thirties". Clearly, this enhanced "view [of] the world" was the platform upon which Phillip could live out his ego ideal and his Dorian Gray-esque rejection of the aging process.

It is clear that Phillip ultimately sought a state of 'perma-adolescence' (Greif, 2017: 84), wherein the experiences of youth could be replicated ad infinitum. As such, his artificially youthful body, hedonistic, jet-setting lifestyle, and love for fast cars reflects Hockey et al's (2010) assertion that youth is no longer defined by age, but through *lifestyle* (Barber, 2007; Brisman and South, 2015). Smith (2014: 93) concludes that 'to be "middle aged" or "old" is not so much defined by years and months, but by "staying in" and succumbing to the more traditional concepts of "adulthood"'. Therefore, under this liberal discourse of *choosing* youth, Phillip elected to deny the biological markers of late adulthood and instead opted for a 'good life' of rekindled adolescence. Smith's (2014) statement can be placed within the process of life stage dissolution (Hayward, 2013), wherein previously delineated stages of maturation have merged to create a homogeneous 'cult of youth'. This has seen adults, who would have previously settled into lives of coherence and responsibility, become *infantilized*, while simultaneously, childhood has been cut short in favour of an elongated adolescence.

The reason for this is quite simple; *youth sells* (Danesi, 2003). Therefore, the advertising instruments of late-capitalism have deliberately cultivated an infantilized state of immaturity in order to maximize the flow of capital (Hayward, 2013). Thus, Phillip's disregard of old age as simply a period of degeneration speaks to his infatuation with the neoliberal system, as he jettisoned all traditionally valuable aspects of older adulthood, such as presiding over multiple generations of family, sustaining a long-term marriage, and reflecting upon cherished memories, in favour of the prolongation of youthful consumption. This depreciation of mature adulthood was present throughout Phillip's construction of the good life, from his rapturous relationship with his sports car, to his smoothed-out face and artificially firm musculature. Crucially, therefore, for Phillip, IPEDs constituted the ultimate youth-affirming commodity, as he effectively purchased the means to unlock the virility and pleasures of youth that are widely advertised under consumer capitalism.

Although he was careful to present his IPED-enhanced perma-adolescence as enviable and idealized, a melancholy ultimately underlay Phillip's description, as what he constructed as the good life was essentially bereft of genuine, fulfilling human relationships. While Phillip's endless stream of youth-affirming products and aesthetics presumably fostered dissatisfaction and consumer desire in his acquaintances (McGowan, 2016), his attempts to enhance his later years appeared to leave him with an objectless anxiety (Hall, 2012a) and an acceptance that he was alone in the world. This captures the fundamentally unfulfilling nature of consumer capitalism and a life of perpetual youth, contoured entirely along the lines of capital extraction and superficial value.

Chapter summary

This chapter has served to consider the role of pleasure as a motivation for IPED consumption through the voice of the project's oldest participant, Phillip. Though initially motivated to use AAS by his instrumental urge to succeed in competitive bodybuilding, Phillip's consumption soon transitioned to being fundamentally lifestyle-oriented, as he employed testosterone firmly within the discourse of anti-aging. Within this, his use encompassed the broader themes of self-medicalization, human mastery of nature, and the contemporary constructions of youth.

While Phillip is somewhat unusual in his academic-minded approach to IPEDs, viewing himself as an experiment in corporeal enhancement, his supplementation of testosterone speaks to something far broader in nature. AAS were imbued with the status of the elixir of youth for Phillip, enhancing his confidence, sex drive, and social life. This ultimately demonstrates the multi-faceted nature of IPED consumption as well as the wider questions that arise when one takes a closer examination.

7

#Ripped: Social Media, Prosumption, and Bodily Desire

Will-to-recognition and performing for the Big Other online

Having explored the lifestyle aspects of IPED consumption, this chapter sets out to examine the role of SNS in perpetuating bodily desire and, by extension, my sample's use of illicit ergogenic aids. Before exploring the SNS under study and my sample's digitally mediated content production, however, it is crucial to map the men's relationship with Facebook and Instagram. Each participant was active on SNS during the study and most interviewees (besides one) indicated that they simultaneously owned a Facebook and Instagram account. They typically spent between two to three hours on the sites daily and most tended to post content at least every other day. As such, through my own researcher Facebook and Instagram profiles, new digitally mediated data was only ever a swipe away and users' content perpetually littered both sites. Given the inherently ocular nature of my participants' posts, it seems futile to rely upon the written word to capture the nature of their content. Instead, towards the close of data collection I contacted the participants with whom I built the greatest rapport to ask for their most-liked images, which are displayed in Figure 7.1.

The men's posts almost exclusively consisted of their sculpted physiques, as they posed for mirror selfies and shared images of their competition triumphs, all the while tensing every sinew under the "anabolic lighting" (Ed) of the gym or a natural beauty spot. Consistent with Tiggemann and Zaccardo's (2018) description of male fitspiration content, the men's posts showcase an over-identification with the male muscular ideal as well as a concerted attempt to self-objectify their physiques (Hakim, 2015). But why do they use social media in this way?

In answer to this question, it is first prudent to unpack the ubiquity of SNS use on contemporary subjectivity and how selfhood, for my sample, is

Figure 7.1: Photomontage of a selection of users' most-liked Instagram and Facebook posts

indelibly bound up in the content they *prosume* (Toffler, 1980; Fuchs, 2021). Yar (2012: 251) explores this within the notion of 'will-to-representation', which describes the 'imperative to represent the self via electronic mediation' and have one's actions observed and validated by others. He contextualizes this within our digitized society, where 'to be' is 'to be seen' (Yar, 2012: 250), arguing that, by sharing self-curated content with one's followers, we demand appraisal in the form of ever more likes and a perpetually increasing friends list. This is supported by Flisfeder (2014: 238) in his reading of social media as he states, 'I tweet, therefore I exist; and the compulsion to (re)tweet is the symptom of our needing to feel affective recognition from the Other'. As such, while it may be their deep bodily desire that drives my sample towards bodywork, it is the need to have this recognized and *seen* that motivates their incessant posting. However, Yar fails to address to *whom* this digital visibility is directed. Given the significant effort the men expend to produce regular, likable content, who is their intended audience, and why is this validation so significant?

Kotzé et al (2020: 4) suggest that 'social media operates as a surrogate [B]ig Other' (see also Raymen, 2018; Kotzé, 2020; Black, 2022). Utilizing their participant's rhetorical question, '"If you didn't take a selfie, did you even train?"' (Kotzé et al, 2020: 4), they contend that it is the act of sharing the workout that makes it real in the Big Other's eyes. This statement begs the question: are SNS now a means through which the subject seeks verification for their actions (or indeed physiques) from the Big Other? Following Flisfeder (2014), Kotzé et al (2020), and Black (2022), it is my contention that these social media represent a means by which my sample created 'content' for the Big Other's verification.

Notably, although Chapter 2 documented the breakdown of belief in the Big Other in Potsford following the collapse of the 'solid' bastions of industrial modernity, the Big Other cannot be said to be 'dead', given that it never truly existed in the first place (Winlow, 2019). Instead, while the institutions and cultures of the past, which formed a stable symbolic order for the subject under industrial modernity, have fallen victim to the onset of globalized neoliberalism, the contemporary subject still requires verification from the Big Other to validate their acts and escape the Real (Kotzé, 2020). In line with the digitization of contemporary society, posting on social media, therefore, represents a means of performing for the Big Other. This point is elaborated upon by Black (2022: 39) as he contends that, despite the collapse of symbolic efficiency in contemporary society, 'we, nonetheless, continue to seek the security of some form of Big Other that can confer meaning and consistency in an era of uncertainty and disillusionment'. As such, according to Flisfeder (2014: 231), 'social media is the platform through which, today, in popular culture, the Big Other continues to be operative'. Therefore, while acts under industrial modernity were verified in terms of one being *known* and respected in the community, the Big Other's validation now comes in the slew of supportive comments, likes, and messages attached to successful SNS posts, validated by this 'secular solution' to the lack of belief in the Big Other by the cynical postmodern subject (Flisfeder, 2014: 236). This was reflected in David's complaint in Chapter 5, where he contended, "I think that there are a lot of people in the gym now who wouldn't be if they couldn't show everyone on social media". Speaking more broadly, Ed noted that "people's happiness and social standing is dictated by likes and following", capturing the relationship between SNS and the Big Other as, using their likes and number of followers as a metric, users can ascertain their "social standing" and feel accepted as part of the contemporary symbolic order. This was elaborated upon by Luke:

> 'Years ago, you had to compete if you wanted to show off what you'd done because otherwise no one else is going to see it. Now you can just post a load of pictures on Instagram and say this is what I've achieved, and people will tell you that you look great and what have you, and you're getting the accolade just by doing that.'

Compared to Luke's experiences of bodybuilding in the 1990s, SNS provide a more immediate form of gratification, more attuned to the hurtling pace of late-capitalism (Crary, 2014). This was also addressed by Ben:

> 'I think with things like Insta[gram], especially the stories that you have now, it's like instant gratification. You can show that you're at the gym at that moment and someone can comment on it like a second later. So you can put something on as you're doing your first couple of sets and then by the end of it you've got ten DMs [direct messages] with people saying you look really good … we don't have to wait for it now. It's almost like me going to the gym and then my trophy's there waiting for me when I get home, you know?'

The "instant gratification" Ben describes illustrates the potency of this technologically mediated means of broadcasting the act for verification as, in place of the long-term accolades and lifetime achievements we once based our selfhood upon, "we don't have to wait for it now". As such, immediate appraisal is offered in the form of complimentary 'DMs', which Ben viewed as akin to virtual trophies. However, unlike the solid silver awards that line athletes like Ben's shelves, the gratification offered by social media melts into air as quickly as it appears. True to the epoch of liquid modernity (Bauman, 2012), the hundreds of likes and tens of swooning messages soon disappear, driving the men to perpetually create bodily content. Further, given the ultra-competitive and atomizing nature of social media, where users clamour to display their cultural and consumer capital (Smith and Raymen, 2018), this transformed means of seeking approval lacks the collectiveness and coherence described in Chapter 2. Instead, my sample were perpetually aware of other users "doing bigger numbers" (Sam) than them, as they were forced to *compete* for the Big Other's approval. This led to some users developing tactics to maximize their exposure, as Scott explained:

S: You are always fishing for more likes, and then you start thinking, 'What gets me the likes then? This picture got likes, why? What was I doing?'. I can't work it out because one picture gets like 150 likes but this one's better, why's that? You can't figure it out.

N: How do you try to make sure you get the most likes?

S: The later at night [you post] the less people see, because by the time anyone gets up in the morning it's already down a lot of people's feeds. So what I would do is, most people are on it at night-time between probably six o'clock and nine o'clock when they're sat at home, so that's when I'll post. I said to Pete the other day as well, because he said his following's gone down, I said share your post on your story. That way you'll get more people seeing it and more people will click on your profile. It's all tactics.

Scott's admission speaks to the pivotal role of social media in facilitating the Big Other's validation of the act. He experienced confusion and anxiety around the apparent disparity between the likes different posts received and, attempting to overcome this, adapted his posting timing and patterns in line with the Big Other's command. Alongside this, Rob noted that the content of posts is also impacted by the need to maximize validation:

> 'I've gone through points where I've put pictures up and I've not got the recognition I expected to get and it's bothered me. … It's bothered me to a point where I've created a more extreme picture and I've been there taking 20 photos from different angles until I got the one that made me look the biggest. … I've been down that rabbit hole of craving likes, been there and got the t-shirt.'

Confronted by a lack of verification from the Big Other, Rob felt forced to accentuate his physical size and the 'extreme' nature of his image. As such, users seeking approval are compelled to share what the Big Other wants, rather than what they necessarily feel comfortable posting.

Finally, it is worth acknowledging the impact upon my sample of conceptualizing likes as their primary means of illustrating their fidelity to the Big Other. Neuroscientific literature has evidenced claims that SNS' quantifiable validation can become addictive to committed users (see Fabris et al, 2020; Priyadarshini et al, 2020; Marengo et al, 2021) and it is important to unpack the psychic implications of being able to numerically measure the Big Other's approval. Scott noted that his perpetual quest for likes "takes it out of you. … I was posting almost every time I went [to] the gym and I actually told myself to stop". His admission speaks to the infinitude of likes as a means of approval, as the dopamine released upon getting a notification (Burhan and Moradzadeh, 2020) makes receiving the Big Other's verification "just a little bit addictive" (Scott). Therefore, given that SNS are engineered to suspend the user in a constant state of expectation and desire so as to maximize advertising revenues (Reisach, 2021), likes as a reflection of the Big Other's approval left my sample in a perpetual state of seeking, and therefore posting, more.

It is at this juncture that we may apply a more critical eye to Yar's concept of will-to-representation and, more specifically, his ascription of the term 'representation'. If 'to be' is 'to be seen' (Yar, 2012: 250), ought we not to re-term my sample's compulsion to perform on SNS as a will-to-*recognition*, given that it is the Big Other's validation that constitutes the endpoint rather than the act of representation itself? Just as a well-trained animal obeys its owner in the knowledge that its behaviour will be rewarded then, so too do the men create content for the Big Other via SNS, craving the recognition as a means of affirming their symbolic order. Thus, SNS, within as well as beyond the hardcore fitness community, are essentially platforms of recognition and any analysis should take this as its starting point.

The digital Lacanian mirror

Understood through the lens of recognition, an acknowledgement existed throughout my sample that, far from providing an accurate portrayal of their lives, the men's use of SNS was analogous to a "highlight reel" (Ed, Ben) where users "only post photos looking their best" (Joe). Bemoaning this, Ben noted, "You see two per cent of people's days. … You don't see the day-to-day reality of it, all the boring bits". In line with this, most of my interviewees admitted to doctoring their images, using various strategies to maximize their bodily and cultural capital.

Principal among these was the practice of taking multiple photos and selecting the image that most captures their ideal self (see Lamp et al, 2019). On this, Ben conceded, "You end up taking 20 selfies and only posting one that you've played around with", while Adam ruefully told me, "I take a load of pictures and I end up only being happy with one, or sometimes none of them, even though I've not really changed". The minuscule differences in images largely depend on "angles and filters and lighting" (Will), as Adam noted "on Instagram you can get a bit of good lighting and take a picture and be like, 'Fucking hell, I look decent there'". My sample also spoke in derogatory tones of gym members misrepresenting themselves by posting images of their physiques in a desirable condition, even if this did not reflect their bodies at the time of the upload. Ben explained, "They'll diet and do a show or a couple of photoshoots and then they just rehash their pictures throughout the year. So they maintain that they're four per cent body fat all year round because that's what gets likes, that's what people like to see". Similarly, Adam described knowing "people who haven't trained for weeks but they say they're in the gym, looking great on social media. Then the next time you see them they're coming in saying that they've got a gut because they've been eating shit for three weeks".

The 'playing around' with selfies hinted at by Ben refers to photo editing, using software like Photoshop and Facetune (Kleemans et al,

2018). My sample commonly doctored their posts to ensure that their images contained "no marks and no blemishes" (Adam), leading Dom to conclude that "you can see so much perfection on Instagram and so much Photoshop, to an untrained eye you don't know what's real and what's not". As such, SNS become spaces of fantasy, where users post enhanced digital versions of themselves to appeal to the Big Other. With this in mind, can the various post-perfecting strategies described here be considered a digitized form of image enhancement? Certainly, the use of platforms such as Photoshop and the built-in filters on Instagram promote the 'excessive naturality' described by Kotzé and Antonopoulos (2019), whereby the natural markers of bodily attractiveness are accentuated, as blemishes are erased and muscle tone is more sharply defined. Though it is beyond the remit of this chapter to address such a claim, it is important to acknowledge the inherently *enhanced* nature of SNS, particularly within the hardcore fitness community.

But what is the impact of sharing these idealized images of the self on SNS? First, we must examine what my sample's posts represent to their selfhood. As touched upon earlier in relation to Phillip, these edited and perfected posts constitute the subject's ego ideal, the 'wish to become like an admired other driven by an ego and superego that have matured as they enter the Symbolic Order' (Hall et al, 2008: 180). Notably, the ego ideal is inherently unattainable and therefore represents the perfect image of oneself in the Big Other's eyes (Žižek, 2006; Hall, 2019). However, by being able to manipulate their digital representation, my sample were able to somewhat attain the unattainable and, in their eyes, meet this ideal. It is here that we can introduce the concept of the *ideal ego* which, although sometimes used interchangeably with the ego ideal, in fact describes the subject's identification with the 'specular other' (Hall et al, 2008: 180) and self-conception as the ideal image. This distinction is pivotal in unpacking the nature of SNS, as the ability to digitally enhance the self enables users to *become* their ideal ego, conflating the formerly unattainable ego ideal with the perfected image they post online.

However, my sample's identification of their digital image as the ideal ego left them with a feeling of discord, as their refined physique stared back at them from their phone screen, undeniably a reflection of themselves, and yet the same image of perfection could not be replicated offline. Just like a child traversing a distorting mirror maze where a different contorted image leers at them from every wall, what can be recognized as the self becomes blurred and obfuscated. On this, Adam confessed:

> 'If someone told me to take my top off, I'd be a bit nervous about doing it, but I do it like every day on social media. But I can control Instagram, if that makes sense. I can control it cus I've taken the picture,

> but I can't control it if somebody's looking at me from a bad angle or whatever. It's all control. What you're showing people is up to you.'

Adam's emphasis on the locus of control is telling, as he is painfully aware that his ego ideal is only achievable through the lens of social media and therefore, to the unfiltered and non-complimentary eye, he feels exposed and self-conscious. His admission evokes Hall's (2019: 171) question, 'Is Facebook or Instagram not the twenty-first-century version of the mirror in which the Lacanian subject sees their idealised image through the eyes of the other, feeling both recognition of it and alienation from it?' Unpacking this, Hall is essentially questioning whether the user truly recognizes their digital 'best self', or if they instead feel estranged from their own manipulated image. This point is expanded upon by Black (2022: 39), as he concludes that 'we are never the online personas we adopt, no matter how close to the "real" me that this identity may seem. [SNS self-representations] are, in effect, a "decaffeinated self": a depiction of us, without the "real" (biological) thing'. Similarly, Penney (2014: 2), describing the effects of digital mediation on users of dating apps, states that '[b]odies as presented under glass surfaces become manipulatable, non-visceral, gaze-oriented visual bodies, for consumption as objects', rather than the fleshy reality that exists offline. This sense of misrecognition was evident, as Adam noted that he "put a false persona on" when posting, while Will told me that he felt as though he "catfished a lot of people, I just think I look a lot better online than I do in person". Referring to the act of catfishing, whereby fake online personas are used as a means of attracting romantic partners, Will viewed his digital self as a separate, idealized entity that was alien to his conventional experience of being in the world. Similarly, Dom's earlier admission that "you don't know what's real and what's not" on SNS is doubly significant here given that every user only posts an idealized version of themselves, and therefore trying to disentangle the real physique from the layers of editing and mediation leaves the subject unable to discern reality from fantasy.

Are SNS dopogenic environments?

While the relationship between SNS and negative body image is well established (see Kim and Chock, 2015; Fardouly and Vartanian, 2016; Kleemans et al, 2018), an application of the true nature of bodily desire is notably lacking in relation to the landscape of idealized images online. The crux of the following argument, therefore, is this: if my sample's bodies represent the *objet petit a*, and their unending journey of bodily dissatisfaction is perpetuated by a fixation on an unattainable ideal, surely the wash of perfected bodies they see each day on SNS functions to exacerbate their desire and increase their drive to enhance their physiques. This contention ties to Girard's (1979) notion of mimetic desire as these physiques exist externally to the user and, therefore, cultivate and mould their notions of bodily perfection. Therefore, the men under study cannot only mimetically identify others' idealized physiques as the *objet petit a* (effectively the ego ideal), but also view their own edited and digitally mediated body (their ideal ego) as an object of bodily desire. Indeed, Dom noted that clients routinely presented him with images of their "dream body" that they encountered on SNS. However, these venerated physiques were essentially unattainable:

> 'You can't look like everybody on Instagram, for the simple fact of (a) enhancement, whether that be anabolic or surgical; (b) Photoshop; or even (c) say it is achievable to look like them without enhancements or Photoshop, the dedication that person has shown over, not 12 weeks, but 12 months and maybe even years to get to the level they're at and to look the way they look.'

Dom captures the potency of SNS as a means of displaying the *objet petit a* given the ubiquitous chemical, surgical, and digital enhancement on display, as well as the sense of instantaneousness that the format promotes. It is no coincidence that the primary platform under study is named *Insta*gram, as the "highlight reel" (Ed, Ben) of physiques present themselves as within immediate reach and yet are ultimately unattainable without long-term commitment. It is this context that generally frames the existing literature's examination of IPED use and SNS-driven bodily dissatisfaction, as illicit ergogenic aids are commonly seen as a means of overcoming the disparity between one's fleshy reality and the fantasy ideals the subject sees on social media (see Melki et al, 2015; Griffiths et al, 2018). This view was echoed by Ed as he stated, "On social media you've got people saying, 'Oh yeah I want that physique', but the only way I can get that physique is if I go on steroids. So I think social media has a massive part to play in [the increased use of AAS]". However, if we understand the subject as perpetually seeking to prolong their dissatisfaction and sabotage any attempts at satiating their desire, Ed's statement is problematic.

While the cacophony of desirable physiques on Instagram and Facebook does ultimately push the subject towards enhancement through the stimulation of bodily dissatisfaction, users actively seek out these images as a means of impairing their sense of completion and keeping their body projects unfinished. Thus, as SNS are designed as 'echo chambers' (Garrett, 2009), reflecting what users wish to see, they represent the ultimate dopogenic environments (Backhouse et al, 2018), as they perpetuate bodily desire through an inexhaustible array of physiques to negatively compare oneself to. The platforms allow users to access bodies from across the world in order to cultivate corporeal desire, unshackling their comparisons from the local bodybuilding scene to encompass a global peer network (Turnock, 2018). Atop this, given users' alienation from their own digitally mediated selves (Hall, 2019), their edited bodies further represent objects of desire which advance the unending cultivation of their fitness. Ultimately, this infinite suspension of desire acts as a "vicious cycle" (Neil) which drives users towards unending bodily enhancement and therefore to the consumption of IPEDs.

Chapter summary

This final consumption chapter has addressed the role of SNS and their relationship to bodily desire and the motivation to use IPEDs. This digital landscape has been shown to stimulate IPED consumption through my sample's compulsion to offer ever more 'likeable' content to the Big Other via their social media posts. This injunction to share one's "highlight reel" (Ed, Ben) makes SNS something of a fantasy space where my sample's ego ideal and ideal ego are conflated and they are ultimately estranged from their own images. The subsequent wash of edited, idealized bodies on social media makes the sites the most compelling dopogenic environments in contemporary life, given that my sample are offered a global peer network of unattainable physiques which stimulate their corporeal dissatisfaction and drive their desire to enhance the body onwards.

PART II

Supply-side

8

Production

Part II, which consists of four chapters, provides an analysis of the 'muscle trade' through the voices of users, sellers, and industry professionals. Various elements of the market – from local gym-based supply chains to online SNS sellers – will be explored, and the interconnections between each highlighted. Starting with an examination of production, the following three chapters explore my participants' experiences of 'traditional' offline closed market supply, before tracking the currents of digitization and commercialization that have accompanied the ascension of the online market.

Before a picture of the distribution of IPEDs can be painted, it is vital to interrogate how and where these compounds are produced. This chapter will, therefore, examine the dual means by which illicit ergogenic aids are made, first unpacking underground laboratory (UGL) operations before turning its attention to licit pharmaceutical production.

Underground laboratories

Operation and market share

Consistent with Turnock's (2020: 2) contention that 'most users are likely buying UGL', 77 per cent of my IPED-using sample acknowledged that most of their substances were manufactured in UGLs. According to Rob, "80 to 90 per cent of steroids [in the UK] are UGL-produced" as well as a selection of fat burners like T5 and DNP. In relation to AAS, Carl told me that although "tablets can be made at home. … Anything oil-based needs to be done properly in a lab. So most of the [UGL owners] buy their raws from China and then they produce them in the labs" (see Llewellyn and Tober, 2010; Denham, 2019; Turnock, 2021a). Therefore, in the words of Aaron, "Ingredients are being imported, but production is predominantly over here". This was reflected in my sample, as 90 per cent of UGL-consuming interviewees stated that their producer was located in the UK.

Throughout data collection, the domestic nature of UGL production was commonly attributed to "the change of law a few years ago" (Aaron), wherein anabolic steroids were stripped of their status as 'medicinal products' in 2012 (Brunsdon, 2012). As a result, importing AAS became a criminal offence, punishable by up to 14 years in prison. Crucially, however, importing raw powders (often sold under the guise of veterinary supplies or agricultural compounds) remains a legal grey area. Therefore, this legislative change allowed domestic UGLs to gain ascendance in the IPED market as, in Aaron's words, "When you weren't allowed to order it in for yourself from abroad, the British labs really took off". However, despite being concentrated in the UK, UGLs cannot be said to be territorial, and may, unbeknown to one another, operate in the same locality. This was addressed by Rob:

N: How [geographically] spaced out are labs would you say?

R: It varies. They don't put 'made in 27 Oxford Street' on the bloody packaging. They're all over the place. Because labs don't sell geographically there is no boundary there. You might have a lab that produces in Bristol that shifts to a wholesaler in Manchester, who then sells back to somebody that lives in Bristol. That happens all the time. A1 were up in Scotland, Energise is based in Bolton but one of their labs was in Birmingham, so it varies massively. There's no real 'you can't have two labs next door to each other'.

Unlike other illicit drugs markets, UGLs do not cover a specific geographic area and do not, as it were, serve their local community. In terms of scale, operations range from "people making stuff up in their garage" (Aaron) through to the most sophisticated outfits "produc[ing] PCT tab[lets] which include proviron [Mesterolone], clomid [Clomifene], [and] arimidex [Anastrozole]" (Rob) with high-specification pharmaceutical equipment. Therefore, underground labs should not be conceptualized as homogeneous in their set-ups, as scale, profitability, and risk-averseness vary from one UGL to the next. Rob demonstrated the relative ease and affordability of setting up a small-scale UGL operation:

N: Do people need a lot of investment to start a UGL?

R: No not necessarily, because to set up a lab it's probably a couple of grand. That would be raw materials, then equipment-wise they only really need a hot plate, an infiltration system, a couple of conical flasks and some scales – I don't really need much else. I buy my vials, I'll buy one thousand or five thousand from China, and if I buy my vials, they'll also send me the labels free

> of charge to my design with the caps. So all I need then is the capping clamps – it's a bit labour intensive that way but it gets me going. I can create a real fancy label design, all I need is Photoshop or a mate who's in graphic design, bung him £200 to do me a website and I'd be all set up for trading.

Rob showcases the initial steps required to set up a viable UGL, which would operate at the most basic end of the market. Conversely, Aaron captured the scope of the larger-scale operations as he described an anonymous UGL he was in regular contact with:

A: I've actually got an invite to go to a UG lab, like a big producer have said they'll let me go along and have a look at the actual lab and look at the manufacturing stuff. … I'm hoping once [lockdown] is all over I can still go and have a look at all that. Some of these huge labs are built out in the middle of nowhere and the numbers that they're producing daily are just phenomenal.

N: In terms of size of the units and stuff, how big are the bigger labs?

A: He was telling me how much they produce in a day, and I'm sure he said that they were pressing 100,000 tablets a day. I think they were doing runs of like a million tablets at a time. Then they would wipe down and reset the lab for whatever they were producing next. They have incredibly proficient, highly skilled chemists working for them – these aren't just Mickey Mouse labs, these are proper people who are very highly qualified. Some of them have spent hundreds of thousands of pounds on the equipment to do it, that's the level we're talking.

Aaron shed light upon the vast scale of the largest UGLs, which possess the means of producing "100,000 tablets a day". Notably, opposing the well-versed narratives of AAS being "cooked up like Super Noodles in the microwave" (Ben), Aaron notes the legitimacy of "proper people" with skills mirroring those of the licit pharmaceutical industry. This influx of such "highly skilled chemists" appears to have bolstered the quality of products on the market, as Aaron explained in relation to his work as a harm reduction practitioner:

> 'Some of the stuff we were interested in ten years ago, we don't focus on too much now. You used to have to really look at your gear and make sure it didn't have bits floating around in it and check if the viscosity is right … but these days they're made pretty well.'

The professionalization of UGLs has also seen a diversification of products, which rely upon the specialist practitioners' aptitude and access to sophisticated facilities. Rob explained:

> 'Some labs have branched into creating generic ancillaries and others have started buying unlabelled kits and putting labels on them selling growth hormone too. Some labs have moved into fat burners as well, particularly stuff like injectable clenbuterol, that have been illicitly manufactured.'

The enhanced capability of these UGLs has meant that, for the largest operations, substances that have traditionally been beyond the remit of UGLs, such as hGH (see Fink et al, 2019; Turnock, 2020), can now be manufactured. Similarly, discussing his involvement in UGL Inception's operations, Carl described how, "We have our own blends [of steroid compounds]. One of those is superb, it's called One Rip. So you get 100 mg of test prop [testosterone propionate], masteron [Drostanolone propionate], and tren ace [trenbolone acetate] all in one-ml jabs". These fusions again illustrate the diversification of UGL products and the sophistication of some labs' production process. However, Rob noted that UGLs' growth was dependent on various factors, and reaching the levels described by Aaron thus represents something of an anomaly:

> 'Some grow naturally and some don't as well because of fear of detection – the larger amounts that you have to import means the greater risk of discovery. Like anything, they develop based on what's going on around them and what resources they have available, and often the supply chains that they have available. Quite often supply chains will limit a lab's development.'

Rob illustrates the barriers UGLs face in their growth and the importance of resources (be it cash flow, storage space, or available expertise) and connections. Given these challenges, Tina noted the turbulence of the UGL landscape, where there is "a new [UGL] coming up every bloody day. One gets shut down and another one will come back as a phoenix company – but they're exactly the same people". Alongside this, UGL owners' level of risk-averseness affects their earning potential, as Rob cautioned that "the larger amounts that you have to import means the greater risk of discovery". For this reason, some labs opt to remain modest in size, operating out of "shipping container[s]" (Rob) or "garages" (Aaron) and selling relatively meagre batches of products.

Having manufactured their substances, differences once again emerge between the various UGLs. Some labs act as traditional wholesalers, selling large batches of their products to local resellers (see Turnock, 2020) and online suppliers. These are then sold by 'retail sellers' (Hall and Antonopoulos, 2016) in spaces like gyms, supplement shops, private residences, online pharmacies, and social media sites. More recently, however, Rob noted a shift in many UGLs' business models, whereby they have begun to sell directly to the IPED-using population:

> 'They never used to sell direct to end users. They used to go through a reseller before the end user. But they realized that the police aren't particularly active on pursuing them and they can sell their product to end users. What they don't do is undercut their resellers, so the end price is still the same price but obviously their profit margin jumps through the roof.'

Rob's description of UGLs selling "direct to end users" is significant as he echoes Laing and Mackey's (2011) findings that illicit pharmaceutical suppliers employ electronic direct-to-consumer advertising (eDTCA) to circumnavigate regulatory authorities. Therefore, given the challenges inherent in overseeing platforms like SNS and online forums, UGLs similarly appear to have discovered the utility of eDTCA as a sales strategy (see also Henning and Andreasson, 2022). Rob attributes this lucrative development to the apathy shown by the authorities in regulating the IPED market. This was supported by my sample, as Sam contended "I just honestly don't think that [the police] care about it", while serving police officer Luke stated, "I've never seen anybody get done [for] steroid dealing". Therefore, where once underground labs could be described entirely in terms of production, some now simultaneously operate as producer-sellers, playing a far more active role in the IPED market.

In light of this, it is worth mapping the main brands encountered during this project's fieldwork. Though by no means exhaustive, Table 8.1 illustrates the UGL 'brands' that dominated the IPED market during data collection.

Brand recognition and the need to appear legitimate

To appeal to end users, UGLs must "build a reputation" (Rob) for their products' potency and the operation's legitimacy (see Gibbs, 2023b). Within this, they face two pressing issues, namely, the necessity to build a distinctive brand and the need to present as trustworthy to their customers. The first of these imperatives was discussed by Rob as he stated, "The thing is with steroid users, what you'll find is they'll go to a lab because it's got a good reputation and it produces good quality drugs", therefore, "UGLs, unlike any other drug, and the closest similarity would be ecstasy, rely on brand recognition". By cultivating a recognizable brand, UGLs can communicate

Table 8.1: Prominent UGL brands encountered during fieldwork

UGL brand	Location
Phoenix Labs	Yorkshire
Energise	Bolton/Birmingham
Inception	Not known
Victory Labs	Not known
EU Pharma	Sheffield
KSI Labs	Not known
King Pharma	Not known
Galactic Pharma	Not known
Astra	Birmingham/Liverpool

Note: In line with this project's research ethics, true brand names have been replaced with pseudonyms.

their legitimacy and trustworthiness, and therefore maximize the sales of the substances they produce, overcoming the inherent untrustworthiness of online illicit drugs markets (Tzanetakis et al, 2016; Bancroft et al, 2020). Basic UGL branding first involves creating a distinctive brand name, typically consisting of an abstract noun or corporate-sounding term, followed by a pharmaceutical or medical descriptor, which functions to both clarify the otherwise obscure lexical item as well as enhancing product legitimacy.

This is furthered by the utilization of polished but intentionally non-descript brand logos. Contradicting Rob's earlier comparison to the ecstasy market, UGL logos do not generally betray the nature of the laboratory's products or mirror the colourful and wacky brands that typify other recreational drug packaging (see Duterte et al, 2009). Instead, they present as more akin to the unremarkable logos of the corporate world and, without insider knowledge, appear entirely legitimate. Though this was not confirmed by the sellers under study, it can be theorized that these muted designs are selected to minimize exposure and attention from the regulatory authorities. Alongside this, they again function to increase the perceived legitimacy of the UGL, allowing prospective customers to conceptualize the laboratory as a licit trader rather than an illegal enterprise where substances are "cooked … up in a bathtub" (Ben). This is furthered by the use of high-quality packaging, as the more successful laboratories replicate licit pharmaceutical products' design and safety features (Fink et al, 2019). Carl discussed this in relation to his choice of brand:

> 'That's how I ended up going with Energise initially, because I was looking at another one called British Street Gear but their stuff all

> comes in bags. Like little zippy bags and you think, "Nah that's not very good. That seems a little bit thrown together, not very professionally done". Whereas Inception, Phoenix, Energise they use proper labelling and the units come sealed and capped off – you know that no one's tampered with it since it's left the lab.'

Carl's choice of UGL brand was, therefore, directly affected by Energise's packaging and a subsequent assumption of quality.

A further dimension to UGLs' product packaging is the use of anti-counterfeiting measures, whereby features like 'security imprints' are added to make their product more challenging to replicate. KSI labs, a large-scale UGL, boast on their website that their products include, 'hot-stamped multiple layer holographic strips and a hidden ultraviolet design'. This high-specification design demonstrates the sophistication of UGL production, as increasingly professionalized packaging leaves products like KSI's virtually indistinguishable from those of many major pharmaceutical companies. The dedication of the lab suggests that their products, which appear well regarded on the market, have been subject to counterfeiting which has negatively affected the operation. However, it is unclear whether this is truly a reaction to their brand being faked, or if the motivation for such tactics is more insidious. On this, Rob suggested, "A lot of this is just marketing ploys as well, it's not necessarily that they're actually getting faked – people think if something's getting faked it must be good". With this in mind, the brand's decision to emphasize this 'issue' could be an example of what Rob referred to as "subversive marketing", whereby they are seeking to bolster their reputation as a product worth faking, utilizing the spectre of counterfeiting to promote their legitimacy.

Pharmaceutical production

Although UGLs constitute the foremost producers of domestic AAS, manufacturing other more complex IPEDs requires facilities that even the most sophisticated UGL cannot assemble. Therefore, although UGLs are beginning to manufacture their own aromatase inhibitors (AIs) such as Mesterolone and Anastrozole, Rob stated that ancillary drugs are "probably 70 per cent pharma" while the fat burner T3 is "99 per cent pharma-produced". As such, these products are manufactured in licensed pharmacies and then either purchased from countries where their sale is legal or siphoned from the licit supply chain in the UK (Fink et al, 2019).

In keeping with Hall and Antonopoulos (2016), Rob advised that these pharmacies are "generally European, so Romanian and Turkish, that sort of thing", while Lee told me that his pharma products were produced in Moldova, given the lax medicinal regulations there. The range of AAS available through these channels is more limited than UGLs' wide selection, given that substances like the blends described by Carl are not approved by regulatory agencies. Similarly, compounds like trenbolone are not legal for human consumption and, therefore, are not produced in licensed medicinal pharmacies. However, users can source these substances through legitimate pharmacies that manufacture products for veterinary use. The import of pharmaceutical substances, provided that they are licensed as medicinal products (MHRA, 2014), is legal in the UK and, therefore, users face no risk through using these channels for most ancillary drugs. However, pharmaceutically produced substances such as hGH fall under the Misuse of Drugs Act (1971) alongside AAS as 'related drugs' (ACMD, 2010). To mitigate this, many users like Ben embark on 'steroid vacations' (Duff, 2012; Dunn et al, 2022; Gibbs, 2023c), taking advantage of a loophole where users can carry a quantity of AAS for personal use into the UK to buy pharmaceutical-grade products in person and transport them into the country. On this, Ben recalled, "I've been abroad to Cyprus and Egypt and things like that, and you can just buy it over the counter, you can go to a chemist and just buy it". Similarly, Josh told me:

> 'I've got a friend who sells, and he knows the guy who owns one of the pharmacies and he goes to Turkey and Egypt a lot, so he brings a lot of the over-the-counter stuff back from there, like your clen[buteral], T3, Arimidex [Anastrozole], Winstrol [Stanozolol] as well. You can get all that over the counter over there … he'll ring them up two weeks before and they'll set stock aside for when he's coming.'

Domestic pharmaceutical-grade products, on the other hand, rely on licensed medicinal products being siphoned from licit medical stock. On this, Ben admitted,

> 'I have all my growth hormone from a supplier at the local hospital, obviously I'm not supposed to have it, but they've sourced it somehow. The stuff that I have is really good, the growth hormone that I have is proper somatropin pens, the nandrolone I use is proper NHS.'

Though I was ultimately unable to locate the source of Ben's NHS supplier, Lee also hinted at the prevalence of this aspect of the market:

> 'There's always going to be someone in the chain that gets to stuff before it gets where it's going. I know a lot of people who are buying large quantities of pharmaceutical-grade AIs and they're paying less than pharmacists pay for it. So that must come straight from source, that's the only way I can imagine you'd be able to do it and make a profit.'

According to Lee, these products are siphoned off at a wholesale level, rather than, as Fink et al (2019) suggest, by individual health practitioners. Unlike the concerns some of my participants raised over the perceived quality of UGL products, Ben told me, "The thing with your pharma stuff, it's made to a certain grade and it's tested because it's used by the NHS, so it has to be a certain standard. I wouldn't just get it from someone's mate who's just cooked it up in a bathtub". This perceived disparity in quality leads users to pay 'several times the retail price' (Fink et al, 2019: 7) for domestic pharmaceutical substances, as Ben explained:

> 'Obviously what I buy is gonna cost a little bit more than the other lads you've spoken to who buy UGL. But these underground labs, if [the vial of AAS] says it's got 50 mg in it you don't know if that's actually the case. It could have 25 mg, but there's people [who are] gonna buy it because it costs five pound less than the pharma stuff.'

Ben captures the sense that pharmaceutically produced IPEDs are inherently more trustworthy than UGL products and attributes UGLs' popularity to users' frugality. Ultimately, although relatively few AAS compounds on the UK market are manufactured in licensed facilities, pharmaceutically produced substances are commonplace within most committed IPED user's stack in the form of PCT and ancillary drugs. Thus, alongside UGLs, licit pharmaceutical production forms the basis of the muscle trade.

Chapter summary

This initial supply-side chapter has focused on the production of IPEDs, presenting the two means by which the drugs that my sample consumed are manufactured. First, it has explored domestic UGLs, which constitute the primary means by which AAS and other more basic compounds are created. The heterogeneity of these labs has been discussed, ranging from extremely modest set-ups to large-scale manufacture employing a range of highly skilled chemists. It has also identified a diversification of the compounds produced in domestic UGLs, as a discernible shift from easily manufactured AAS to multi-compound substances and even some PCT drugs was evident in the fieldwork. The importance of brand recognition and the need to present as legitimate has also shone through, as UGLs rely on customer loyalty and attempt to build an image of professionalism through their packaging and logos. It is clear that this emphasis on appearing legitimate is a reaction to the well-versed narratives permeating the IPED-using community that UGL products are unhygienic and poorly produced.

Conversely, pharmaceutically produced products, although generally more expensive, garner a great deal more legitimacy given the safeguards and regulation of the licit industry. This market appears to be the source of most of the ancillary drugs in circulation, either used alongside AAS or as part of users' PCT. Although users like Ben siphon pharmaceutical products from the UK medical supply chain, the most common origin of pharmaceutical-grade IPEDs appears to be European nations with laxer regulations than the UK. As a result, users partake in 'steroid holidays', taking advantage of the loophole in domestic legislation to source these products over the counter in places such as Egypt and Cyprus. Ultimately, it is clear that the production of IPEDs, while broadly split into two channels, is in flux, with domestic UGLs diversifying and pharmaceutical products flooding the market in response to users' increased demand.

9

The Offline IPED Marketplace

Following the interrogation of IPED production in Chapter 8, we can now turn to the localized, offline supply chains that exist within Potsford. Importantly, this section does not claim to provide a definitive account of all the various supply networks in Potsford's fitness scene. Instead, it serves as a glimpse into the different means by which my sample leant upon their gym-based community to source IPEDs, highlighting the significance of peer networks and unpacking the most prominent features of offline supply.

"It's always people you know": the importance of community and peer networks

In line with the existing literature on offline IPED supply, the significance of peer networks in Potsford's local fitness scene played a substantial role in facilitating my sample's acquisition. Of my IPED-using sample, 77 per cent relied upon their contacts in the hardcore fitness scene – be it fellow bodybuilders, coaches, or close friends – to access the market, while 62 per cent collected their products in person, either from a UGL supplier or from a friend who was also a reseller. As such, many of their primary experiences of the market physically occurred in the spaces of the gyms under study. It is crucial here to note the normalization of consumption within these sites and how the widespread acceptance of illicit enhancement in both gyms facilitated their centrality in the supply chain. Scott, although not an IPED user himself, captured the ubiquity of consumption in Muscle Sanctuary:

> 'Ninety per cent of people in [Muscle Sanctuary] I would say use some sort of gear, and they're very open about it. I was actually working out once in front of the mirrors on the dumbbells and I got talking to a lad next to me. He was saying, "How long [have] you been training?", I told him I used to be 18 stone and I'd been training about a year and a half. He said, "You'd do it much quicker with some steroids in you". That open. I just said, "I'm alright ta mate", honestly it was that open.'

Scott's experience speaks to the openness of both gyms' members and the perception that the sites of bodily labour were safe spaces within which the men could discuss and, crucially, source their drugs. Given this culture of normalization, I encountered something of a 'closed market' (Coomber and Turnbull, 2007) during my offline fieldwork, wherein supply was premised upon participants' peer relationships. Turnock (2021a) describes how, in the gyms he studied, the local closed IPED market relied upon tight-knit peer networks, mutual trust and informal 'introductions' to facilitate supply. Operating within the broader illicit IPED market, Potsford's hardcore fitness scene somewhat echoes this description as a 'partial' supply chain (Fincoeur et al, 2015), wherein only those with the prerequisite bodily and cultural capital can enter, and transactions heavily depend on sustained trust. This was reflected in Andy's account of first accessing IPEDs in Muscle Sanctuary:

N: So in terms of acquisition, how did you source [your IPEDs]? Online or the gym?

A: Through personal contacts. … I trust my source who I get my stuff from, more so I think because I'm in here 10/12 hours a day and everyone knows me. If someone was to give me some stuff that was rubbish, they'd have to face up to me in here.

As demonstrated in Andy's veiled threat, his supply is premised on trust and familiarity (Coomber, 2003) as, in place of any regulatory oversight, the informal social bonds act as a guarantor of quality. This reflects Fincoeur et al's (2015: 242) finding that these culturally embedded IPED markets rely upon an 'enduring relationship' between the buyer and seller, and therefore suppliers must cultivate a long-term affinity with their customers by sharing the same spaces and cultural practices. Salinas et al (2019) capture this in their characterization of their main fieldsite, a hardcore 'spit and sawdust' gym (Brighton et al, 2020), which they describe as simultaneously being a space of communality and commerce. Therefore, particularly as Muscle Sanctuary also constituted Andy's place of work, his cultural embeddedness in the gym was indelibly tied to both his consumption and his means of supply. This was supported by Phillip, who emphasized the significance of the gym in the closed market when recounting his initial experiences of sourcing his IPEDs:

P: It was a matter of having a word with someone at the gym. At other gyms that I have trained in, if you want to get hold of gear, they'll say to you, 'Oh it's so and so who does the gear in this gym'. It's not necessarily the owner of the gym, it's one of the guys in the gym and everybody knows who that person is.

N: Is that the case with Muscle Sanctuary?
P: I don't know who the supplier is in Muscle Sanctuary, I've never enquired. But clearly in Muscle Sanctuary there is a lot of it going on, so there must be sellers in the gym. I don't know, so I've stuck with the person I started with.

Phillip captures the ubiquity of gym-based culturally embedded supply beyond the context of Potsford and contends that prominent 'faces' hold a monopoly over certain gym-based supply chains. This was supported by Josh, who, talking generally about IPED suppliers in gyms, told me, "It's always people you know that have used and train for a long time that are involved in getting gear for other people". However, Phillip's estimate that a single actor "does the gear" in Muscle Sanctuary was inconsistent with my findings, which indicate that, although certain networks surrounded prominent 'faces', both gyms under study more closely represented IPED 'trading bazaars' (Salinas et al, 2019: 48), wherein various subgroups and loyalties meant that they each hosted several illicit supply networks. Phillip's admission that "I stuck with the person I started with" despite having moved regions speaks to this factional loyalty where, once a level of trust and custom is established, users remain bound to their suppliers beyond simple market forces or geographic convenience. Phillip's long-standing relationship with his supplier is consistent with Coomber et al's (2014) emphasis on peer-to-peer relationships within local supply chains. Indeed, Moyle et al's (2013) contention that such community-based drug supply privileges aspects of communality and respect over any great financial imperative was also evident in Ben's relationship with his supplier:

N: So supply-wise, how do you source your stuff?
B: I have a guy that I have it off and I've used him for years. He's a close personal friend, I'd probably say he's one of my best friends.
N: Do you get that delivered by post then?
B: Nah, I just go round to his house; he doesn't live far away. I just go and grab it. I think he generally supplies a lot of the bigger guys that are competitive bodybuilders.
N: Is he in the bodybuilding community himself then?
B: Yeah he is, he uses and competes just like I do. That's why everyone trusts him I think.

Ben's admission that his supplier is "one of [his] best friends" illustrates the centrality of his peer network and the local bodybuilding community in his experiences of supply. The seller's dual status as someone who "uses [IPEDs] and competes" speaks to the cultural proximity between both parties which affords him an otherwise unattainable degree of trust within the bodybuilding community. Also notable is Ben's statement that he collects the substances from the seller's home. Although this is unsurprising given the geographic proximity of Potsford's hardcore fitness community, Ben's actions again demonstrate how embedded such sellers are within their customers' lives. This was further exemplified in Ed's relationship with the UGL producer from whom he purchased his IPEDs:

N: Do you know the supply chain of what you're buying? Do you know where it's made?

E: Like I say I've met the guy and I've been to his house loads of times, I don't think he makes it at his house, I think he has some kind of workshop for that. But it is quite a small lab and he does have a pharmaceutical licence so he is obviously able to make it correctly and reliably. But there isn't a lot of people in the operation so that's why it's quite a small-town thing.

Echoing Ben, Ed's knowledge of his UGL producer's home, operation, and background illustrates the accountability that users can expect in the closed, local market. Unlike the accounts of scamming and counterfeit products in the wider, open market (Graham et al, 2009), the personal connection and level of access to their suppliers afforded by the closed market set-up allows users to feel secure that they are safe from any bad faith actors. Thus, through being culturally embedded and accessible to their customers, these sellers demonstrate 'responsible vending' strategies (Van Hout and Bingham, 2014), investing in genuine relationships with their clients rather than being wholly motivated by short-term sales (see also van de Ven and Mulrooney, 2017; Turnock, 2020).

Barriers to entry

However, the closed nature of the localized, offline market and its reliance upon peer networks created certain barriers to entry. Simply put, if a potential customer does not hold the prerequisite social ties or bodily capital then they are essentially precluded from the partial markets described here. This is discussed by Maycock and Howat (2005) in their study into the initial barriers to AAS use. They found that access to the localized market was contingent on 'making the right contacts' (Maycock and Howat, 2005: 321), as prospective consumers were indoctrinated into a mindset of IPED normalization and schooled in how to address the stigma of AAS use in wider society (Coquet et al, 2018; Svedsäter et al, 2021). More poignantly, Maycock and Howat (2005) note that culturally embedded suppliers perform a risk assessment on potential users prior to extending their custom to them in order to minimize the risk of regulation. This was reflected in Rob's comment on the influence of my bodily capital on my potential to engage in this closed market:

> 'If you are a face-to-face seller, you wouldn't sell your drugs to someone you thought would fuck up because it would come back to you. No disrespect, but if I was a seller and you came to me wanting steroids [I'd say], "Piss off, I don't have none of them, I don't sell them – don't know what you're on about". Because you're a risk, you're too normal. It's like Freemasons, steroid users always know another one and you don't fit the profile so you're not getting anything because you might be Old Bill.'

Rob's statement captures these in-built barriers, as he branded my physique "too normal" and therefore a risk to any culturally embedded supplier's operation. Therefore, to have access to community-embedded sellers, one must "fit the profile" (Carl), both physically and culturally. This ties into the narrative around users reaching their natural limit before initiating use as access to the closed market required, as it were, the potential user to have graduated from an apprenticeship of unassisted gym work to a threshold where they could be said to need IPEDs. This was true in the case of Ed, who was widely praised for his approach within the community, as he relied upon his bodily and cultural capital to be introduced to his coach's supply chain. Further, Jake, discussing his involvement in the same social supply network as Ed, emphasized these barriers through his acknowledgement that he need not look beyond the community-based offline market due to his localized cultural capital:

> 'I've got no reason to [engage in the online market] now, I've got enough contacts to never have to go online for things. What usually happens in person is that someone sparks up a conversation and you just go from there. I suppose the only reason why I'd go online is if I was frightened of asking someone, because it is a taboo subject. It takes bollocks to walk up to someone in the gym and say, "Do you know where I can get this?", because you're making the assumption that they use something and they know [where to buy IPEDs]. But I'm at a point now where people know me and ask me about gear and I even get people trying to sell me stuff in the gym that I've not even asked for [laughs].'

Jake's words are telling, as he rejected the need to engage in the online market given his contacts and standing in the local bodybuilding community and was in fact involuntarily solicited in Muscle Sanctuary. His account illustrates how his physique and popularity in the community delivered him to a position where he was considered worth approaching by users looking to establish market connections. He effectively became a gatekeeper for the partial market in Potsford's hardcore fitness scene, capable of ushering in those who enquired about supply chains or leaving them unconnected. He also noted that "[i]t takes bollocks to walk up to someone in the gym" to make the initial enquiries without having built up a relationship with other community members. I encountered this same trepidation when enquiring about my sample's consumption and subsequent involvement in the market as an outsider as, lacking bodily capital or any meaningful gatekeeper in the community, I was aware that some users may feel wary of judgement or stigma as a result of my questions (see Van Hout and Kean, 2015). It was only after I was known by several influential 'faces' in Potsford's hardcore fitness scene that I was able to uncover several of my sample's UGL supply chains. This again illustrates the barriers that inhibit non-community members from accessing the market.

The case of Dom and Astra

Late in my offline fieldwork, immediately prior to the first national coronavirus lockdown, I stumbled upon the most coherent example of a 'local' IPED supply chain within Potsford, which encompassed both gyms under study and was built around Dom, a PT and prominent community member. Dom, whose decade of high-end personal training experience and IPED-related expertise made him a well-known figure in Potsford's hardcore fitness scene, can be described as a 'steroid mentor' (van de Ven and Mulrooney, 2017) and, in some sense, an 'anabolics coach' (Gibbs et al, 2022b). Van de Ven and Mulrooney (2017) describe steroid mentors as experienced IPED users who voluntarily help novice consumers with injecting techniques, dosing, and harm reduction. As such, Sam described how Dom, who coached him as a young trainer, "has come out with stuff that I never think about, he's obviously not university educated but he's that level, he'd definitely get a Master's [degree] in anabolics [laughs]". As Sam alludes to, this is manifested in his personal training services, imbuing Dom with the status of an anabolics coach given his formalized paid-for advice to his clients. Dom, therefore, was a figure who enjoyed substantial cultural capital within the hardcore fitness community and acted as something of an authority figure in Predator.

Dom's IPEDs, typifying the UK marketplace, were produced in a domestic UGL which he had used for several years prior to our interview. He had built up an 'enduring relationship' (Fincoeur et al, 2015: 242) with the UGL owner and was exceedingly complimentary of the lab's legitimacy:

N: So from your personal perspective, how do you go about getting [your IPEDs]?

D: For me, I'm gonna be honest, I only use one person, because I know exactly where it comes from and exactly what's in it. That's a health thing for me, I don't want to buy something that somebody's made in a bathtub in a shed in their garden. I specifically use this guy for a reason. I will pay more than probably a couple of lads do to get it off the street but for me I like it to be pure if that makes sense, even though I'm taking drugs.

N: Is that local to here then?

D: No [pauses for a couple of seconds] West Midlands. Well I've got one in the West Mids and one up in Liverpool.

Illustrating Rob's assertion in the previous chapter in regard to the geographic location of UGLs, Dom locates his supplier's facilities in the West Midlands and the North West, both of which he regularly visited to collect his orders in person. He noted that, alongside visiting the UGL, their relationship was mainly carried out on WhatsApp, through which he would request his order and arrange pick up. Though Dom was reticent to name this UGL, Sam identified them as Astra, a relatively small-scale but well-established operation who, according to several online forums, 'have been around a while' (anonymous contributor to a popular UK-based bodybuilding forum). Thus far, Dom's involvement appears highly typical, however it is his role in facilitating his clients' and fellow gym users' consumption that elevates his significance in this research. In line with his role as a steroid mentor and anabolics coach, Dom acted as a focal point in allowing Astra to sell to Sam, Ed, and Jake, whom he introduced to the UGL owner and even acted as a social supplier or user-seller (Coomber et al, 2014; Antonopoulos and Hall, 2016; Begley et al, 2017), functioning as an intermediary between the lab and his clients by picking up on their behalf and storing the products at his home. He conceptualized this behaviour as simply part of his coaching service:

N: Say if you've got a client who's clean and reached their natural potential, would you carry out a consultation with them before advising them on performance enhancers? What's your process?

D: So nine out of ten times they'll train for a period of however many months and then I'll get a message through, 'Dave down the gym said I should take this, I don't know what it is, do you?' Then I'll explain it's this compound and it does X, Y, and Z. Then it'll either go 'I don't think you're at a point where you need to take them' or 'Where do you want to go with your fitness goals?' is my question. And then they tell me and it's

> either 'You don't need steroids to get there' or 'Over time you may need steroids to get there but it's your choice.' Then if they come back to me like, 'I've thought about it for a few days or a few weeks, I've done my research or I've read this' or whatever then I will point them in the direction of my guys because it's what I use and I'd recommend it compared to other stuff on the market. But obviously I don't sell them anything or make any money from it, it's their choice where they go at the end of the day.

Dom's informal role as a steroid mentor, as well as his more formalized position as an anabolics coach, allows him to 'drift' into the role of a social supplier, as his advice about compounds and suitability soon blurs with the recommendation of his UGL brand. Fincoeur et al (2015) note that social suppliers typically do not envision themselves as 'real dealers' and often substitute economic benefits for less tangible gains like reputation or an acknowledgement of expertise. As such, when Dom stresses that he holds no financial stake in his clients' choice of supplier, this does not necessarily mean that he does not benefit from their loyalty to his brand. Further, given that Dom is paid by these clients for his licit services, he may reap a financial reward in the longer term through their continued custom. Given Chapter 5's identification of the precarity of the health and fitness economy, this enduring custom takes on some significance, particularly as Sam and Ed are some of his long-term clients. Thus, a hazy distinction emerges between Dom's role as a PT, a steroid mentor, an anabolics coach, and a social supplier.

After speaking to several of Dom's clients during my fieldwork, the significance of his involvement in their access to his supply chain became increasingly clear. Sam, for example, recalled Dom's role in his initiation into IPED use:

S: Then in terms of sourcing [my IPEDs] and finding information about them, I was training at Muscle Sanctuary at the time under the coach who I've been with now ever since my second ever show. He was one of the top trainers at that gym, a guy called Dom, I went through him. I trusted him. He was a relatively young guy at the time, but going back to image, he was the biggest guy in Muscle Sanctuary. He was sponsored by the gym and was with Muscle Future [a well-known supplement company] at the time so I thought he was the guy to go to. So I contacted him, went from there and I managed to source them through one of his contacts.

N: How did that work with logistics? Did you drive to a house and meet someone or a postal order? What did you do?

S: I basically just went to Dom's [house] and he gave them [to] me there and then. Obviously, I wasn't going to reveal to anybody that he's breaking the law, but yeah. It's just the way things are done as well in terms of how readily available they are. I trusted the source though, trusted the lab, researched the lab and asked Dom as many questions as I could. It's always a risk, you've got to trust the source and the guy you're working with … with Dom I knew he had my best interests at heart and I've been working with him ever since and I've never had any bad side effects besides what I was telling you about before.

Sam's recollection captures Dom's influential role in granting his clients access to the partial market, as he sought his counsel after making the decision to graduate on to using IPEDs. Sam cites Dom's enhanced bodily and cultural capital as a compelling factor in his choice to enquire about IPED supply through him, as his status as "the biggest guy in Muscle Sanctuary", alongside his sponsorship deal, positioned Dom as a prominent 'face' in the gym. Linking this to this book's earlier analysis about the role of PTs' physiques as the object of desire for their clients, clearly Sam had identified that to emulate Dom's desirable physique he needed to begin using IPEDs, and Dom was therefore simultaneously part of the drive to use the substances as well as the practical means of supply. Also notable is Sam's emphasis on Dom's altruistic motivation for assisting him, as he acknowledges that "I knew he had my best interests at heart". This again speaks to Moyle et al's (2013) conceptualization of social supply, as Sam suggests that Dom simply wanted to share his source as a means of ensuring that Sam was taking reputable substances from a trusted supplier.

More practically, Dom physically facilitated Sam's engagement with Astra's supply chain by holding the products at his private residence, presumably having picked up Sam's order alongside his own. In this sense, he could be conceptualized as a 'designated buyer' (Moyle and Coomber, 2015), given that he absorbed the risk of meeting the supplier on behalf of Sam as well as making the novice user's initial experiences of purchase as uncomplicated as possible. Both Ed and Jake also relied upon Dom to make the initial 'introduction' (Turnock, 2021a). Ed, who had been a long-term client of Dom's when I met him, explained this, stating, "Dom put me in touch [with Astra]. He's the guy to know in terms of that because he knows the person who runs the lab, which again was my incentive to trust where the source was from". Ed's trust in Dom's recommendation illustrates the influence such actors have in the closed market as, were Dom to have endorsed a different brand, his clients would have inevitably followed his lead. Therefore, from Astra's perspective, maintaining a long-term relationship with Dom appears to be a vital part of their business model.

Finally, Jake, although not one of Dom's clients, entered the Astra supply chain on account of the PT's connections and community standing, as he explained when I enquired about his involvement in the IPED market:

N: So in terms of how you source [your IPEDs] now, is that through your coach or through a friend or what?
J: I speak directly to the people; I get it myself. I've built up a relationship over time with them so I source it all myself, I don't go through people.
N: How did you go about making that contact?
J: So one of the guys in Muscle Sanctuary [Dom] knows the main proprietor of the brand and he's quite in with him, [he has] been to see it all. That's how I know all about it, he's been and had a tour and all that. So he put me onto these guys and then subsequently I dropped off to one of my friends.

Although Jake was initially adamant that he did not rely on resellers or middlemen, he acknowledged Dom's instrumental role in establishing his long-standing relationship with Astra's owner. Again, this speaks to the importance for Astra of having a 'face' like Dom within Potsford's hardcore fitness community and, it can be assumed, the effort the lab went to in giving Dom a trust-building 'tour' of their facilities has paid off. Jake further admits that, due to his enduring relationship with Astra's owner, he "dropped off to one of [his] friends". This demonstrates how such community-based supply chains can grow organically by word-of-mouth and, by extension, how pivotal Dom's role in bringing Jake in was to Astra's continuing success.

Ultimately, this supply chain is demonstrative of the wider workings of the offline, community-based market, with its reliance upon trust, cultural embeddedness, and peer networks. As such, the importance of community 'faces' like Dom cannot be overstated in these partial markets and, more poignantly, to the UGL brands themselves.

Chapter summary

This chapter has examined the offline IPED market in Potsford, highlighting the sanctity of peer networks and informal contacts in the hardcore fitness community for those seeking to purchase IPEDs. As has been demonstrated, insiders in the community are able to tap into the partial, offline market in a manner that someone like myself could not. As such, barriers are deliberately erected to preclude those who lack the cultural embeddedness required to engage in the local market, which typically takes place in gyms, users' and sellers' homes, and through mutual acquaintances. This led to consumers like Jake feeling no need to source substances online or through unfamiliar networks, as a level of trust and perceived authenticity was already established within his immediate peer group.

The tight-knit nature of such supply chains has been illustrated with PT and anabolics coach Dom's relationship with UGL Astra, through whom he facilitated Sam, Jake, and Ed's supply. Demonstrating the common conflation between PTs and IPED supply, Dom's value to Astra is clear as both a verification of authenticity and as a means of increasing custom. Similarly, for the novice users, Dom's steroid mentorship allowed them access to a trusted source and shielded them from the torrid online market, which will be discussed in Chapter 11. Ultimately, as Salinas et al (2019) counsel, localized offline markets still represent the primary means by which those in the hardcore fitness community source their drugs and, therefore, any dialogue around IPED supply ought to recognize the importance of these networks and peer relationships.

10

The IPED Market in Transition: Commercialization, Normalization, and Digitization

Turning to recent developments in the broader illicit ergogenic aids market, this chapter follows Fincoeur et al's (2015) contention that the IPED market is experiencing a number of significant shifts and cannot now exclusively be understood in line with the notion of offline minimally commercial and social supply.

Commercialization and community breakdown

Despite the culturally embedded supply chains employed by most of my community-based sample, I became increasingly aware of some simmering tensions in the broader IPED market as I spent longer in the field. Even those who engaged in Potsford's local closed market expressed a perception that the 'good old days' of IPED supply as a community enterprise were numbered and appeared resigned to the fact that increased profitability and scale of production were fundamentally altering the market. This sentiment was voiced by non-IPED user Scott who, deriding the notion of social supply, scoffed:

> 'Why would you sell anything just for a social benefit? … If you're selling anything there's always money in it, not just because you feel like it, it's money. … Nah, I can't see the social side of it, it's not like they're going round with an ice cream cart [saying], "Come and get your steroids".'

Scott captures the general cynicism that my sample expressed regarding the motivations of most actors in the market, despite the fact that many of them used the supply chains that he critiques. Fincoeur et al (2015) echo this in their finding that the market for recreational weight trainers and bodybuilders in the Netherlands and Belgium has experienced a move away from minimally commercial and social-commercialist supply, towards what they call 'market-oriented dealers'. They describe how these actors lack the community ties that underlie closed markets and are instead entirely motivated by maximizing their revenues. The authors attribute this to growing regulatory oversight and the associated increase of risk for sellers, arguing that the otherwise law-abiding culturally embedded suppliers have essentially been forced out of the market as a result of the 'war on doping'. However, I found the IPED market to be extremely poorly regulated (Gibbs, 2022). Why then, if it is not the risk of prosecution that has deterred community-based suppliers, has this shift towards commercialization and away from cultural embeddedness occurred? This troubling direction, I argue, is largely rooted in the increased profitability of the UGL market, resulting from labs' new-found direct-to-consumer approach. UGLs' realization that they could effectively cut out the middleman has seen "their profit margin jump through the roof" (Rob), flooding their operations with finance that would otherwise be siphoned off by associated actors. Rob elaborated:

N: Does that make it a decent industry to be in if you own a UGL and sell direct [to end users]?

R: Oh yeah, mega money, mega money. I'll give you an example, he's a knobhead and I can't stand him, but a gentleman I know started selling, set up his own lab and within 18 months he had 350 grand going through his bank account and at least £100,000 in cash, but I suspect it might be more, and he was a one-man operation. Mega bucks.

Similarly, Aaron commented that the larger UGLs "make an absolute fucking killing". Whereas labs have traditionally been run by culturally embedded figures given their relatively meagre profit margins, following the increased market share of domestic UGLs, running a UGL now represents a potentially lucrative enterprise. This is not to say that all UGL actors are not culturally embedded, a point Aaron hastened to make clear when he discussed his relationship with the UGL owner who had promised him a guided tour. Neither does it discount the reality that lab operations take dedicated time and expertise to run. However, the increased potential for profitability appears to have attracted a wave of market-oriented dealers and drastically altered the communal atmosphere of the wider market (Turnock, 2021b).

An effect of this has been a new-found disharmony between the UGL suppliers themselves. Whereas existing literature paints the UGL market as essentially amicable (see Turnock, 2020, 2021a), an undercurrent of one-upmanship and competitiveness was evident as I delved deeper into these supply chains. Capturing this, Rob spoke candidly about what he saw as a sea change in the atmosphere of the UGL landscape:

> 'Generally speaking, the steroid market has always been very placid, so labs have never really bashed each other, they've all got along. In fact, there was a period of time where a lot of labs were sharing information and helping each other out when they were struggling. UGLs like Galactic Pharma and A1 all worked within each other as well. Then Phoenix came along and they've been very standalone, very loud, very aggressive and as a result there's been some disharmony within the other labs. We've never seen this, generally speaking the community will police itself so if a lab's shit it'll soon get called out. Energise tried this years ago but they were a couple of jumped-up fucking knobheads from over Bolton way and no one ever really listened to them and as a result they settled down. … But Phoenix have marketed [themselves] in such a big and aggressive way that it's sort of caught everybody's attention. So I don't know if we're gonna see, for the first time, a little bit of a doping war almost where other labs might start getting aggressive back in their marketing or they might start mudslinging, or they might start just ringing the Old Bill and reporting them. So it's unusual, I'm interested to see how it goes.'

Rob demonstrates the ill-feeling that a newly ascendant lab, Phoenix, has brought to the market. He describes Phoenix as antithetical to the 'placid' mutually respectful UGL landscape described in the current literature and, in line with Fincoeur et al (2015), suggests that the previous culturally embedded pro-social ethos of the labs is being undermined by this new actor. Although acknowledging that "Energise tried this years ago", Rob presents Phoenix's impact as something of a watershed moment which, according to him, could result in pronounced in-fighting and even UGLs informing on one another (see Dickinson, 2017). Turnock (2021a), in his exploration of IPED supply on a prominent internet forum, similarly found that the two main suppliers on the platform, having been mutually respectful at the outset of his work, were ultimately involved in a highly public dispute which resulted in the protagonist being reported to the Drug Enforcement Agency by his rival. As such, it appears that Rob's suggestion that other UGLs "might start ringing the Old Bill" would not be unprecedented if the informal self-policing efforts continue to be unsuccessful. This in-fighting was also discussed by Carl when I brought up Rob's comments to him:

N: I've spoken to a few people around this topic, and they've said that UGLs as a marketplace were quite amicable, they all got on with each other, but in recent times it's become a lot more competitive and petty. Does that echo your experience?

C: That's exactly how it is. They no longer ask guys who are bodybuilders to sell for them they simply ask anybody who's interested in making money – they don't respect the community and actually try and upset the other labs. Phoenix in particular have not made many friends with the way they've gone about it, but give them some credit, it's worked.

As Carl alludes to, despite Phoenix Labs' poor social standing in the UGL community, they appeared to be one of the most profitable operations in the UK muscle trade. Therefore, they seem to hold little regard for the norms of IPED supply and simply wish to assert their dominance in the marketplace. Carl further noted that "Phoenix is just based on sales, you could contact them and say, 'I'm not interested in diet, I'm not interested in training, what can I take to get big?'. And they'll send you stuff". This, again, speaks to the UGL's disregard for the sanctity of 'graduating' onto IPEDs that was central to Potsford's partial market. Discussing the impacts of an increase in the culturally distant sellers described by Carl, Luke stated, "If you actually know the person who's supplying you personally and they can see you progress and you can go to them for advice, that's got to be better than somebody on the end of a phone that you've never met". Luke's words speak to the potential harms of a move towards market-oriented dealers as the pastoral aspect of steroid mentorship and social supply appears to be seeping away from the community in favour of unfettered capital gain.

This influx of market-oriented dealers also appears to have brought about a reconceptualization of the IPED market itself, from something of a standalone niche economy to being part of the broader illicit drugs market. Salinas et al (2019) observed that IPEDs are commonly sold alongside conventional recreational drugs like cocaine and cannabis in the gym they studied. Echoing this, Aaron remarked:

> 'Back in the day you used to have like a crack dealer, a heroin dealer, a cannabis dealer, a coke dealer and a steroid dealer. But now it's a fucking one-stop shop. It's like the old cliché of somebody opening up their big coat and saying, "What do you want?". You get your cocaine for the weekend, then your cannabis to come down, you get your steroids to get big and your Viagra to help you with the Mrs [laughs] all in one place.'

Although the suppliers Aaron describes here are clearly resellers not UGLs, his comments are nonetheless telling of the general market's trajectory and, as will be explored in the next section, the mainstreaming of the consumer base following the broader logic of commercial markets. Aaron's description of a "one-stop shop" demonstrates an acute versatility in a market that was once highly specialized and community-centred (Antonopoulos and Hall, 2016). Lee similarly expressed this sentiment as he shared his prediction for the longevity of the market:

> 'I can't see it slowing down with so many more people getting into fitness, more people wanna look good, you know? The younger generation, most of them are out there banging god knows what into their systems over the weekend anyway with pills and coke, so putting in a bit of gear as well, I don't think they see it as being much different.'

Lee's assertions speak to both the normalization of IPEDs as illicit lifestyle substances and the illicit ergogenic aids market's amalgamation with broader illicit supply chains. The engulfment of the IPED market into these wider illicit drug economies again illustrates their profitability and a move away from the community supply model, in line with other drugs markets (Ruggiero and Vass, 1992; Densley et al, 2018; Harding, 2020). Turnock (2021b: 6), however, contends that the contemporary IPED economy ought to be conceptualized as 'two markets', where localized supply chains have seen an influx of market-oriented polydrug dealers. This two-pronged picture is helpful in reconciling my offline culturally embedded sample's experience of supply and this new-found evidence of animosity and commercialization in the UGL economy. Therefore, while polydrug suppliers have entered the market in pursuit of commercial gain, this does not mean that the community-embedded suppliers no longer function in the offline spaces of hardcore fitness. Instead, what I have observed is a general shift away from these traditional forms of supply as the market has grown and mainstreamed. This can be seen to broadly echo the changing conception of IPEDs as normalized lifestyle drugs and the broader trends of medicalization and human enhancement described in Chapter 6.

Though this general transition appears entirely negative, several of my participants suggested that the increased profitability of the market has, in fact, necessitated an improvement in the quality of the products. Aaron, for example, told me, "Generally speaking, underground labs are pretty bloody good these days". As was explored in Chapter 8, the sophistication of UGL production has dramatically improved at the upper end of the market and, therefore, provided they are committed to producing a well-dosed product, suppliers can offer substances of a higher quality than ever before. Alongside this, reminiscent of the well-worn myth that privatization and free-market economics ultimately benefits the consumer, Lee argued that UGLs have been compelled to improve their substances:

> 'I think the quality of gear has improved massively over the last few years. The old trick was they'd dose it up nicely to start with then

after a few months they'd drop it right down just to make a shit load of money on it. Then it would generally just disappear and a different brand would come back again at a later date, again fully dosed. I think that sort of era's gone, with social media now they can't get away with that. People are lab-testing gear as well, that's a lot more available. So I think now what a lot of the labs are doing is they're trying to emphasize and put out quality gear and go off the back of having good continued sales rather than making a quick buck. It's easy enough to get and quality-wise there's a lot of good gear out there at the moment because it's in their best interest to keep it good and keep making money.'

Lee contends that the increased financial imperative has encouraged labs to create consistently well-dosed products, altering their business models from short- to long-termist. Though he also attributes this to suppliers not being "able to get away with" poor service in the wake of SNS reviews and private testing, a free-market logic underpins his statement, perhaps reflecting his own positionality as a supplement shop owner and, according to Rob, IPED supplier.[1] Similarly, Carl decried the popular assumption that UGL-produced IPEDs are under-dosed:

'There's still a massive problem in the market where people think they need to take a fuck-tonne of gear but they don't, not with the quality of stuff on the market these days. I've had some of my stuff tested and found it to be overdosed and that's because the labs know they'll make more money if they offer a decent product, just like any other industry.'

Carl's argument explicitly attributes this apparent improvement in product quality to the increased profit motive of the influx of market-oriented dealers as, following the libertarian free-market logic described by Turnock (2021a) in his sample of illicit ergogenic aid users, he characterizes the IPED market as "just like any other industry". However, it should be noted that, like Lee, Carl was himself involved in the IPED supply chain and therefore would be unlikely to criticize the products he otherwise promoted. Ultimately, without the ability to quantitatively test the quality of products on the market, Aaron's, Lee's, and Carl's claims are mere anecdotal speculation. What is most striking in the men's assertions, however, is that the apparent increase in quality is a result of the commercialization of the market.

Mainstreaming and digitization

This commercialization is intimately bound up with the swell of new users looking to purchase illicit ergogenic aids and the subsequent growth in demand unpacked throughout this book's consumption chapters. Chapter 6 argued that IPEDs can now be more readily conceptualized as lifestyle drugs (Hall, 2019), having transcended their formerly exclusive presence in hardcore fitness and sporting contexts to become unequivocally mainstream. This is reflected empirically in Zahnow et al's (2018) finding that Christiansen et al's (2017) 'Well-being' and 'YOLO' (You Only Live Once) user types constitute 38.6 per cent and 11.1 per cent of the IPED-consuming population, respectively. Antonopoulos and Hall (2016: 702) term this burgeoning population 'occasional users' and note that they exist outside the hardcore fitness community (and presumably its partial markets). This transition was articulated by Carl as he compared attitudes around IPEDs in his early years in the gym (in the late 1990s) to the present day:

> 'Back in the day it was very hush hush, very quiet. People didn't speak about it. Someone would come up in the gym and give your vest a tug [and say], "Come and have a chat with me over here, mate". But nowadays people are walking into the gym and they're asking what gear they should be on. It's a different ball game now. I know there are natural competitions and that's fine, but otherwise, everybody's on it.'

The general market has adapted to facilitate this new-found normalization by lowering its barriers of entry and ushering in a broader demographic of users. However, is this a fair statement or, on the other hand, has the market in fact encouraged more gym users to consume IPEDs? Considering the former contention that the market has adapted to an expanded user base following the normalization of IPEDs, Chapter 4's finding that enhancement drugs function to prolong bodily desire seems to suggest that, as the health and fitness industry has grown, consumer demand has reached unprecedented levels. Similarly, the earlier exploration of IPEDs as pleasurable drugs for lifestyle enhancement and elixirs of youth would suggest that the market has seen an increase in its user base in line with the broader trends of medicalization and the repudiation of old age. However, situating the shifting user demographics entirely within the demand-side omits any discussion of the role of the altering nature of the market in allowing less culturally embedded consumers to purchase and use IPEDs.

According to Antonopoulos and Hall (2016: 704), the global process of digitization allows 'virtually anyone to become a steroid distributer' and, more poignantly, allows anyone with access to the internet to become a customer. The online IPED market, which will be unpacked in the next chapter, therefore, undermines the barriers erected by the various localized partial markets and allows culturally alienated consumers to enter the supply chain. Rob put forward this argument in characteristically robust tones:

> 'Steroids would never have boomed the way they have if it wasn't for the internet, because people wouldn't have had access to the information and they wouldn't have had access to the drugs because [culturally embedded suppliers] wouldn't have sold it to them. … There were a few unscrupulous dealers but a lot of dealers wouldn't sell them to you unless you knew what you were doing in the sense of training and diet. So unless you were training hard you didn't ask for them, which is why all steroid users back then looked like steroid users. … Fifty per cent of steroid users now don't even look like they've seen the inside of a gym, they look like they've been to Greggs. I have fucking clients galore who look like that because they haven't got a clue how to train, and that's one of the problems that the exposure to the internet has caused is that it's given access to these people who really don't deserve them. That's probably a little bit snobby to say, but the point is that half the people involved in weight training and gyms today that use steroids would not go to the gym if steroids didn't exist, because it's the steroids that keep them there and allow them to make progress. … Now people get their drugs before they even get their memberships, people go to the gym because they have to get the drugs to work.'

Rob captures the sense of resentment that I encountered throughout the 'old-school' hardcore fitness population as he derided the online market for allowing an influx of IPED users who are not deserving of access to enhancement substances. He situates the rise in these outsider users wholly within the digitization of the market, arguing that "people get their drugs before they even get their memberships" rather than needing to graduate onto IPED consumption. Supporting Rob's claim, Dom stated, "[IPEDs are] so accessible and the simple reason for that is the internet", while Lee conceded that "[y]ou only have to jump on Facebook or Instagram or whatever at the moment and you'll get friend requests pop up off people wanting to sell you stuff or you'll get added to groups – access to gear is fucking easy". Thinking back to Jake's description of it taking "bollocks to walk up to someone in the gym", for those who are not culturally embedded, the impediments that hamper their supply can, therefore, be bypassed by moving online. This was further discussed by Luke:

> 'Back in the day you just basically spoke to somebody at the gym and they'd be able [to] get it for you. But I think nowadays, I've had people add me on Facebook and send me friend requests and I've accepted them because they look like they're involved in the fitness industry. Then as soon as I've accepted them it's immediately followed by a private message saying, "I sell good quality gear", with a price list

> asking me if I'm interested. So I think people are selling it like that now, online. The capacity to be able to sell it like that's grown, whereas at one time I think you had to know somebody. You couldn't really just walk into a gym if you didn't know the guy who ran the gym, or you didn't know people in there. You couldn't just walk up to somebody in there and say, "I wanna buy some steroids". You'd probably get your head punched in – it was very much being in the circle. Whereas now a complete stranger will sell it to you over the internet.'

The digitization of the market has allowed those for whom supply was previously out of reach to make contact with 'a complete stranger' despite their lack of bodily or cultural capital. This was also discussed by Carl as he complained about the uptake in IPED use within the non-hardcore training community:

> 'There's always been a culture within gyms of, if you're there long enough, if you know a few faces, if people see you regularly, if you look like you train hard and you're taking it seriously – you only have to wait a few months and someone will approach you. But these people who come in and fanny about for a couple of hours they probably wouldn't get approached, so [the online market] is their avenue in. There used to be an ethos of "If you don't compete you shouldn't be on gear", but nowadays everybody's taking it just to look better.'

Carl's words capture the reality that this broader demographic of lifestyle users who train "just to look better" have been allowed a means of accessing the otherwise obscure and network-reliant supply chain. His comments again speak to a sense of nostalgia for the previous era of cultural embeddedness, as Carl heavily judges those who "come in and fanny about for a couple of hours", inferring that they have not earned their IPEDs in the same "snobby" (Rob) manner as Luke and Rob. However, it is still unclear whether these users – who are reminiscent of Turnock's (2018) characterization of 'hedonic' IPED consumers – would have used illicit ergogenic aids regardless of the market's accessibility, or whether their consumption only occurs because of the availability of IPEDs online. What is important, however, is that a discernible shift appears to have occurred in the general market towards digitization and the associated increase in accessibility for those outside of the 'traditional' IPED-using population. Therefore, as the market 'has in some respects moved online' (Hall and Antonopoulos, 2016: 64), it appears that, although minimally commercial and social supply is rife in the partial offline market in Potsford, the broader trajectory of supply is moving towards this culturally estranged customer base.

Chapter summary

This chapter has highlighted some recent shifts in the supply of IPEDs, broadly conceptualized as the commercialization and digitization of the market, and the attendant mainstreaming of product availability. I first explored the growing tensions among domestic UGLs that were reported by my sample, wherein a consensus emerged that labs – influenced by the likes of relatively new players such as Phoenix – appear to have started in-fighting. This is a far cry from the traditionally amicable UGL marketplace and, I have contended, has been fuelled by the increased revenues available to labs as a result of direct-to-end user sales tactics. In line with Fincoeur et al (2015), the influx of culturally estranged 'market-oriented' sellers has also been noted, whose disregard of community norms has encouraged the use of polydrug sales and collapsed the barriers that were formerly built into the UGL market (Turnock, 2021b). However, due to increased community testing and quality safeguards as well as enhanced financial stakes, narrative evidence points to an increase in overall product quality.

Relatedly, the mainstreaming of the IPED market, stimulated by an increase in lifestyle use as well as the removal of many cultural barriers to supply, has allowed many 'occasional users' (Antonopoulos and Hall, 2016), who would otherwise lack the necessary peer networks, to purchase AAS and other substances. As the following chapter will detail, despite not holding the prerequisite cultural capital to engage in actors like Dom's localized supply chain, amateur users can simply turn to social media to source their drugs. I have presented something of a chicken and egg problem here, as it remains unclear whether an increase in lifestyle use has fed the expansion of the online market, or indeed whether the ease with which substances can be purchased has encouraged consumption in a wider demographic of users who may not 'deserve' to be engaging in chemical performance enhancement. This chapter has ultimately served to underpin what follows and track the rapid changes in IPED supply that explicate the growth of SNS markets and a new generation of less culturally embedded users.

11

The Online IPED Market

Now we turn to the online supply chains that have played a role in allowing a host of less culturally embedded actors to enter the UK muscle trade. Signalling the prominence of this market, Rob concluded our interview by stating that "The marketplace for steroids is probably more so internet-based and social media-based than anything. That's the way it's gone". While the operation of online pharmacies, sales forums, and dark net sites has been expertly navigated within the current literature (Hall and Antonopoulos, 2016; Antonopoulos and Hall, 2016; Moore and Rid, 2016; Turnock, 2021a), during my time in the field it became increasingly obvious that the surface web online IPED market is mainly concentrated on SNS (see Cox et al, 2023). As such, although I acknowledge the heterogeneity of online supply and its numerous messy intersections with different platforms, the following analysis will principally focus on 'retail' selling on Facebook and Instagram as a burgeoning part of the online IPED ecosystem.

Mapping the SNS market

Customer base

Before outlining the structure of Facebook and Instagram as sites of IPED supply, it is worth noting the widespread derision and mistrust of both platforms' sellers by my offline sample. Understood within the context of their reliance upon community-embedded closed market supply, most of my gym-based participants were highly sceptical of utilizing these platforms as spaces of illicit commerce. This was summed up by Johnny as we discussed what he saw as the inevitability that he would begin using IPEDs as his lifting journey progressed:

N: [If you were to begin using IPEDs], would you look in the gym or would you look online, what would be your way of sourcing them?

J: I wouldn't look online. There's lots of people that I know of, none personally, but there's people that I would approach who have helped other people I know, so yeah I wouldn't go online. It's a science at the end of the day and it is incredible how many people are taking performance enhancing drugs that have no idea what they're taking. They'll go on a forum, look at what doses other people are taking, then they'll buy it off somebody on Facebook that they don't know and they'll just start doing it. Why would you not go through someone you know, who can actually give you a bit of guidance rather than ghosting you once they've sold you some shit gear?

Johnny's words demonstrate how the SNS marketplace is essentially superfluous for my culturally embedded sample. This captures the reality that the supply chains described in this chapter do not serve these 'traditional' IPED-using communities, but instead provide a means of accessing the general market for culturally distant would-be consumers. It is this population, therefore, on whom the SNS market is mainly reliant. This was summed up by Carl who, although being a long-standing weight trainer, was drawn to the SNS IPED market after having been "out of the steroids game" for several years:

> 'So [upon my return to the gym] after about three or four months of clean training I was approached. A guy in the gym said, "Wow mate, you've got a great frame, you could be really big, have you ever thought about taking gear?" I said, "Well I've tried it before but I really wouldn't know the way in now. Normally people come up to you in the gym and offer it to you, you know?" So this guy said, "Well you need to check out Facebook, it's all over Facebook. Just search for groups on Facebook". Wow, I mean I just didn't realize it was such a big thing – I searched on there and put an order in within about a week.'

Carl's astonishment at the accessibility of the online IPED market is telling as, although he "wouldn't know the way in" to the offline closed market that he previously engaged in, his fellow gym user's advice led him to the Facebook market as a means of re-entering the supply chain without the need for existing contacts. Although Carl could not be described as a typical 'occasional' or YOLO user (Antonopoulos and Hall, 2016; Christiansen et al, 2017), the effortlessness with which he was able to contact a supplier and place an order starkly contrasts with the long-term nature of Dom's closed market network. Buttressing this, David shrugged as he told me, "I could probably get 150 bottles of [AAS] here by tomorrow just by going through a few Facebook groups". However, aside from the accessibility of SNS for non-connected users, why have these platforms become so popular as a means of purchasing IPEDs? Addressing this, Turnock (2021a) highlights the significance of the 'aesthetic culture' of SNS, contending that because so much of the fitness industry's content is prosumed online, it is unsurprising that online sellers seeking custom should be drawn to these sites of digital fitness. Therefore, as social media platforms constitute some of the most dopogenic environments in contemporary society, it follows that they double-up as a means of commerce for their users.

SNS sellers

Before unpacking the structure of the social media IPED market, the two types of retail SNS IPED sellers that I encountered – 'UGL representatives' and 'independent resellers' – ought to be explored (see also Gibbs, 2023b). Although this typology does not necessarily capture the heterogeneity of actors involved in the SNS supply chain, it represents the most straightforward means of understanding the operations I observed and interacted with online.

First, UGL representatives – who exist most prevalently on Facebook – sell exclusively on behalf of the UGL they are affiliated with, acting to promote a specific brand and foster a sense of familiarity within the consumer. In reward, they are offered commission for their sales. Certain brands opt to be more visible than others on SNS and, therefore, during my time in the field, the UGL representatives I encountered were mainly from Phoenix Labs, Energise, Victory Labs, and KSI. Further, unlike the actors that Hall and Antonopoulos (2016) identified in the illicit medicines trade, these representatives tend to be British owing to the domestic nature of the UGL economy. Unlike most recreational drug sellers on social media, they are open about their identity within the groups they operate, commonly using what appear to be their genuine photographs and names as a means of building familiarity and trust. However, their affiliation to their brand is often subtle, as is evident in Box 11.1 where UGL representative Pete Simms describes himself as a 'supplement' seller despite identifying his relationship with Phoenix in his Facebook bio. Without my situated knowledge of the UGL market, I would have been unaware of his illicit status, therefore allowing him to hide in plain sight from those lacking the prerequisite cultural capital.

Unlike UGL representatives, independent IPED resellers may carry various different UGL brands and therefore do not necessarily represent a specific producer. This is demonstrable in Figure 11.1 where @paul_greaves' bio boasts that he stocks '[d]ifferent steroids labs' as well as growth

Box 11.1: UGL representative Pete Simms' Facebook bio (27/02/21)

Official Phoenix Supplements! DM for great prices ✉ Bodybuilder 💪

Figure 11.1: Instagram reseller @paul_greaves' profile advertising the range of products and brands that he sells (12/08/20)

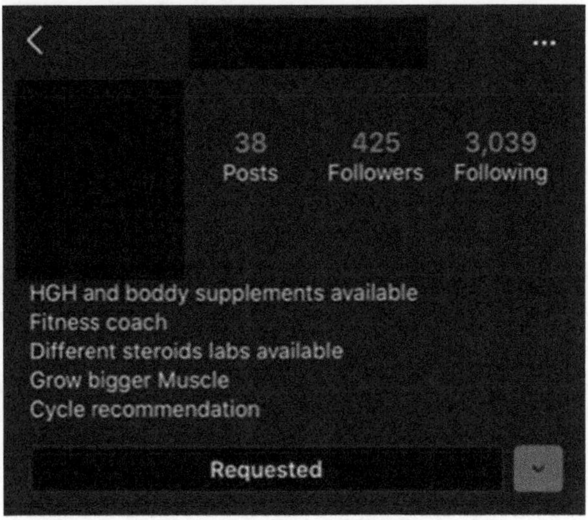

hormone. With that said, most of these suppliers appeared to have long-standing relationships with certain online pharmacies or UGLs and (although not exclusively) stocked and advertised their products. These actors appear more drawn to Instagram as a platform rather than the largely UGL-operated Facebook groups. Further, in distinction to the UGL representatives' apparent disregard for their anonymity, independent resellers typically conceal their identity with generic profile pictures of bodybuilders or pharmaceutical imagery and employ IPED-related pseudonyms. For this reason, their nationality is unclear from their profiles. However, following numerous interactions with such sellers, my data suggest that most operate from nations such as China, Pakistan, and Turkey. The differences between these two types of sellers are summed up in Table 11.1 for further clarity.

Table 11.1: Types of SNS IPED sellers and their characteristics

Seller type	Preferred platform	Anonymity	Products sold	Geographic location
UGL representative	Facebook (specifically the Groups feature)	Typically use authentic images and names	One specific UGL brand	Britain
Independent reseller	Instagram	Typically anonymize images and names	Range of UGL brands and (counterfeit or genuine) pharmaceutical-grade products	Large variance, typically Southeast Asia and Eastern Europe

Market structure

Unlike the online pharmacies described by Hall and Antonopoulos (2016) and Mackey and Nayyar (2016), with their 'direct-order' structure, SNS are best understood as 'peer-to-peer' platforms (Turnock, 2021a) wherein sales are negotiated and non-standardized. Whereas online pharmacies use infrastructures reminiscent of major online retailers like Amazon (see, for example, Turnock and Gibbs, 2023), SNS transactions more closely resemble that of an online haggle (Terwiesch et al, 2005). Turnock (2021a) further draws distinction between what he terms 'open' and 'closed' sellers online, the former of which are indiscriminate in their operation and advertise publicly in the hope of attracting a broad range of customers, while the latter – echoing the closed offline market – sell only to those with whom they have cultivated a trusting relationship. This dualism can crudely be applied to illustrate the differences between the Facebook IPED market and Instagram's role in the supply chain. As will be demonstrated, Facebook IPED supply occurs mainly within private or semi-private groups, hidden from view and dependent on customers being 'accepted' by the UGL representative. Instagram, on the other hand, plays host to extremely open, public IPED solicitation more in line with the general perception that the online market is 'open to anyone' (Antonopoulos and Hall, 2016: 708).

Facebook

A consensus was apparent within my sample that Facebook constitutes the main arena of IPED commerce on social media. Summing this up, Aaron told me, "I think Facebook [is the most prominent SNS for IPED supply]. I think because you can add people to groups without needing to invite them. Instagram's the same, I could probably scroll down five times and I'll come across someone selling gear on there. But Facebook has more".

Facebook's role in the social media IPED market is predominantly played out on the platform's private or semi-private groups, which users can request to join, and either be accepted or denied access by the admin. These admins, far from the community moderators described by Turnock (2021a) on bodybuilding forums, are UGL representatives who use these 'backstage' (Goffman, 1959) digital spaces away from the site's general traffic to advertise and solicit their operations. Therefore, although Hall and Antonopoulos (2016: 39), in their description of the illicit pharmaceutical trade on SNS, note that, 'Friends tend to post stock available directly on their walls or on the page of a group, often with photographic evidence of the product alongside their names and the date', my data point to more of a top-down dynamic, where groups are created and moderated by sellers, who subsequently hold a monopoly over these micro closed markets. This is evident in Box 11.2 where Phoenix representative Danny Knowles sets out some 'community rules' for his public (soon to be private) group.

Box 11.2: Phoenix representative Danny Knowles' welcoming message to members of a newly created Facebook IPED selling group (17/06/20)

What's up guys!

This is the new group for all existing and new clients. It's also a place to motivate one another, share progress, tips, training, diet or even just to get that something off your chest if needed. 😛

I'd like to keep community rules simple. Racism, hate or any other form of abuse will not be tolerated. I'll make a show of you and you'll be blocked. I'm the owner and ONLY trusted source. My track record speaks for itself. Openly talking about PEDs and advice is accepted but please no photos of products. If you need a menu, you'll need to WhatsApp me.

Going forward I aim to support the community and will be sponsoring people I see who fit the shoe. I've already spoken to one or two of you about this. I'm not a money hungry c**t or a tight arse I will always try to accommodate people and support as best I can. I will be adding in some great people moving forward and some top coaches from abroad who you can also pick their brains.

For now, the group is on public but will be made private after a few days. I'd rather quality people than numbers in here. So for now the person who adds the most people who can be vouched for will be sent free product at end of the week. Yes, FREE, get adding 😎

Also, if you guys could leave some feedback on myself or services I'd appreciate it 😃

Any questions ask away👍

As demonstrated in Danny's introductory post, UGL representatives claim to cultivate a 'community' space, wherein members can 'motivate one another, share progress, tips, training [and] diet'. Supporting this seemingly virtuous undertaking, Danny makes clear that he is not overtly profit-driven and presents his role as something of a community leader, aiding consumers in their perpetuation of bodily desire by providing them access to 'top coaches' and other resources. His focus on community here is important as, given the widespread mistrust of the online market and its lack of cultural embeddedness (Fincoeur et al, 2015; van de Ven and Koenraadt, 2017), Danny's efforts mitigate the inherent untrustworthiness of the space. In doing this, he somewhat emulates Dom's role as a steroid mentor (van de Ven and Mulrooney, 2017) within his group, replicating the offline closed market's appeal as a site of support and communality (see Gibbs, 2023b). While this is perhaps an example of genuinely well-intentioned customer service, like the responsible vending strategies described by van de Ven and Mulrooney (2017) in the online pharmacy market, the impersonality of Facebook and openness of the market (demonstrated by my access to his post) belies this communal presentation's true motive. Unlike the culturally embedded offline closed market actors, Carl also noted that Phoenix is indiscriminate when recruiting its representatives, stating:

> 'The lads who sell for Phoenix aren't like your old-school lifters in the gym. Phoenix basically say, "If you want to set up a Facebook group to sell this stuff and make some money, then get in touch", and they're not interested if you've ever lifted a weight before, they're just interested in whether you can manage the job.'

According to Carl, although a façade of mentorship and communality is present, these actors need not be culturally embedded in any true sense. Instead, this superficial proximity is recreated in line with the market-oriented ethos of the UGL economy (Fincoeur et al, 2015) and UGL representatives are ultimately recruited by virtue of their ability to "manage the job". Demonstrating this, Danny's categorical statement 'I'm the owner and ONLY trusted source', coupled with an express ban on product photos (presumably either to prevent negative reviews or simply to mitigate the risk of being shut down), exposes his commercial intentions. This is compounded by his determination to rapidly populate the group and build a substantial prospective client base before taking the community private. Motivated by this, Danny promises to send free products to the most prolific community-builder. This speaks to another important aspect of the SNS market for suppliers – the need to remain vigilant of law enforcement (Tzanetakis et al, 2016). Carl stated that "the only risk in terms of jail time and criminal record is if you're a seller". Therefore, while group members face little to no

Box 11.3: Part of Galactic Pharma's price list (07/04/20)

Oxymetholone 60 × 50 mg £40
Winstrol 60 × 50 mg £40
Anavar 50 × 50 mg £40
Proviron 50 × 50 mg £40
Methandienone 100 × 20 mg £30
Clenbuterol 100 × 0.4 mg £30
Clenbuterol 50 × 0.2 mg sopharma £10
Prengyl 5000 iu £20

risk in being part of a public community on Facebook, as a seller, Danny is conscious to protect himself by moving the group into a more private space.

Following the establishment of these groups, users message the UGL representative on an encrypted platform such as WhatsApp, Kik, or Wikr (Moyle et al, 2019) to request a 'price list' and, if necessary, haggle to negotiate a favourable deal. Demant et al (2019) describe a similar pattern in the SNS recreational drugs market wherein encrypted messaging services are employed for conversations concerning financial transactions and logistical information. WhatsApp appears to be the most popular platform through which UGL representatives converse with customers from their Facebook groups, as Rob explained:

> 'Wikr and WhatsApp are probably the most commonly used … but Wikr is a pain in the arse. So WhatsApp is the more common one, and WhatsApp isn't easy for the police to get into once a phone's been shut. If the police pay more interest, then you'll see encryption become more important but because police involvement and investigation is minimal … then there's not really been the need.'

Following a peer-to-peer negotiation of the price list (see Box 11.3), the customer's order is placed. Payment, depending on the buyer and seller's preference, is generally made through PayPal, MoneyGram, or direct bank transfer and orders are posted to the user.

Instagram

Unlike Facebook's relatively closed infrastructure, Instagram reflects the more common perception of the open-to-all online market. For this reason, I was able to gain a substantial data set from numerous interactions with

Box 11.4: An example of a typical independent reseller's Instagram profile showing the products on offer as well as pro-IPED advice and marketing (02/07/19)

38 posts	425 followers	3,039 following

HGH and body supplements available

Fitness coach

Different steroids labs available

Grow bigger muscle

Cycle recommendation

independent resellers on the platform, commonly not even needing to initiate the conversation. Without the 'Group' feature, resellers' Instagram profiles constitute their primary advertising spaces and therefore particular attention is paid to cultivating a polished, pharmaceutical-looking page (Cox et al, 2023). As well as cultivating a convincing user 'bio' (Box 11.4), this typically involves "post[ing] pictures of gear" (Carl) to exemplify the range and legitimacy of the products on offer or sharing pseudo-scientific or fitness-related content with a 'pro-drug bias' (Brennan et al, 2013: 159).

Given the platform's asymmetric nature (Hu et al, 2014), resellers must rely on prospective customers following them before they can initiate contact. As a result, these accounts appear to search specific gym and fitness-related hashtags and subsequently follow a large volume of accounts in the hope that some will follow them back. As my fieldwork progressed, I was frequently followed by such sellers without needing to search them out due to the 'Recommended follow' feature on the app. Cognizant of the relative sanctity of being followed back, Instagram independent resellers typically made contact with me almost immediately, as demonstrated in Figure 11.2.

Carl described the strategies of flattery and ingratiation that often accompany such messages, where "[Instagram resellers] will friend you and then they'll contact you and say, 'Oh you look great, your physique's fantastic. How long have you been training? Where are you based?'. Then you know what's coming, it always comes back to, 'I've got stuff that will make you bigger'". This speaks to the need to immediately built rapport and overcome the innate mistrust that SNS sellers are subject to. Therefore, in the same way that UGL representatives attempt to foster a sense of mutuality and

Figure 11.2: An example of an independent reseller making first contact immediately after I followed his account back (04/02/20)

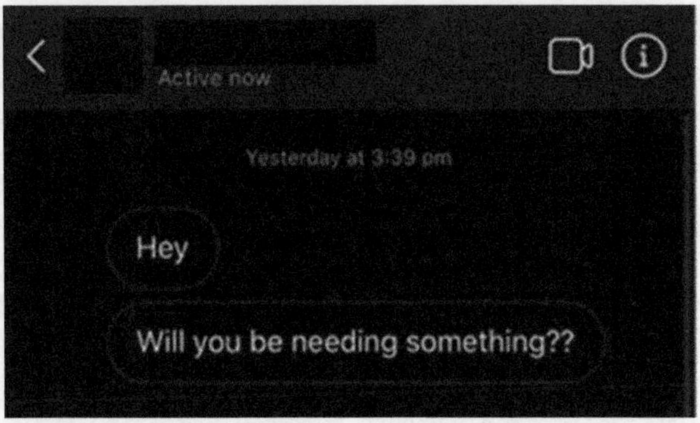

community, Instagram resellers must endeavour to come across as personable and legitimate despite the platform's limited affordances. This mandate was further evident in the practice of 'prescription' (see Gibbs et al, 2022b), where some independent resellers enquired about my goals (often reduced to 'bulking' or 'cutting'), height, and weight before counselling me on the most effective and (in their eyes) safe cycle (see Figure 11.3).

This is just one example of many similar interactions I had during my time in the field, where I was 'prescribed' compounds that a first-time user would be extremely unlikely to purchase under the supervision of an offline mentor such as Dom. Therefore, it appears that these faux-mentor relationships are simply a tool through which to maximize sales to unsuspecting novice consumers. Supporting this, independent reseller @supplementsandmore (Figure 11.4) candidly stated 'I sell to everyone', regardless of their level of experience or apparent suitability. This opposes the offline closed market's emphasis on 'graduating' onto IPEDs and again illustrates the lack of barriers present to entering the SNS market. However, attempting to mitigate this, the seller claims that, as 'amateurs need a lot of coaching', they receive a 'manual booklet and video CD' alongside their cycle. Though I never saw proof of such products, @supplementsandmore's willingness to provide these services again speaks to an attempt to play the role of an online steroid mentor or coach.

Following this, resellers typically offer a pricelist detailing their brands and products before engaging in the same electronic haggling process described earlier. While some were swift to transfer this more sensitive part of the interaction onto an encrypted platform such as WhatsApp or Telegram, most of these discussions were situated within Instagram's in-built messaging feature. These suppliers also generally accept most third-party payment methods as well as bank transfer.

Figure 11.3: Independent reseller @biggearofficial 'prescribing' an eight-week AAS bulking cycle to me (04/02/20)

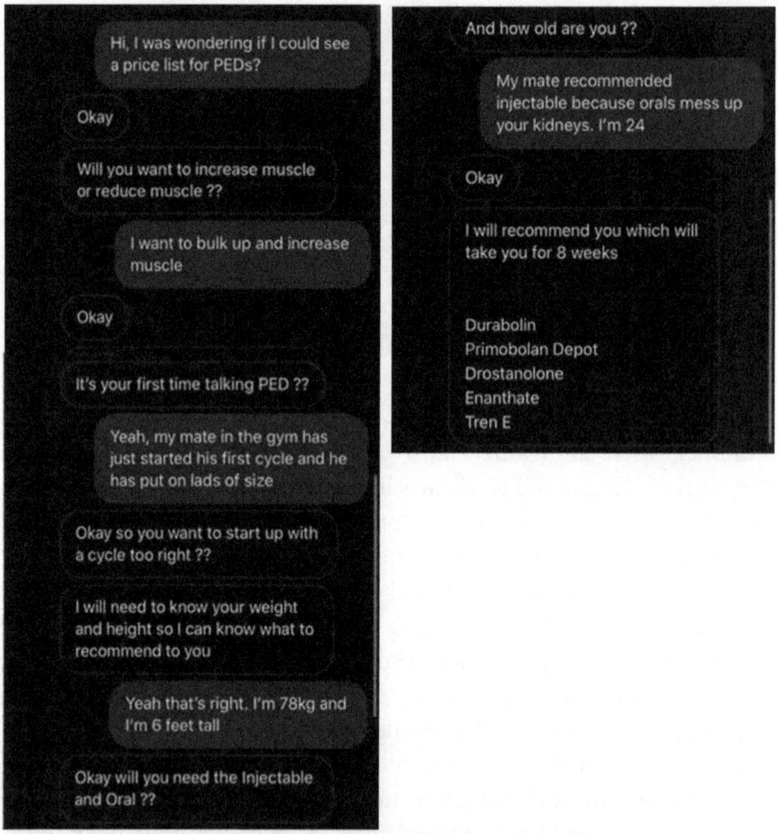

Shipping and discreet packaging

Though the Facebook and Instagram market are distinct in their set-up, both share a reliance on postal services to deliver their products. Given the domestic nature of most UGLs, products procured through lab representatives are typically delivered using Royal Mail. Independent resellers, on the other hand, rely on services such as FedEx to ship their products internationally. Particularly within this latter practice, sellers frequently employ risk-mitigation tactics whereby packages are disguised to avoid detection and confiscation (see Turnock, 2021a; Cox et al, 2023). As demonstrated in Figure 11.5, independent resellers on Instagram repeatedly vied for consumer trust by presenting their products as books or Amazon packages to ensure their safe passage through customs.

Figure 11.4: Independent reseller @supplementsandmore discussing his differing strategies for selling to novice and long-term customers (11/10/19)

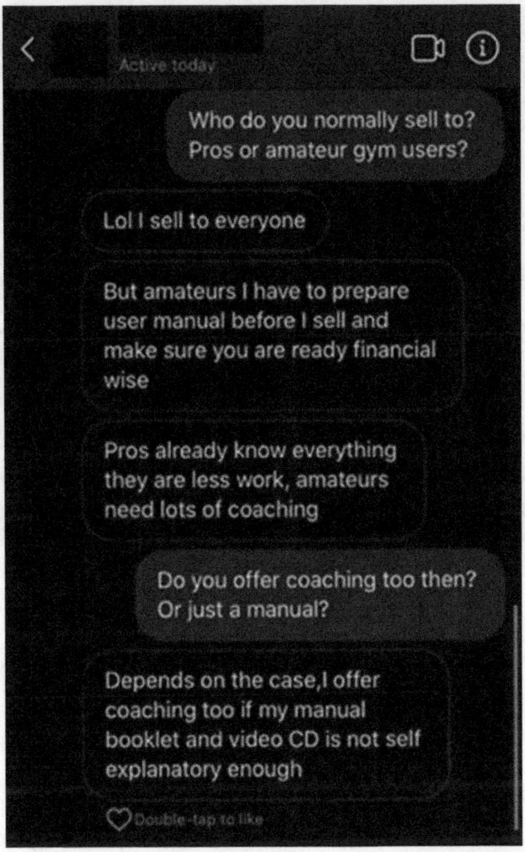

Similarly, for bulk orders @ragin_roids (Box 11.5) described how they insert 'thin aluminium sheets to prevent any X-ray from getting to the parcel' as well as placing the products in air-sealed bags to lessen the risk from sniffer dog detection. Ultimately covering the items in a further layer of disguise, @ragin_roids' triple-protected system functions not only to lessen the likelihood of detection, but also as a means of reassurance for the consumer. Though this is a relatively extreme example, it illustrates the added considerations in the online market compared with many of my offline sample's experiences of simply picking up their IPEDs in person. Ultimately, this represents the final, and most high-risk, hurdle for suppliers, who must deliver the products if they wish to gain repeat business.

Figure 11.5: Examples of two Instagram independent resellers discussing the discreet nature of their packaging (11/10/19)

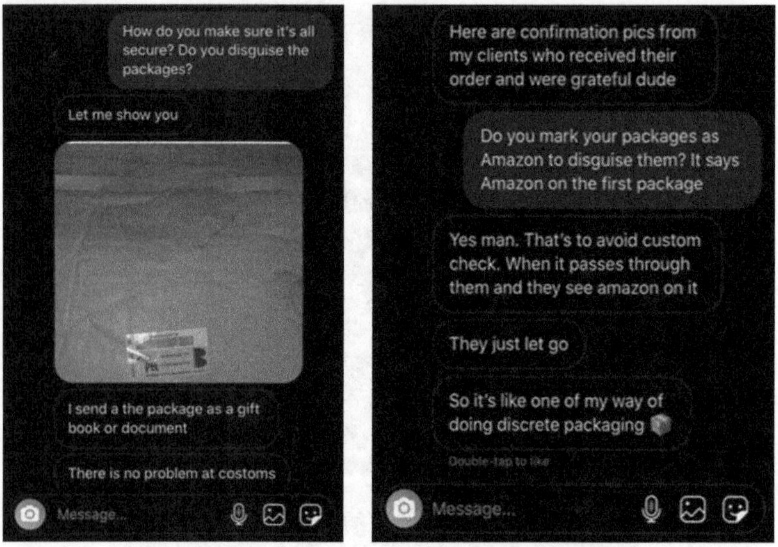

Box 11.5: @ragin_roids describing the lengths they go to in order to protect bulk orders from detection (11/10/19)

NG: Is there anything else you do to make it discreet?

RR: I use a very simple but yet sophisticated method. We put the products in thin aluminium sheets to prevent any X-ray from getting to the parcel, then put the products in 2x vacuum sealed polythene bag to prevent any scent (smell) from going out so no dog can sniff the parcel. After that I then put in another bag and we fill it with some cocoa beans to make the parcel look like a chocolate package. I now do the final parcelling and proceed to have your parcel shipped over to you.
I use this other method but only for huge bulk orders!

Chapter summary

This final analysis chapter has explored the SNS IPED market, focusing on retail sellers on Facebook and Instagram. Though superfluous for the offline culturally embedded sample, these platforms – among surface websites, forums, and other social media sites – represent a means for those lacking cultural capital to purchase IPEDs on the very same dopogenic media that stimulate their bodily desire. These sellers have broadly been split into two types: UGL representatives and independent resellers. As I have expounded, UGL representatives mainly operate on private or semi-private groups and only sell on behalf of a specific UGL brand. These actors are generally British and make no effort to disguise their identity. In terms of their modus operandi, UGL reps create groups through which to advertise their lab's products and, after sharing their pricelist, engage in an online haggling process on an encrypted platform such as WhatsApp, before accepting payment on platforms like PayPal and discreetly posting their products to customers via Royal Mail.

Independent resellers, on the other hand, embody the 'open to anyone' (Antonopoulos and Hall, 2016: 708) nature of the SNS market, proactively soliciting for business on Instagram and using hashtags and recommended follows to target prospective customers. Though their identities are generally anonymized, effort is made to produce a polished profile as a means of bolstering their legitimacy. Similarly, my interactions with these sellers involved a high level of flattery, faux advice, and IPED prescription as the sellers attempted to overcome the inherent untrustworthiness of SNS. Notably, though qualitatively different in their approach, this chapter found a similar pattern of outsourcing conversations around sales to apps such as WhatsApp and Wikr. These dialogues frequently included assurances of the sophisticated strategies employed to avoid detection when shipping internationally, again illustrating the parallels between these two categorizations of seller.

Ultimately, we can see that the SNS market exists not for the hardcore bodybuilders, strongmen, and powerlifters, but instead acts as an online portal through which the burgeoning population of lifestyle users can access a traditionally closed drugs market. It need come as no surprise that the same platforms that promote the swell of muscled selfies that often act as a source of corporeal dissatisfaction somewhat complete the circle in allowing the cultivation of chemical dissatisfaction through IPED supply.

12

Conclusion

This final chapter will summarize this book's findings and answer the fundamental questions of why my sample used IPEDs, and how they engaged with the market. Though these are rather lofty aims for a single study, it is hoped that what has been presented in this book will go some way towards shedding light on these key questions and adding some much-needed theoretical nuance to this burgeoning area of study.

Why use IPEDs?

A primary focus of this monograph has been to address the question of what motivates IPED users to consume substances that are often accompanied by a panoply of harms, expenses, and ascetic protocols. Aiming to move beyond basic accounts of aesthetic motivation, sporting attainment, and deficient body image, this book has, to paraphrase Winlow (2019), examined what lies beneath my sample's compulsion to chemically enhance their physiques. I have argued that the fundamental drive to consume IPEDs lies within the Lacanian notion of desire, wherein the subject is psychically compelled to prolong a state of dissatisfaction and lack by perpetually striving for, but never attaining, the *objet petit a* (Lacan, 1958; McGowan, 2016). For my sample, this relentless search for the lost object is manifested in fitness and muscular growth as a result of the inherently unending nature of bodywork (Bauman, 2012). As such, the physical form becomes the *objet petit a* and corporeal improvement is the unattainable promise that the subject can aim for. Therefore, the orthodox accounts of bodily dissatisfaction fuelling IPED consumption ought to be reinterpreted in light of the reality that the subject fundamentally seeks to perpetuate a state of bodily desire. By extension, IPEDs provide users with a means of erecting further barriers to their corporeal satisfaction, so that the *objet petit a* remains tantalizingly out of grasp. From this, we can better understand the acts of bodily jouissance that accompany IPED consumption as well as the addictive nature of substances such as AAS, whose illusory promise draws the subject to continually seek chemical enhancement, potentially to the point of abuse.

I have also sought to ground analysis in the meso and macro politico-economic contexts of this work, and therefore, sitting atop this psychic draw to bodily enhancement, I contend that a host of external factors have contributed to the recent swell in IPED consumption. Although Brennan et al's (2017) suggestion that sporting motivation plays a pivotal role in many athletes' compulsion to use IPEDs is correct, following Kotzé and Antonopoulos (2019) this book has uncovered broader instrumental drives that promote IPED use among Potsford's health and fitness professionals. For participants like Ed, Sam, and Dom, using illicit enhancement substances is necessitated by their physical embodiment of their fitness 'brand' (Khamis et al, 2017), and the potential financial consequences of losing their 'boosted' bodily capital. In post-industrial towns and cities like Potsford, where the burgeoning health and fitness industry provides a more rewarding alternative to the low-paid menial labour that characterizes the local economy, I have therefore argued that this state of 'permanent recession' (Hall et al, 2008) acts as a 'dopogenic environment' (Backhouse et al, 2018), pushing those for whom physical size and strength function as marketable assets towards illicit enhancement.

Another key finding has been the conceptualization of IPEDs as lifestyle drugs, explored through the case study of Phillip. Following Mulrooney et al (2019), this book has argued that the question of why users consume IPEDs cannot be divorced from an exploration of the pleasurable effects they provide. Therefore, although my sample were captivated by IPEDs' role in prolonging the body as the *objet petit a*, they also enjoyed the anti-aging, confidence-boosting, and well-being-bolstering aspects of drug use. For Phillip, injecting testosterone was akin to an elixir of youth and represented a means of prolonging the good life of travel, sports cars, and masculine virility. Motivation to consume IPEDs can, therefore, be understood as much in relation to the enhancement of one's life – particularly in old age – as one's performance in the gym.

Finally, given the increasingly digitized nature of contemporary society and the attendant practice of digital prosumption (Hall, 2019; Fuchs, 2021), the role of social media platforms should not be overlooked when addressing the question of motivation. I have argued that social media sites such as Facebook and Instagram allow users to perform for the Big Other by sharing their physiques and receiving validation in the form of likes, comments, and messages. In this pursuit of verification, they employ exposure-maximizing tactics, which create a landscape of idealized and perfected bodies akin to a Lacanian mirror (Hall, 2019), wherein users ultimately feel alienated from their own image as their ideal ego and ego ideal become subverted to present a hyper-real fantasy space. This digital landscape is indelibly impacted by the technological platforms that host it, as the architecture of the SNS push users to post more and more often and decree the success of content according to their metrics. As such, users are propelled into a frenzy of self-promotion and aesthetic representation. This wash of perfected bodies therefore acts as a digital dopogenic environment given that the global peer network that users are exposed to further fuels their bodily desire, with each chiselled physique constituting the *objet petit a* that they can (unsuccessfully) attempt to emulate. As such, scrolling past a multitude of semi-nude, idealized physiques, the lack that drives the subject is stimulated and the likelihood of IPED consumption increases.

As the multi-faceted nature of this response illustrates, the motivation to consume IPEDs, far from being reducible to a standardized set of risk factors, is informed by numerous highly contextual, interconnected layers of influence. My sample's motivation to engorge their physiques and use illicit ergogenic aids should therefore be understood as an interplay of psychoanalytic, instrumental, and experiential factors, and embedded in the meso and macro processes of digitization and post-industrial decline.

Potsford's local closed market structure

Potsford's local IPED market was explored at length in Chapter 7 and, although users were aware of the growing online marketplace, supply was shown to mostly occur within community-embedded peer groups where consumers' bodily and cultural capital facilitated access to IPEDs. Underlying this was a normalization of drug consumption in the local sites of hardcore fitness, which facilitated a 'partial' market (Fincoeur et al, 2015) where trust and peer network played a substantial role. This echoes previous scholarship on similar 'traditional' offline supply chains, where enduring relationships with UGL suppliers are premised on a sustained affinity and brand loyalty, alongside a commercial imperative. On a practical level, this involved users such as Ben and Sam collecting products from their suppliers' home addresses, as a hybrid model of social supply and minimally commercialist supply operated within these well-connected networks.

However, owing to the culturally embedded nature of localized supply, Potsford's offline market can also be characterized as fundamentally 'closed' (Coomber and Turnbull, 2007) as certain barriers precluded non-community members from entering. Principal among these are bodily capital and community connections, as users such as Ed and Jake were expected to undergo an apprenticeship in hardcore training before being permitted to progress onto IPEDs. The parameters of this closed market were policed by community gatekeepers like Dom who, in his role as a 'steroid mentor' and 'anabolics coach' (van de Ven and Mulrooney, 2017; Gibbs et al, 2022b), was able to grant or deny access to the supply chain and, as was demonstrated in the case study of his relationship with UGL Astra, make introductions to his brand as a middleman or social supplier. Above all else, Dom's mutually beneficial relationship with Astra illustrates the importance of building localized community connections for UGLs who can benefit from informal word-of-mouth marketing and introductions, establishing them as a trusted source within these partial markets.

Market trajectory: commercialization and SNS supply

This monograph has identified a number of processes that are fundamentally altering the nature of IPED supply. Chapter 10 followed Fincoeur et al (2015) in noting a general shift towards 'market-oriented' dealers entering the IPED market, who hold far less regard for the notions of communality and cultural embeddedness than those operating in Potsford's closed supply chains, and are instead driven by commercial gain. Opposing Fincoeur et al (2015) however, I have argued that this concerning transition can be explained by the increased profitability of the marketplace and UGLs' tactic of electronic direct-to-consumer advertising (Laing and Mackey, 2011). Given the lucrative nature of IPED supply, I have also shown how newer market-oriented actors such as Phoenix Labs have eroded the formerly amicable relationships between the various UGLs and created a sense of disharmony. In turn, this shift appears to have pushed the market closer to other 'mainstream' poly drug economies (Salinas et al, 2019) as these new actors, in line with their commercial imperative, are not limited to IPEDs but instead also offer a "one-stop shop" (Aaron) of recreational drugs.

The digitization of the market and its subsequent accessibility has further widened the user base to include those who are prohibited from the local partial market due to their lack of bodily or cultural capital. This, I have argued, somewhat explains the burgeoning number of IPED users nationally, alongside the multi-faceted drivers to consumption described earlier in this book. However, the question of causation – that is, whether the increased accessibility has led to more use or vice versa – is unclear, and appears symbiotic in nature, with consumption being both facilitated and driven by this digitized accessibility. This does, however, support the notion of lifestyle or 'occasional' use (Antonopoulos and Hall, 2016), with 'YOLO' and 'Well-being' types (Christiansen, 2020) being offered a means of sourcing IPEDs away from the localized partial market. As such, trainers need not graduate onto IPEDs in the wake of these shifts and may, as Rob suggested, "get their drugs before they even get their memberships". It should be emphasized, however, that this transition is not universal and, as my analysis of Potsford's partial market demonstrates, culturally embedded use and supply still dominate in many sites of hardcore fitness despite the general market's trajectory. Additionally, I noted a widespread derision from my offline sample towards the social media market, which further emphasizes the disconnect between the traditional user base and the new-found digital means of supply.

Addressing the social media market, this book has focused on Facebook and Instagram and found two types of sellers: UGL representatives and independent resellers. Operating mainly on Facebook semi-private groups, UGL representatives sell on behalf of a specific (usually UK) producer and tend to be relatively open about their identity. Independent resellers, on the other hand, carry various brands and advertise their products more overtly, mainly on Instagram. Overall, SNS supply can be described as peer-to-peer in nature (Turnock, 2021a), opposing online pharmacies and instead representing more of a negotiation. On Facebook, prospective customers are added to specific groups before being solicited by UGL reps who hold a monopoly over the digital space. Lacking such an affordance, Instagram resellers generally approach members of the digital fitness community specifically and offer their services via the messaging feature. Both types of sellers rely on price lists to display their range of products and conversation is generally moved onto a more secure encrypted platform like WhatsApp or Telegram at the point of order. Unlike the partial market, orders are sent out via the postal service or courier, and risk-mitigation strategies are employed to reduce the likelihood of regulatory interception.

Recommendations for future research and conclusion

While this monograph has endeavoured to make a unique and timely contribution to the existing literature on IPEDs, a great deal more scholarship is required. Following the efficacy of my connective ethnographic approach, I encourage scholars seeking to further map the interconnections between the processes of 'traditional' offline supply, digital prosumption, and the online IPED market to similarly reject the online/offline dualism. With some notable exceptions (see Hall and Antonopoulos, 2016; Demant et al, 2020; Turnock, 2021a), IPED research has tended to overlook the utility of digital ethnography and the value of researchers immersing themselves in sites like Facebook, Instagram, and online forums. Therefore, research into digital spaces beyond Facebook and Instagram would be a welcome addition to the literature, perhaps focusing on platforms like Snapchat, Telegram, and Wikr, which were frequently indexed by digital suppliers as well as my IPED-consuming sample during my fieldwork.

In terms of the IPED market more generally, although this work has established the primacy of domestic UGL production and sales, further exploration is required into the scale of UGL operations and how the trends of commercialization and the influx of market-oriented dealers has shaped UK IPED supply. Ultimately, although access into a small-scale UGL has been achieved elsewhere (see Turnock, 2020), research conducted inside a large-scale commercial lab would shed light upon the nascent trends that have been uncovered in this book. Similarly, while pharmaceutical-grade production was briefly explored in Chapter 8, future scholarship should aim to interrogate this supply chain more rigorously and identify how the substances that Ben and Josh consumed were siphoned off licit supply chains or legally imported via 'steroid holidays' (Dunn et al, 2022; Gibbs, 2023c).

In terms of user motivation and the 'demand-side', future research should advance this book's interrogation of Lacanian desire and bodily dissatisfaction and apply the concept of the physical form as the *objet petit a* to other gym-using populations. For example, given my exclusive focus on hardcore and competitive users, further work should address the burgeoning IPED-consuming population who do not necessarily commence use when they reach a natural plateau, as well as female users. Finally, Chapter 7's analysis of my sample's relationship with social media led me to ask the question: can the various like-increasing strategies such as filters, photo editing, and deliberately angled images be considered a digitized form of enhancement? This is an area ripe for future scholarship, particularly given the ubiquity of digital prosumption and bodily culture on social media (Hakim, 2015; Richardson et al, 2019).

Ultimately, this work can draw three overarching conclusions. First, in the words of Rob, "steroid use isn't going away". Broadening Rob's supposition to include the other IPEDs explored in this work, it can be surmised that the macro, meso, and micro contexts that lead to consumption are unlikely to alter any time soon. Given the all-encompassing sense of capitalist realism (Fisher, 2009) that has weathered even the ravages of the COVID-19 global pandemic (Briggs et al, 2020), IPEDs' status as a form of hyper-conformity to the incumbent political system and a means to compete in the post-industrial spaces of towns and cities like Potsford looks set to continue unabated. Neither is the mass use of social media showing any signs of halting as the Global North becomes increasingly digitized and our identities are played out more fully online, maintaining the sites' potency as globalized dopogenic environments. As such, we must look to transcend the 'narrative of harm' (Mulrooney et al, 2019) inherent throughout anti-doping research and instead foster an honest dialogue about IPED consumption.

Second, we should acknowledge that IPEDs, far from representing subcultural, niche substances, can now best be conceptualized as 'lifestyle' drugs (Hall, 2019) given their availability and normalization. Exemplified through my case study of Phillip, although substances like AAS still predominate in spaces of fitness, their lifestyle-enhancing effects are now experienced far beyond the traditional milieus of the hardcore bodybuilding gym. As such, the IPED-using population is fundamentally altering from a culturally embedded sub-group to a far broader and less knowledgeable consumer base. This represents a substantial challenge for harm reduction practitioners given the long-term health consequences of IPED use and how to best target this increasingly disparate population (Bates et al, 2022).

Finally, I have presented something of a causality dilemma in relation to the mainstreaming of the IPED market, where it is not obvious whether the rise in lifestyle IPED use has been driven by, or simply accommodated by, the market. What is clear, however, is that the UK muscle trade has experienced a profound shift from an amicable, predominantly offline closed space to a hybrid model where 'traditional' community-based supply now sits alongside a highly accessible online market that is largely played out on SNS. This process appears to have been accelerated by the increased profitability of the illicit economy and the poor regulation of these new spaces of commerce that exist beyond regulatory oversight. Though I can offer no great counsel as to how to better regulate this mutation in IPED supply, such a development echoes the wider challenges facing the policing of illicit drug markets on social media (Moyle et al, 2019). On a more intellectual level, in this book I hope to have made a convincing case that the topic of IPEDs ought to be addressed with the theoretical and political rigour that it demands. Ultimately, far from simply representing a means of 'getting ripped' in the gym, the substances, as well as the market infrastructure that facilitates their use, evoke a multitude of profound criminological and philosophical debates that can serve as a lens to examine far larger shifts and trends within contemporary society.

Notes

Introduction

1 The name of the city has been anonymized to ensure participant confidentiality.

2 Any readers from a practitioner background or less well-versed in criminological theory may wish to skip the sections on the book's ontological and epistemic commitments and move ahead to the chapter's main focus on the gym as a site of deviant leisure.

Chapter 2

1 This refers to those who are employed as managers, directors, technical, and learned professionals.

2 Unfortunately, I have been unable to verify this claim, although a search on the website Hussle (2020) located at least 36 gyms in the area.

3 This is the rather full-throttle chorus of former AC/DC guitarist Rob Bailey's song 'BEAST'. This tune was a regular fixture at Muscle Sanctuary and could be heard at around 6 pm each night.

4 'Spotting' refers to the act of supporting another gym user as they perform a strenuous resistance lift. This occurs when a member wants to safely push their muscles to the point of failure or when they are attempting a substantial lift (see Rothmann (2022) for a fuller exploration of this practice).

Chapter 4

1 DNP, short for 2,4-dinitrophenol, is an extremely efficacious fat burner (Grundlingh et al, 2011) and one of the most dangerous IPEDs on the illicit market.

2 In line with the body's imperative of hormonal homeostasis.

Chapter 6

1 I have decided to omit Phillip's area of academic expertise in order to protect his anonymity.

2 World Anti-doping Agency.

3 BCAAs are a popular sports supplement that claims to boost muscular growth and reduce fatigue in users.

Chapter 10

1 During our two interviews Lee did not indicate any involvement in the supply of IPEDs, however Rob informed me that he was in fact a small-scale reseller and, given my outsider status, was unwilling to share this information with me.

References

ACMD (2010). *Consideration of the Anabolic Steroids.* London: Home Office.

Alhabash, A. and Ma, M. (2017). 'A tale of four platforms: motivations and uses of Facebook, Twitter, Instagram, and Snapchat among college students?' *Social Media and Society*. 3 (1), pp 1–13.

Amin, A. (1994). *Post-Fordism: A Reader.* London: Blackwell Publishing.

Ancrum, C. (2013). 'Stalking the Margins of Legality: Ethnography, participant observation and the post-modern underworld'. In: S. Winlow and R. Atkinson (eds), *New Directions in Crime and Deviancy.* Abingdon: Routledge, pp 113–127.

Andersson, A., Jensen, T.K., Juul, A., Petersen, J., Jorgensen, T., and Skakkebaek, N. (2007). 'Secular decline in male testosterone and sex hormone binding globulin serum levels in Danish population surveys'. *Journal of Clinical Endocrinology*. 93 (12), pp 4696–4705.

Andreasson, J. and Johansson, T. (2019). 'Bodybuilding and fitness doping in transition: historical transformations and contemporary challenges'. *Social Sciences*. 8 (80), pp 1–14.

Angell, P.J., Chester, N., Sculthorpe, N., Whyte, G., George, K., and Somauroo, J. (2012). 'Performance enhancing drug abuse and cardiovascular risk in athletes: implications for the clinician'. *British Journal of Sports Medicine*. 46, pp 78–84.

Antonopoulos, G. and Hall, A. (2016). '"Gain with no pain": anabolic-androgenic steroids trafficking in the UK'. *European Journal of Criminology*. 13 (6), pp 696–713.

Askew, R. and Williams, L. (2021). 'Rethinking enhancement substance use: a critical discourse studies approach'. *International Journal of Drug Policy*. 95, p 102994. doi: https://doi.org/10.1016/j.drugpo.2020.102994.

Aubel, O. and Ohl, F. (2014). 'An alternative approach to the prevention of doping in cycling'. *International Journal of Drug Policy*, 25(6), pp 1094–1102. doi: https://doi.org/10.1016/j.drugpo.2014.08.010.

Ault, R. (2020). *'Our toxic air is a public health emergency ...': Air pollution predicted to kill 660 Stoke-on-Trent residents in next decade.* Available at: https://www.stokesentinel.co.uk/news/stoke-on-trent-news/our-toxic-air-public-health-3746748. Last accessed 12 November 2022.

Ayres, T. (2019). 'Substance Use in the Night-Time Economy: Deviant leisure?' In: T. Raymen and O. Smith (eds), *Deviant Leisure: Criminological Perspectives on Leisure and Harm*. London: Palgrave Macmillan UK, pp 135–160.

Ayres, T. (2022). 'Traversing the fantasy of drugs: drugs, consumerism and everyday life'. *Drugs: Education, Prevention and Policy*. 13 (1), pp 17–30. [Online]. Available at: https://doi.org/10.1080/09687637.2022.2070056.

Backhouse, S., Griffiths, C., and McKenna, J. (2018). 'Tackling doping in sport: a call to take action on the dopogenic environment'. *British Journal of Sports Medicine*. 52, pp 1485–1486.

Bancroft, A., Squirrell, T., Zaunseder, A., and Rafanell, I. (2020). 'Producing trust among illicit actors: a techno-social approach to an online illicit market'. *Sociological Research Online*. 25 (3), pp 456–472. doi: 10.1177/1360780419881158.

Barber, B. (2007). *Consumed: How Markets Corrupt Children, Infantilize Adults and Swallow Citizens Whole*. London: Norton.

Bartolini, N., MacKain, S., and Pile, S. (2019). 'Spirit knows: materiality, memory and the recovery of Spiritualist places and practices in Stoke-on-Trent'. *Social & Cultural Geography*. 20 (8), pp 1114–1137.

Bates, G., Ralphs, R., Walker Bond, V., Boardley, I., Hope, V., Van Hout, M., and McVeigh, J. (2022). 'Systems mapping to understand complexity in the association between image and performance enhancing drugs (IPEDs) and harm'. *International Journal of Drug Policy*. 107, p 103801. [Online]. Available at: https://doi.org/10.1016/j.drugpo.2022.103801.

Bauman, Z. (1997). *Postmodernity and its Discontents*. Cambridge: Polity Press.

Bauman, Z. (2009). *Does Ethics Have a Chance in a World of Consumers?* Boston: Harvard University Press.

Bauman, Z. (2012). *Liquid Modernity*. 11th ed. Cambridge: Polity Press.

Bauman, Z. (2015). *Intimations of Postmodernity*. 2nd ed. London: Routledge.

Beck, U. (1992). *Risk Society: Towards a New Modernity*. London: SAGE Publications Ltd.

Begley, E., McVeigh, J., Hope, V., Bates, G., Glass, R., Campbell, J., and Smith, J. (2017). *Image and Performance Enhancing Drugs 2016 National Survey Results*. Liverpool: Liverpool John Moores University.

Beissel, A., Giardina, M., and Newman, J. (2014). 'Men of steel: social class, masculinity, and cultural citizenship in post-industrial Pittsburgh'. *Sport in Society*. 17 (7), pp 953–976.

Beynon, H., Hudson, R., and Sadler, D. (1994). *A Place Called Teesside: Locality in a Global Economy*. Edinburgh: Edinburgh University Press.

Bhaskar, R. (1997). *A Realist Theory of Science*. London: Verso.

Black, J. (2022). 'The Appearance of Authority in Health and Wellbeing Media: Analysing digital guru media through Lacan's "Big Other"'. In: S. Lawrence (ed) *Digital Wellness, Health and Fitness Influencers Critical Perspectives on Digital Guru Media*. Abingdon: Routledge, pp 35–51.

Bloor, M., Monaghan, L., Dobash, R.P., and Dobash, R. (2005). 'The Body as a Chemistry Experiment: Steroid use amongst South Wales bodybuilders'. In: S. Nettleton and J. Watson (ed) *The Body in Everyday Life*. London: Routledge, pp 27–44.

Boepple, L. and Thompson, J. (2016). 'A content analytic comparison of fitspiration and thinspiration websites'. *International Journal of Eating Disorders*. 49 (1), pp 98–101.

Boer, R. (2007). 'Skin gods: circumcising the built male body'. *Journal of Men, Masculinities and Spirituality*. 1 (1), pp 35–44.

Bourdieu, P. (1985). 'The genesis of the concepts of habitus and field'. *Sociocriticism*. 2 (2), pp 11–24.

Bourke, J. (1994). *Working Class Cultures in Britain 1890–1960: Gender, Class and Ethnicity*. London: Routledge.

Brennan, B., Kanayama, G., and Pope, H. (2013). 'Performance-enhancing drugs on the web: a growing public-health issue'. *The American Journal on Addictions*. 22 (2), pp 158–161.

Brennan, R., Wells, J., and Van Hout, M.C. (2017). 'The injecting use of image and performance-enhancing drugs (IPED) in the general population: a systematic review'. *Health and Social Care in the Community*. 25 (5), pp 1459–1531.

Briggs, D., Ellis, A., Lloyd, A., and Telford, L. (2020). 'New hope or old futures in disguise? Neoliberalism, the COVID-19 pandemic and the possibility for social change'. *International Journal of Sociology and Social Policy*. 40 (9/10), pp 831–848.

Brighton, J., Wellard, I., and Clark, A. (2020). 'Gym Spaces'. In: J. Brighton, I. Wellard, and A. Clark, *Gym Bodies: Exploring Fitness Cultures*. Abingdon: Routledge, pp 65–97.

Brimblecombe, P. (2006). 'The Clean Air Act after 50 years'. *Weather*. 61 (11), pp 311–314.

Brisman, A. and South, N. (2015). '"Life-stage dissolution", infantilization and antisocial consumption: implications for de-responsibilization, denial and environmental harm'. *YOUNG*. 23 (3), pp 209–221.

Brower, K., Blow, F., Young, J., and Hill, E. (1991). 'Symptoms and correlates of anabolic androgenic steroid dependence'. *British Journal of Addiction*. 86, pp 759–768.

Brownsword, N. and Mydland, A. (2017). 'Topographies of the Obsolete: Exploring the site specific and associated histories of post industry'. In: N. Brownsword and A. Mydland, *Topographies of the Obsolete: Ashmolean Papers*. Crewe: Obsolete Publications, pp 10–17.

Brunsdon, N. (2012). *Changes to steroid laws*. Available at: https://www.injectingadvice.com/v4/index.php/articles/harm-reduction-practice/188-changes-to-steroid-laws. Last accessed 29 March 2022.

Buchanan, A. (2011). *Beyond Humanity? The Ethics of Biomedical Enhancement.* Oxford: Oxford University Press.

Burchill, F. and Ross, R. (1977). *A History of the Potters' Union.* Stoke-on-Trent: Ceramic & Allied Trades Union.

Burhan, R. and Moradzadeh, J. (2020). 'Neurotransmitter dopamine (DA) and its role in the development of social media addiction'. *Journal of Neurology & Neurophysiology.* 11 (7), p 507.

Burrell, J. (2009). 'The field site as a network: a strategy for locating ethnographic research'. *Field Methods.* 21 (2), pp 181–199.

Buxton, P. (2017). *Stoke has a day out on the tiles.* Available at: https://www.ribaj.com/culture/stoke-architecture-day-ceramic-stoke-on-trent#:~:text=As%20late%20as%201938%2C%20half,role%20of%20ceramics%20within%20architecture. Last accessed 12 November 2022.

Canning, V. and Tombs, T. (2021). *From Social Harm to Zemiology: A Critical Introduction.* London: Routledge.

Cederström, C. and Spicer, A. (2015). *The Wellness Syndrome.* Cambridge: Polity Press.

Chaline, E. (2015). *The Temple of Perfection: A History of the Gym.* London: Reaktion Books.

Chandler, M. and McVeigh, J. (2013). *Steroids and Image Enhancing Drugs 2013 Survey Results.* Liverpool: Liverpool John Moores University Centre for Public Health.

Christiansen, A.V. (2020). *Gym Culture, Identity and Performance-Enhancing Drugs: Tracing a Typology of Steroid Use.* Abingdon: Routledge.

Christiansen, A.V., Vinther, A.S., and Liokaftos, D. (2017). 'Outline of a typology of men's use of anabolic androgenic steroids in fitness and strength training environments'. *Drugs Education Prevention & Policy.* 24 (3), pp 295–305.

Clarke, R. and Cornish, D. (1985). 'Modelling Offenders' Decisions: A framework for policy and research'. In: M. Tonry and N. Morris (eds) *Crime and Justice: An Annual Review of Research 6.* Chicago: University of Chicago Press, pp 147–185.

Clement, J. (2020a). *Facebook: number of monthly active users worldwide 2008–2020.* Available at: https://www.statista.com/statistics/264810/number-of-monthly-active-facebook-users-worldwide/#:~:text=With%20over%202.7%20billion%20monthly,network%20ever%20to%20do%20so. Last accessed 30 November 2022.

Clement, J. (2020b). *Number of monthly active Instagram users 2013–2018.* Available at: https://www.statista.com/statistics/253577/number-of-monthly-active-instagram-users/. Last accessed 30 November 2022.

Clement, J. (2020c). *Distribution of Facebook users worldwide as of October 2020, by age and gender.* Available at: https://www.statista.com/statistics/376128/facebook-global-user-age-distribution/. Last accessed 1 December 2020.

Cohen, J., Collins, R., Darkes, J., and Gwartney, D. (2007). 'A league of their own: demographics, motivations and patterns of use of 1,955 male adult non-medical anabolic steroid users in the United States'. *Journal of the International Society of Sports Nutrition*. 4, p 12.

Conrad, P. and Potter, D. (2004). 'Human growth hormone and the temptations of biomedical enhancement'. *Sociology of Health & Illness*. 26 (2), pp 184–215.

Constine, J. (2016). *Instagram launches 'Stories,' a Snapchatty feature for imperfect sharing*. Available at: https://techcrunch.com/2016/08/02/instagram-stories/. Last accessed 3 September 2022.

Coomber, R. (2003). 'There's no such thing as a free lunch: how 'freebies' and 'credit' operate as part of rational drug market activity'. *Journal of Drug Issues*. 34 (4), pp 939–962.

Coomber, R. and Turnbull, P. (2007). 'Arenas of drug transactions: adolescent cannabis transactions in England—social supply'. *Journal of Drug Issues*. 37 (4), pp 845–865.

Coomber, R., Pavlidis, A., Santos, G., Wilded, M., Schmidte, W., and Redshaw, C. (2014). 'The supply of steroids and other performance and image enhancing drugs (PIEDs) in one English city: fakes, counterfeits, supplier trust, common beliefs and access'. *Performance Enhancement & Health*. 3 (3), pp 135–144.

Coquet, R., Roussel, P., and Ohl, F. (2018). 'Understanding the paths to appearance- and performance-enhancing drug use in bodybuilding'. *Frontiers in Psychology*. 9 (1431), pp 1–14.

Corrigan, P. (2018). *Is Stoke-on-Trent's workforce really the least productive in the whole country?* Available at: https://www.stokesentinel.co.uk/news/stoke-trents-workforce-really-least-1495451. Last accessed 14 May 2021.

Cox, L., Gibbs, N., and Turnock, L.A. (2023). 'Emerging anabolic androgenic steroid markets: the prominence of social media'. *Drugs: Education, Prevention and Policy*, pp1–14. doi:https://doi.org/10.1080/09687637.2023.2176286.

Crary, J. (2014). *24/7 Late Capitalism and the Ends of Sleep*. London: Verso.

Cullinane, P. (2018). *Bogus security guard who opened shutters to reveal this massive cannabis factory told cops: 'This will make your day'*. Available at: https://www.stokesentinel.co.uk/news/stoke-on-trent-news/bogus-security-guard-who-opened-1819967. Last accessed 23 November 2022.

Dalsgaard, S. (2016). 'The ethnographic use of Facebook in everyday life'. *Anthropological Forum*. 26 (1), pp 96–114.

Danesi, M. (2003). *Forever Young: The 'Teen-Aging' of Modern Culture*. Toronto: Toronto University Press.

Davies, W. (2011). 'The political economy of unhappiness'. *New Left Review*. 71, pp 65–80.

Davies, W. (2015). *The Happiness Industry: How the Government and Big Business Sold Us Well-Being*. London: Verso.

de Grey, A. (2005). 'Resistance to debate on how to postpone ageing is delaying progress and costing lives'. *EMBO Rep.* 6 (Suppl 1), pp S49–S53.

Demant, J., Bakken, S., and Hall, A. (2020). 'Social media markets for prescription drugs: platforms as virtual mortars for drug types and dealers'. *Drug and Alcohol Today*. 20 (1), pp 36–49.

Demant, J., Bakken, S., Oksanen, A., and Gunnlaugsson, H. (2019). 'Drug dealing on Facebook, Snapchat and Instagram: a qualitative analysis of novel drug markets in the Nordic countries'. *Drug and Alcohol Review*. 38, pp 377–385.

Deneen, P. (2018). *Why Liberalism Failed*. London: Yale University Press.

Denham, B. (2008). 'Masculinities in hardcore bodybuilding'. *Men and Masculinities*. 11 (2), pp 234–242.

Denham, B. (2019). 'Anabolic steroid cases in United States District Courts (2013–2017): defendant characteristics, geographical dispersion, and substance origins'. *Contemporary Drug Problems*. 46 (1), pp 41–57.

Densley, J., McLean, R., Deuchar, R., and Harding, S. (2018). 'An altered state? Emergent changes to illicit drug markets and distribution networks in Scotland'. *International Journal of Drug Policy*. 58, pp 113–120.

Derrida, J. (1998). 'Plato's Pharmacy'. In: J. Drakakis and N. Conn Liebler, *Tragedy*. Abingdon: Routledge, pp 338–360.

Dickinson, T. (2017). 'Non-violent threats and promises among closed-market drug dealers'. *International Journal of Drug Policy*. 42, pp 7–14.

Ditton, J. (1979) *Controlology: Beyond the New Criminology*. London: Macmillan.

Duff, E. (2012). *'Steroid vacations' a dangerous rage for the ripped*. Available at: https://www.traveller.com.au/steroid-vacations-a-dangerous-rage-for-the-ripped-1zbto. Last accessed 30 March 2022.

Dunn, M., Mulrooney, K.J.D., Biddau, D., McKay, F.H., and Henshaw, R. (2022). '"Bali over the counter": exploring the overseas use and acquisition of anabolic-androgenic steroids'. *Deviant Behavior*. 43(4), pp 447–460. doi: 10.1080/01639625.2020.1806452.

Duterte, M., Sales, P., and Murphy, S. (2009). 'What's in a label? Ecstasy sellers' perceptions of pill brands'. *Journal of Psychoactive Drugs*. 41 (1), pp 27–37.

Eagleton, T. (2008). *Trouble with Strangers: A Study of Ethics*. Chichester: Wiley-Blackwell.

Edensor, T. (ed) (2000). *Reclaiming Stoke-on-Trent: Leisure, Space and Identity in the Potteries*. Stoke-on-Trent: Staffordshire University Press.

Elias, N. (1991). *The Society of Individuals*. Oxford: Basil Blackwell.

Ellis, E., Briggs, D., Winlow, S., Esquinas, A., Verdugo, R., and Suárez, S. (2018). 'Liberalism, lack and living the dream re-considering youth, consumer sovereignty and the attractions of night-time leisure in Magaluf'. *Journal of Extreme Anthropology*. 2 (2), pp 1–19.

Evans, G. (2017). 'Brexit Britain: why we are all postindustrial now'. *American Ethnologist*. 44 (2), pp 215–219.

Evans-Brown, M., McVeigh, J., Perkins, C., and Bellis, M. (2012). *Human Enhancement Drugs: The Emerging Challenges to Public Health*. Liverpool: Liverpool John Moores University Centre for Public Health.

Fabris, M., Marengo, D., Longobardi, C., and Settanni, M. (2020). 'Investigating the links between fear of missing out, social media addiction, and emotional symptoms in adolescence: the role of stress associated with neglect and negative reactions on social media'. *Addictive Behaviors*. 106, pp 1–6.

Facebook. (2020). *Company info*. Available at: https://about.fb.com/company-info/. Last accessed 1 December 2020.

Fardouly, J. and Vartanian, L. (2016). 'Social media and body image concerns: current research and future directions'. *Current Opinion in Psychology*. 9, pp 1–5.

Fatt, S., Fardouly, J., and Rapee, R. (2019). '#malefitspo: links between viewing fitspiration posts, muscular-ideal internalisation, appearance comparisons, body satisfaction, and exercise motivation in men'. *New Media & Society*. 21 (6), pp 1311–1325.

Featherstone, M. (1982). 'The body in consumer culture'. *Theory, Culture & Society*. 1 (2), pp 18–33.

Featherstone, M. (1991) *Consumer Culture and Postmodernism*. London: Sage.

Ferrell, J. (1996). *Crimes of Style: Urban Graffiti and the Politics of Criminality*. Boston: Northeastern University Press.

Ferrell, J. (1999). 'Cultural criminology'. *Annual Review of Sociology*. 25, pp 395–418.

Fincoeur, B., van de Ven, K., and Mulrooney, K. (2015). 'The symbiotic evolution of anti-doping and supply chains of doping substances: how criminal networks may benefit from anti-doping policy'. *Trends in Organized Crime*. 18 (3), pp 229–250.

Fink, J., Schoenfeld, B., Hackney, A., Matsumoto, M., Maekawa, T., Nakazato, K., and Horie, S. (2019). 'Anabolic-androgenic steroids: procurement and administration practices of doping athletes'. *The Physician and Sports Medicine*. 47 (1), pp 10–14.

Fisher, M. (2009). *Capitalist Realism: Is There No Alternative?* Winchester: Zero Books.

Fleming, A. (2019). *The science of senolytics: How a new pill could spell the end of ageing*. Available at: https://www.theguardian.com/science/2019/sep/02/the-science-of-senolytics-how-a-new-pill-could-spell-the-end-of-ageing. Last accessed 25 February 2022.

Flisfeder, M. (2014). 'Enjoying Social Media'. In: M. Flisfeder and L. Willis (eds) *Žižek and Media Studies*. London: Palgrave Macmillan, pp 229–240.

Fox, J. and Moreland, J. (2015). 'The dark side of social networking sites: an exploration of the relational and psychological stressors associated with Facebook use and affordances'. *Computers in Human Behavior*. 45, pp 167–176.

Fuchs, C. (2021). *Social Media: A Critical Introduction*. 3rd ed. London: SAGE Publications Ltd.

Fussell, S. (1992). *Muscle: Confessions of an Unlikely Bodybuilder*. New York: Ny Avon Books.

Gammon, E. and Palan, R. (2006). 'Libidinal International Political Economy'. In: M. de Goede (ed) *International Political Economy and Poststructural Politics*. London: Palgrave Macmillan UK, pp 97–114.

Garrett, R. (2009). 'Echo chambers online? Politically motivated selective exposure among internet news users'. *Journal of Computer-Mediated Communication*. 14 (2), pp 265–285.

Geiger, R. and Ribes, D. (2011). 'Trace ethnography: following coordination through documentary practices'. In *2014 47th Hawaii International Conference on System Sciences*. IEEE, pp 1–10.

Giannoulakis, S. and Tsapatsoulis, N. (2016). 'Defining and Identifying Stophashtags in Instagram'. In: P. Angelov, Y. Manolopoulos, L. Iliadis, A. Roy, and M. Vellasco, *Advances in Big Data. INNS 2016. Advances in Intelligent Systems and Computing, 529*. New York: Springer, 304–313.

Gibbs, N. (2021). '"No one's going to buy steroids for a home workout": the impact of the national lockdown on hardcore gym users, anabolic steroid consumption and the image and performance enhancing drugs market'. *Journal of Contemporary Crime, Harm, and Ethics*. 1(1), pp 45–62.

Gibbs, N. (2022). *The regulation of anabolic-androgenic steroids in the UK: Priority, provision, and problems. HED Matters*, [online] pp 12–14. Available at: https://humanenhancementdrugs.com/wp-content/uploads/HED-Matters-Vol-5-Issue-1_Aug-2022-1.pdf. Last accessed 13 January 2023.

Gibbs, N. (2023b). 'Sponseredathlete: The marketing of image and performance enhancing drugs on Facebook and Instagram'. *Trends in Organized Crime*. doi: https://doi.org/10.1007/s12117-023-09491-4. Last accessed 13 January 2023.

Gibbs, N. (2023c). 'Steroid Holidays: Sharm El Sheikh, Sinai Peninsula, Egypt'. In: A. Lynes, C. Kelly and J. Treadwell (eds) *50 Dark Destinations: Crime and Contemporary Tourism*. Bristol: Policy Press, pp 187–193.

Gibbs, N. and Hall, A. (2021). 'Digital Ethnography in Criminology: Some notes from the virtual field'. In: A. Lavorgna and T. Holt (eds) *Researching Cybercrimes: Methodologies, Ethics, and Critical Approaches*. London: Palgrave Macmillan UK, pp 283–299.

Gibbs, N. and Piatkowski, T. (2023). 'The Liver King lie: misrepresentation, justification, and public health implications'. *International Journal of Drug Policy*, 114, p 103979. doi: https://doi.org/10.1016/j.drugpo.2023.103979.

Gibbs, N., Turnock, L., and Salinas, M. (2022a). 'Post-industrial masculinities and gym culture: graft, craft and fraternity'. *The British Journal of Sociology*. 73(1), pp 220–236.

Gibbs, N., Cox, L., and Turnock, L. (2022b). 'Anabolics coaching: emic harm reduction or a public health concern?' *Performance Enhancement & Health*. 10 (3), p 100227. doi: 10.1016/j.peh.2022.100227.

Gillette, M. (2017). 'Deindustrialisation and Heritage in Three Crockery Capitals'. In: N. Brownsword and A. Mydland, *Topographies of the Obsolete: Ashmolean Papers*. Crewe: Obsolete Publications, pp 18–49.

Girard, R. (1979). *Violence and the Sacred*. Baltimore: Johns Hopkins University Press.

Goffman, E. (1959). *The Presentation of Self in Everyday Life*. Harmondsworth: Penguin.

Graham, M., Ryan, P., Baker, J.S., Davies, B., Thomas, N., Cooper, S., Evans, P., Easmon, S., Walker, C., Cowan, D., and Kicman, A. (2009). 'Counterfeiting in performance- and image-enhancing drugs'. *Drug Testing and Analysis*. 1 (3), pp 135–142.

Greenslade, M. (1993). 'The Potteries: A question of regional identity'. In: A. Phillips (ed) *The Potteries: Continuity and Change in a Staffordshire Conurbation*. Stroud: Alan Sutton, pp 164–173.

Greenway, C. and Price, C. (2018). 'A qualitative study of the motivations for anabolic-androgenic steroid use: the role of muscle dysmorphia and self-esteem in long-term users'. *Performance Enhancement & Health*. 6 (1), pp 12–20.

Greif, G. (2008). *Buddy System: Understanding Male Friendships*. Oxford: Oxford University Press.

Greif, M. (2017). *Against Everything*. New York: Knopf Doubleday Publishing Group.

Griffiths, S., Murray, S., Krug, I., and McLean, S. (2018). 'the contribution of social media to body dissatisfaction, eating disorder symptoms, and anabolic steroid use among sexual minority men'. *Cyberpsychology, Behavior, and Social Networking*. 21 (3), pp 149–156.

Grogan, S., Shepard, S., Evans, R., Wright, S., and Hunter, G. (2006). 'Experiences of anabolic steroid use: in-depth interviews with men and women body builders'. *Journal of Health Psychology*. 11 (6), pp 845–856.

Gruman, J. (2003). *A History of Ideas About the Prolongation of Life*. New York: Springer.

Grundlingh, J., Dargan, P., El-Zanfaly, M., and Wood, D. (2011). '2,4-dinitrophenol (DNP): a weight loss agent with significant acute toxicity and risk of death'. *Journal of Medical Toxicology*. 7, pp 205–212.

Hakim, J. (2015). '"Fit is the new rich": male embodiment in the age of austerity'. *Soundings*. 61 (11), pp 84–94.

Hall, A. (2019). 'Lifestyle Drugs and Late Capitalism: A topography of harm'. In: T. Raymen and O. Smith (eds) *Deviant Leisure: Criminological Perspectives on Leisure and Harm*. London: Palgrave Macmillan UK, pp 161–186.

Hall, A. and Antonopoulos, G. (2016). *Fake Meds Online: The Internet and the Transnational Market in Illicit Pharmaceuticals*. London: Palgrave Macmillan UK.

Hall, S. (2012a). *Theorising Crime and Deviance: A New Perspective*. London: SAGE Publications Ltd.

Hall, S. (2012b). 'The Solicitation of the trap: on transcendence and transcendental materialism in advanced consumer-capitalism'. *Human Studies*. 35 (3), pp 365–381.

Hall, S. (2020). 'Consumer Culture and English History's Lost Object'. In: A. Hall, T. Kuldova, and M. Horsley (eds) *Crime, Harm and Consumerism*. Abingdon: Routledge, pp 21–38.

Hall, S. and Winlow, S. (2015). *Revitalizing Criminological Theory: Towards a New Ultra-realism*. Abingdon: Routledge.

Hall, S. and Winlow, S. (2018). 'Ultra-realism'. In: W. DeKeseredy (ed) *Routledge Handbook of Critical Criminology*. 2nd ed. Abingdon: Routledge, pp 43–56.

Hall, S., Winlow, S., and Ancrum, C. (2008). *Criminal Identities and Consumer Culture: Crime, Exclusion and the New Culture of Narcissism*. Abingdon: Routledge.

Hammarén, N. and Johansson, T. (2014). 'Homosociality: in between power and intimacy'. *SAGE Open*, 4(1), pp 1–11.

Hanley Santos, G. and Coomber, R. (2017). 'The risk environment of anabolic–androgenic steroid users in the UK: examining motivations, practices and accounts of use'. *International Journal of Drug Policy*. 40, pp 35–43.

Hanna, E., Gough, B., and Markham, S. (2020). 'Masculinities in the construction industry: a double-edged sword for health and wellbeing?'. *Gender, Work and Organization*. 27 (4), pp 632–646.

Hansard. (2007). *Parliamentary Debates, House of Commons, January 8th to January 26th*, vol. 455. London: Her Majesty's Stationery Office.

Harding, S. (2020). *County Lines: Exploitation and Drug Dealing among Urban Street Gangs*. Bristol: Policy Press.

Hart, E. (2005). 'Anthropology, class and the "big heads": an ethnography of distinctions between "rough" and "posh" amongst women workers in the UK pottery industry'. *The Sociological Review*. 53 (4), pp 710–728.

Harvey, D. (2007). *The Limits to Capital*. London: Verso.

Harvey, O., Parrish, M., van Teijlingen, E., and Trenoweth, S. (2021). 'Libido as a motivator for starting and restarting non-prescribed anabolic androgenic steroid use among men: a mixed-methods study'. *Drugs: Education, Prevention and Policy*. 29 (3), pp 267–288. [Online]. Available at: https://doi.org/10.1080/09687637.2021.1882940.

Hayward, K. (2013). '"Life stage dissolution" in Anglo-American advertising and popular culture: Kidults, Lil' Britneys and Middle Youths'. *The Sociological Review*. 61 (3), pp 525–548.

HEDN. (2020). *HED profiles*. [Online]. Human Enhancement Drugs Network. Available at: https://humanenhancementdrugs.com/hed-profiles/. Last accessed 17 February 2023.

Henning, A. and Andreasson, J. (2022). 'Preventing, producing, or reducing harm? fitness doping risk and enabling environments'. *Drugs: Education, Prevention and Policy*. 29 (1), pp 95–110. doi: 10.1080/09687637.2020.1865273.

Hine, C. (2007). 'Connective ethnography for the exploration of e-science'. *Journal of Computer-mediated Communication*. 12 (2), pp 618–634.

Hirschi, T. (1998). 'A Control Theory of Delinquency'. In: F. Williams and M. McShane (eds) *Criminology Theory: Selected Classic Readings*. 2nd ed. Cincinnati: Anderson Publishing Co., pp 289–306.

Hobbs, D. (1998). 'Going down the glocal: the local context of organised crime'. *The Howard Journal of Criminal Justice*. 37 (4), pp 407–422.

Hoberman, J.M. (2005). *Testosterone Dreams: Rejuvenation, Aphrodisia, Doping*. Berkeley; London: University of California Press.

Hockey, J., Robinson, V., and Hall, A. (2010). 'Chronologising Adulthood/Configuring Masculinity'. In: J. Burnett (ed) *Contemporary Adulthood*. London: Palgrave Macmillan UK, pp 88–103.

Hollands, R. and Chatterton, P. (2002). 'Changing times for an old industrial city: hard times, hedonism and corporate power in Newcastle's nightlife'. *City*. 6 (3), pp 291–315.

Holman, G. (2020). *The works brass band – a historical directory of the industrial and corporate patronage and sponsorship of brass bands*. Available at: https://hcommons.org/deposits/item/hc:28155/. Last accessed 31 January 2023.

Hope, V.D., McVeigh, J., Marongui, A., Evans-Brown, M., Smith, J., Kimergard, A., Croxford, S., Beynon, C., Parry, J., Bellis, M., and Ncube, F. (2013). 'Prevalence of, and risk factors for, HIV, hepatitis B and C infections among men who inject image and performance enhancing drugs: a cross-sectional study'. *British Medical Journal Open*. 3 (9), pp 1–11.

Horst, A. and Miller, D. (2012). *Digital Anthropology*. London: Berg Publishers.

Hu, Y., Manikonda, L., and Kambhampati, S. (2014). 'What we Instagram: A first analysis of Instagram photo content and user types', in *Proceedings of the 8th International Conference on Weblogs and Social Media, ICWSM*. Ann Arbor: The AAAI Press, pp 595–598.

Hughes, B. and Coakley, J. (1991). 'Positive deviance among athletes: the implications of over conformity to the sports ethic'. *Sociology of Sport Journal*. 8 (4), pp 307–325.

Hunt, T. (2013). *Stoke-on-Trent travel tips: Wedgwood and the industrial revolution.* Available at: https://www.theguardian.com/travel/2013/feb/04/stoke-on-trent-travel-tips-industrial-revolution#:~:text=Stoke%2Don%2DTrent%20is%20one,brick%20Manhattan%20of%20bottle%2Dkilns. Last accessed 12 November 2022.

Hussle. (2020). *Gyms in Stoke-on-Trent.* Available at: https://www.hussle.com/gyms-in-stoke-on-trent. Last accessed 27 November 2022.

Hutson, D. (2013). '"Your body is your business card": bodily capital and health authority in the fitness industry'. *Social Science & Medicine.* 90, pp 63–71.

Imrie, R. (1989). 'Industrial restructuring, labour, and locality: the case of the British pottery industry'. *Environment and Planning A: Economy and Space.* 21 (1), pp 3–26.

Jackson, M. (2020). *Police discover hundreds of cannabis plants inside North Staffordshire industrial unit.* Available at: https://www.stokesentinel.co.uk/news/stoke-on-trent-news/police-discover-hundreds-cannabis-plants-4484501. Last accessed 23 November 2022.

Jayne, M. (2004). 'Culture that works? Creative industries development in a working-class city'. *Capital and Class.* 28 (3), pp 199–210.

Jenkins, J.G. (1963). *A History of the County of Stafford: Volume 8.* Available at: https://www.british-history.ac.uk/vch/staffs/vol8. Last accessed 25 November 2022.

Johnson, D. (2008). *Tie Me to the Mast: The Football Season Has Begun.* York: SportsBooks.

Johnston, A. (2008). *Žižek's Ontology: A Transcendental Materialist Theory of Subjectivity.* Chicago: Northwestern University Press.

Jones, M. (1961). *Potbank: A Social Enquiry into Life in the Potteries, Life in Britain.* London: Secker & Warburg.

Kanayama, G., Brower, K., Wood, R., Hudson, J., and Pope, H. (2009). 'Anabolic-androgenic steroid dependence: an emerging disorder'. *Addiction.* 104 (12), pp 1966–1978.

Kashkin, K. and Kleber, H. (1989). 'Hooked on hormones? An anabolic steroid addiction hypothesis'. *JAMA.* 262 (22), pp 3166–3170.

Keane, H. (2005). 'Diagnosing the male steroid user: drug use, body image and disordered masculinity'. *Health: An Interdisciplinary Journal for the Social Study of Health, Illness and Medicine.* 9 (5), pp 189–208.

Kelly, J. (1990). *Leisure Identities and Interactions.* London: Associated University Presses.

Khamis, S., Ang, L., and Welling, R. (2017). 'Self-branding, "micro-celebrity" and the rise of social media influencers'. *Celebrity Studies.* 8 (2), pp 191–208.

Kim, J. and Chock, M. (2015). 'Body image 2.0: associations between social grooming on Facebook and body image concerns'. *Computers in Human Behavior.* 48, pp 331–339.

Kimergård, A. (2015). 'A qualitative study of anabolic steroid use amongst gym users in the United Kingdom: motives, beliefs and experiences'. *Journal of Substance Use.* 20 (4), pp 288–294.

Kimmel, M. (1996). *Manhood in America.* New York: Free Press.

Kleemans, M., Daalmans, S., Carbaat, I., and Anschütz, D. (2018). 'Picture perfect: the direct effect of manipulated instagram photos on body image in adolescent girls'. *Media Psychology.* 21 (1), pp 93–110.

Klein, A. (1993). *Little Big Men.* New York: State University of New York Press.

Kotzé, J. (2018). 'Criminology or Zemiology? Yes, please! On the refusal of choice between false alternatives'. In: A. Boukli and J. Kotzé (eds), *Zemiology: Reconnecting Crime and Social Harm.* London: Palgrave Macmillan, pp 85–106.

Kotzé, J. (2019). *The Myth of the 'Crime Decline': Exploring Change and Continuity in Crime and Harm.* Abingdon: Routledge.

Kotzé, J. (2020). 'The Commodification of Abstinence'. In: S. Hall, T. Kuldova, and M. Horsley, *Crime, Harm and Consumerism.* Abingdon: Routledge, pp 54–70.

Kotzé, J. and Antonopoulos, G.A. (2019). 'Boosting bodily capital: maintaining masculinity, aesthetic pleasure and instrumental utility through the consumption of steroids'. *Journal of Consumer Culture.* doi: 10.1177/1469540519846196.

Kotzé, J. and Lloyd, A. (2022). *Making Sense of Ultra-realism: Contemporary Criminological Theory through the Lens of Popular Culture.* Bingley, UK: Emerald Publishing Limited.

Kotzé, J., Richardson, A., and Antonopoulos, G. (2020). 'Looking "acceptably" feminine: a single case study of a female bodybuilder's use of steroids'. *Performance Enhancement & Health.* 8 (2–3), pp 1–7.

Kraska, P., Bussard, C., and Brent, J. (2010). 'Trafficking in bodily perfection: examining the late-modern steroid marketplace and its criminalization'. *Justice Quarterly.* 27 (2), pp 159–185.

Kremenik, M., Onodera, S., Nagao, M., Yuzuki, O., and Yonetani, S. (2006). 'A historical timeline of doping in the Olympics (Part 1 1896–1968)'. *Kawasaki Journal of Medical Welfare.* 12 (1), pp 19–28.

Lacan, J. (1958). 'Desire and the interpretation of desire in Hamlet'. *Yale French Studies.* 55/56, pp 11–52.

Lacan, J. (1974) *Seminar XXII of Jacques Lacan, R.S.I., text established by J.-A. Miller.* Paris: Editions du Seuil.

Lacan, J. (1997). *The Seminar of Jacques Lacan: Book III.* New York: Norton.

Lacan, J. (2013). *The Ethics of Psychoanalysis 1959–1960: The Seminar of Jacques Lacan*. 2nd ed. Abingdon: Routledge.

Laing, B. and Mackey, T. (2011). 'Prevalence and global health implications of social media in direct-to-consumer drug advertising'. *Journal of Medical Internet Research*. 13 (3), p e64.

Lair, D., Sullivan, K., and Cheney, G. (2005). 'Marketization and the recasting of the professional self'. *Management Communication Quarterly*. 18 (3), pp 307–343.

Lamp, S., Cugle, A., Silverman, A., Thomas, T., Liss, M., and Erchull, M. (2019). 'Picture perfect: the relationship between selfie behaviors, self-objectification, and depressive symptoms'. *Sex Roles*. 81, pp 704–712.

Lapadat, J. and Lindsay, A. (1999). 'Transcription in research and practice: from standardization of technique to interpretive positionings'. *Qualitative Inquiry*. 5, pp 64–86.

Large, J. (2019). 'Conspicuously "Doing" Charity: Exploring the relationship between doing good and doing harm in tourism'. In: T. Raymen and O. Smith (eds) *Deviant Leisure: Criminological Perspectives on Leisure and Harm*. London: Palgrave Macmillan UK, pp 325–346.

Lasch, C. (1979). *The Culture of Narcissism: American Life in an Age of Diminished Expectations*. New York: W.W. Norton.

Lash, S. and Urry, J. (1987). *The End of Organized Capitalism*. Cambridge; Madison: University of Wisconsin Press.

Leander, K. and McKim, K. (2003). 'Tracing the everyday "sitings" of adolescents on the internet: a strategic adaptation of ethnography across online and offline spaces'. *Education, Communication, Information*. 3 (2), pp 211–240.

Lee, E., Lee, J., Ho Moon, J., and Sung, Y. (2015). 'Pictures speak louder than words: motivations for using Instagram'. *Rapid Communication*. 18 (9), pp 552–556.

Llewellyn, W. and Tober, M. (2010). *Underground Anabolics*. Florida: Molecular.

Lloyd, A. (2013). *Labour Markets and Identity on the Post-Industrial Assembly Line*. Abingdon: Routledge.

Lloyd, C. (2007). *Qualifications and an employer-led system: recruitment practices in the UK fitness industry*. Available at: https://ora.ox.ac.uk/objects/uuid:2a499757-f188-41d2-aeb4-0b9ad6244413. Last accessed 14 October 2022.

Lyng, S. (1990). 'Edgework: a social psychological analysis of voluntary risk-taking'. *American Journal of Sociology*. 95 (4), pp 851–886.

Lyon, P. and Colquhoun, A. (1999). 'Selectively living in the past: nostalgia and lifestyle'. *International Journal of Consumer Studies*. 23 (3), pp 191–196.

Macho, J., Mudrak, J., and Slepicka, P. (2021). 'Enhancing the self: amateur bodybuilders making sense of experiences with appearance and performance-enhancing drugs'. *Frontiers in Psychology*. 12. doi: 10.3389/fpsyg.2021.648467.

Mackey, T. and Nayyar, G. (2016). 'Digital danger: a review of the global public health, patient safety and cybersecurity threats posed by illicit online pharmacies'. *British Medical Bulletin*. 118, pp 115–131.

Mah, A. (2013). *Industrial Ruination, Community and Place: Landscapes and Legacies of Urban Decline*. London: University of Toronto Press.

Mahoney, I. (2015). *Graftin' up 'anley duck: narrating the influence of unemployment upon identity and crime in Stoke-on-Trent*. Available at: https://www.semanticscholar.org/paper/Graftin%27-up-%27anley-duck-%3A-narrating-the-influence-Mahoney/57556f64858c35c6f2c88d57d79995283f60b56f. Last accessed 25 November 2022.

Mann, J. (2021). 'Cognitive enhancing drug use by students in the context of neoliberalism: cheating? Or, a legitimate expression of competitive entrepreneurialism?' *International Journal of Drug Policy*. 95, pp 102907.

Mann, J. (2022). 'Cognitive enhancing drug use amongst students in (neoliberal) higher education: a functional response'. *Drugs: Education, Prevention and Policy*. [Online]. Available at: https://doi.org/10.1080/09687637.2022.2064268. Last accessed 8 December 2022.

Marcellin, F. (2022). State of the Fitness Industry Report 2022 finds UK industry building back to pre-pandemic levels. [Online]. *Leisure Opportunities*. Last updated: 26 May 2022. Available at: https://www.leisureopportunities.co.uk/news/Club-closure-stats-reveal-impact-of-Covid-on-fitness-ind. Last accessed 2 September 2022.

Marengo, D., Montag, C., Sindermann, C., Elhai, J., and Settanni, M. (2021). 'Examining the links between active Facebook use, received likes, self-esteem and happiness: a study using objective social media data'. *Telematics and Informatics*. 58, pp 1–11.

Marshall, K., Chamberlain, K., and Hodgetts, D. (2020). 'Male bodybuilders on Instagram: negotiating inclusive masculinities through hegemonic masculine bodies'. *Journal of Gender Studies*. 29 (5), pp 570–589.

Marwick, A. (2015). 'Instafame: luxury selfies in the attention economy'. *Public Culture*. 27 (1), pp 137–160.

Matthews, C. and Jordan, M. (2020). 'Drugs and supplements in amateur boxing: pugilistic amateurism and ideologies of performance'. *Qualitative Research in Sport, Exercise and Health*. 12 (5), pp 631–646.

Mauss, M. (1973). 'Techniques of the body'. *Economy and Society*. 2 (1), pp 70–88.

Maycock, B. and Howat, P. (2005). 'The barriers to illegal anabolic steroid use'. *Drugs: Education, Prevention and Policy*. 12 (4), pp 317–325.

McDowell, L. (2003). *Redundant Masculinities*. Oxford: Blackwell Publishing.

McGee, A. (2020). 'Using the therapy and enhancement distinction in law and policy'. *Bioethics*. 34 (1), pp 70–80.

McGowan, T. (2003). *The End of Dissatisfaction? Jacques Lacan and the Emerging Society of Enjoyment*. New York: State University of New York Press.

McGowan, T. (2016). *Capitalism and Desire: The Psychic Cost of Free Markets*. New York: Columbia University Press.

McVeigh, J. and Begley, E. (2017). 'Anabolic steroids in the UK: an increasing issue for public health'. *Drugs: Education, Prevention and Policy*. 24 (3), pp 278–285.

McVeigh, J., Evans-Brown, M., and Bellis, M. (2012). 'Human enhancement drugs and the pursuit of perfection'. *Adicciones*. 24 (3), pp 185–190.

Melki, J., Hitti, E., Oghia, M., and Mufarrij, A. (2015). 'Media exposure, mediated social comparison to idealized images of muscularity, and anabolic steroid use'. *Health Communication*. 30 (5), pp 473–484.

MHRA. (2014). *MHRA – Information about buying prescription drugs from Internet Pharmacies (UD)*. Available at: https://www.tpauk.com/main/article/mhra-information-about-buying-prescription-drugs-from-internet-pharmacies-ud/#:~:text=There%20are%20no%20formal%20restrictions,authorisation%20to%20aid%20personal%20. Last accessed 30 March 2021.

Milbank, J. and Pabst, A. (2016). *The Politics of Virtue: Post-liberalism and the Human Future*. London: Rowman & Littlefield Ltd.

Millington, B. (2016). 'Fit for prosumption: interactivity and the second fitness boom'. *Media, Culture & Society*. 8 (38), pp 1184–1200.

Mitchell, W. and Fazi, S. (2017). *Reclaiming the State*. London: Pluto Press.

Monaghan, L. (2002). 'Vocabularies of motive for illicit steroid use among bodybuilders'. *Social Science & Medicine*. 55 (5), pp 695–708.

Mooney, R., Simonato, P., Ruparelia, R., Roman-Urrestarazu, A., Martinotti, G., and Corazza, O. (2017). 'The use of supplements and performance and image enhancing drugs in fitness settings: an exploratory cross-sectional investigation in the United Kingdom'. *Human Psychopharmacology*. 32, pp 1–6.

Moore, D. and Rid, T. (2016). 'Cryptopolitik and the darknet'. *Survival*. 58 (1), pp 7–38.

Morgan, D. (1992). *Discovering Men*. London: Routledge.

Morris, S. (2018). *Up to a million Britons use steroids for looks not sport*. Available at: https://www.theguardian.com/society/2018/jan/21/up-to-a-million-britons-use-steroids-for-looks-not-sport. Last accessed 10 December 2022.

Mould, O. (2015). *Urban Subversion and the Creative City*. Abingdon: Routledge.

Moyle, L. and Coomber, R. (2015). 'Earning a score: an exploration of the nature and roles of heroin and crack cocaine "user-dealers"'. *The British Journal of Criminology*. 55 (3), pp 534–555.

Moyle, L., Coomber, R., and Lowther, J. (2013). 'Crushing a walnut with a sledge hammer? Analysing the penal response to the social supply of illicit drugs'. *Social & Legal Studies*. 22 (4), pp 553–573.

Moyle, L., Childs, A., Coomber, R., and Barratt, M. (2019). '#Drugsforsale: an exploration of the use of social media and encrypted messaging apps to supply and access drugs'. *International Journal of Drug Policy*. 63, pp 101–110.

Muehlebach, A. and Shoshan, N. (2012). 'Post-Fordist affect: introduction'. *Anthropological Quarterly*. 85 (2), pp 317–343.

Mullen, C., Whalley, B., Schifano, F., and Baker, J. (2020). 'Anabolic androgenic steroid abuse in the United Kingdom: an update'. *British Journal of Pharmacology*. 177 (10), pp 2180–2198.

Mulrooney, K., van de Ven, K., McVeigh, J., and Collins, R. (2019). 'Steroid Madness: Has the dark side of anabolic-androgenic steroids (AAS) been over-stated?'. In: K. van de Ven, K. Mulrooney, and J. McVeigh (eds) *Human Enhancement Drugs*. Abingdon: Routledge. pp 54–67.

Nash, M. (2018). '"Let's work on your weaknesses": Australian CrossFit coaching, masculinity and neoliberal framings of "health" and "fitness"'. *Sport in Society*. 21 (9), pp 1432–1453. doi: 10.1080/17430437.2017.1390565.

Nayak, A. (2006). 'Displaced masculinities: chavs, youth and class in the post-industrial city'. *Sociology*. 40 (5), pp 813–831.

Nettleton, S. (2013). *The Sociology of Health and Illness*. 3rd ed. Cambridge: Polity Press.

Nomis. (2022). Labour Market Profile – Stoke-On-Trent. [Online]. Nomis. Available at: https://www.nomisweb.co.uk/reports/lmp/la/1946157171/report.aspx#. Last accessed 2 September 2022.

Orbach, S. (2009). *Bodies*. London: Profile Books Ltd.

Outka, E. (2009). *Consuming Traditions: Modernity, Modernism, and the Commodified Authentic*. Oxford: Oxford University Press.

Parker, H., Aldridge, J., and Measham, F. (1998). *Illegal Leisure: The Normalisation of Adolescent Recreational Drug Use*. London: Routledge.

Partington, R. (2018). *Stoke is debt capital of England and Wales – followed by Plymouth*. Available at: https://www.theguardian.com/money/2018/jul/13/stoke-is-debt-capital-of-england-and-wales-followed-by-plymouth. Last accessed 20 October 2022.

Pemberton, S. (2015). *Harmful Societies: Understanding Social Harm*. Bristol: Policy Press.

Penney, T. (2014). 'Bodies under glass: gay dating apps and the affect-image'. *Media International Australia*. 135 (1), pp 107–117.

Perls, T. (2009). 'Growth hormone and anabolic steroids: athletes are the tip of the iceberg'. *Drug Testing and Analysis*. 1 (9–10), pp 419–425.

Pineau, T., Schopfer, A., Grossrieder, L., Broséus, J., Esseiva, P., and Rossy, Q. (2016). 'The study of doping market: how to produce intelligence from internet forums'. *Forensic Science International*. 268, pp 103–115.

Plehwe, D. (2015). 'Introduction'. In: P. Mirowski and D. Plehwe (eds) *The Road from Mont Pèlerin: The Making of the Neoliberal Thought Collective*. Cambridge, MA: Harvard University Press, pp 1–42.

Pope, H., Wood, R., Rogol, A., Nyberg, F., Bowers, L., and Bhasin, S. (2014). 'Adverse health consequences of performance-enhancing drugs: an Endocrine Society scientific statement'. *Endocrine Reviews.* 35 (3), pp 341–375.

Posner, E. (1973). 'John Thomas Arlidge (1822–99) and the Potteries'. *British Journal of Industrial Medicine.* 30 (3), pp 266–270.

Postill, J. and Pink, S. (2012). 'Social media ethnography: the digital researcher in a messy web'. *Media International Australia.* 12 (145), pp 123–134.

Prince, S. (2019). '(Re)tracing the everyday "sitings": a conceptual review of internet research 15 years later'. *Issues and Trends in Educational Technology.* 7 (1), pp 45–60.

Priyadarshini, C., Dubey, R., Kumar, Y., and Jha, R. (2020). 'Impact of a social media addiction on employees' wellbeing and work productivity'. *The Qualitative Report.* 25 (1), pp 181–196.

Quaglio, G., Fornasiero, A., Mezzelani, P., Moreschini, S., Lugoboni, F., and Lechi, A. (2009). 'Anabolic steroids: dependence and complications of chronic use'. *Internal and Emergency Medicine.* 4, pp 289–296.

Raymen, T. (2018). *Parkour, Deviance and Leisure in the Late-Capitalist City.* Bingley: Emerald Group Publishing.

Raymen, T. (2022). *The Enigma of Social Harm.* London: Taylor & Francis.

Raymen, T. and Smith, O. (2016). 'What's deviance got to do with it? Black Friday sales, violence and hyper-conformity'. *The British Journal of Criminology.* 56 (2), pp 389–405.

Raymen, T. and Smith, O. (2017). 'Lifestyle gambling, indebtedness and anxiety: a deviant leisure perspective'. *Journal of Consumer Culture.* 20 (4), pp 1–19.

Raymen, T. and Smith, O. (2019a). 'Introduction: Why leisure?'. In: T. Raymen and O. Smith (eds) *Deviant Leisure: Criminological Perspectives on Leisure and Harm.* London: Palgrave Macmillan UK, pp 1–14.

Raymen, T. and Smith, O. (2019b). 'Deviant leisure: a critical criminological perspective for the twenty-first century'. *Critical Criminology.* 27, pp 115–130.

Reisach, U. (2021). 'The responsibility of social media in times of societal and political manipulation'. *European Journal of Operational Research.* 291 (3), pp 906–917.

Rice, M. (2010). *The Lost City of Stoke-on-Trent.* London: Frances Lincoln Limited.

Richardson, A., Dixon, K., and Kean, J. (2019). 'Superheroes: image and performance enhancing drug (IPED) use within the UK, social media and gym culture'. *Journal of Forensic and Legal Medicine.* 64, pp 28–30.

Ridgway, J. and Clayton, R. (2016). 'Instagram unfiltered: exploring associations of body image satisfaction, Instagram #selfie posting, and negative romantic relationship outcomes'. *Cyberpsychology, Behavior and Social Networking*. 19 (1), pp 2–7.

Riley, S., Griffin, C., and Morey, Y. (2013). 'The Rise of the "Pleasure Citizen": How leisure can be a site for alternative forms of political participation'. In: K. Demetriou (ed) *Democracy in Transition*. Berlin: Springer, pp 61–75.

Roberts, K. (1978). *Contemporary Society and the Growth of Leisure*. London: Longman.

Roberts, S. (2018). *Young Working-Class Men in Transition*. Abingdon: Routledge.

Rosenmann, A., Kaplan, D., Gaunt, R., Pinho, M., and Guy, M. (2018). 'Consumer masculinity ideology: conceptualization and initial findings on men's emerging body concerns'. *Psychology of Men & Masculinity*. 19 (2), pp 257–272.

Rothmann, J. (2022). *Macho Men in South African Gyms*. London: Palgrave Macmillan.

Ruggiero, V. and Vass, A. (1992). 'Heroin use and the formal economy: illicit drugs and licit economies in Italy'. *British Journal of Criminology*. 32 (3), pp 273–291.

Sagoe, D., Molde, H., Andreassen, C., Torsheim, T., and Pallesen, S. (2014). 'The global epidemiology of anabolic-androgenic steroid use: a meta-analysis and meta-regression analysis'. *Annals of Epidemiology*. 24 (5), pp 383–398.

Salinas, M., Floodgate, W., and Ralphs, R. (2019). 'Polydrug use and polydrug markets amongst image and performance enhancing drug users: implications for harm reduction interventions and drug policy'. *International Journal of Drug Policy*. 67, pp 43–51.

Sandel, M. (2007). *The Case Against Perfection*. Cambridge, MA: Harvard University Press.

Santarossa, S., Coyne, P., Lisinski, C., and Woodruff, S. (2016). '#fitspo on Instagram: a mixed-methods approach using Netlytic and photo analysis, uncovering the online discussion and author/image characteristics'. *Journal of Health Psychology*. 24 (3), pp 376–385.

Sassatelli, R. (2010). *Fitness Culture: Gyms and the Commercialisation of Discipline and Fun*. Basingstoke: Palgrave Macmillan UK.

Sattler, F. (2013). 'Growth hormone in the aging male'. *Best Practice & Research Clinical Endocrinology & Metabolism*. 27 (4), pp 541–555.

Sekers, D. (1981). *The Potteries*. Buckinghamshire: Shire Publishing.

Sheldon, P. and Bryant, K. (2016). 'Instagram: motives for its use and relationship to narcissism and contextual age'. *Computers in Human Behavior*. 58, pp 89–97.

Shilling, C. (2003). *The Body and Social Theory*. 2nd ed. London: SAGE Publications Ltd.

Skeggs, B. (1997). *Formations of Class and Gender: Becoming Respectable*. London: SAGE Publications Ltd.

Slobodian, Q. (2018). *Globalists*. London: Harvard University Press.

Smith Maguire, J. (2008). *Fit for Consumption: Sociology and the Business of Fitness*. Abingdon: Routledge.

Smith, O. (2014). *Contemporary Adulthood and the Night-Time Economy*. London: Palgrave Macmillan UK.

Smith, O. and Raymen, T. (2018). 'Deviant leisure: a criminological perspective'. *Theoretical Criminology*. 22 (1), pp 63–82.

Southwood, I. (2011) *Non-Stop Inertia*. Winchester: Zero.

Sprangler, L. (1992). 'Buddies and pals: a history of male friendships on prime-time television'. In: S. Craig (ed) *Men, Masculinity and the Media*. London: SAGE Publications Ltd, pp 93–110.

Squires, K. (2020). 'All work and no play? The well-being of children living and working in nineteenth-century Staffordshire, England'. *Childhood in the Past*. 13 (1), pp 60–77.

Stebbins, R. (2007). *Serious Leisure: A Perspective for Our Time*. New Jersey: Transaction Publishers.

Svedsäter, G., Svennberg, L., Westfelt, L., Qvarfordt, A., and Lilja, M. (2021). 'Performance and image enhancing substance use among young people in Sweden'. *Performance Enhancement & Health*. https://doi.org/10.1016/j.peh.2021.100194.

Tan, R. and Scally, M. (2009). 'Anabolic steroid-induced hypogonadism: towards a unified hypothesis of anabolic steroid action'. *Medical Hypotheses*. 72 (6), pp 723–728.

Telford, L. (2021). '"There is nothing there": deindustrialization and loss in a coastal town'. *Competition & Change*. Available at: https://doi.org/10.1177/10245294211011300. Last accessed 17 October 2022.

Telford, L. (2022). *English Nationalism and Its Ghost Towns*. Abingdon: Taylor & Francis.

Telford, L. and Lloyd, A. (2020). 'From "infant Hercules" to "ghost town": industrial collapse and social harm in Teesside'. *Critical Criminology*. Available at: https://doi.org/10.1007/s10612-020-09523-3. Last accessed 18 October 2022.

Terwiesch, C., Savin, S., and Hann, I. (2005). 'Online haggling at a name-your-own-price retailer: theory and application'. *Management Science*. 51 (3), pp 339–351.

Thurnell-Read, T. and Monaghan, M. (2023). *Intoxication: Self, State and Society*. London: Palgrave Macmillan.

Tiggemann, M. and Zaccardo, M. (2015). '"Exercise to be fit, not skinny": the effect of fitspiration imagery on women's body image'. *Body Image*. 15, pp 61–67.

Tiggemann, M. and Zaccardo, M. (2018). '"Strong is the new skinny": a content analysis of #fitspiration images on Instagram'. *Journal of Health Psychology*. 23 (8), pp 1003–1011.

Toffler, A. (1980). *The Third Wave: The Classic Study of Tomorrow*. New York: Bantam.

Tomlinson, P. (2015). *How England's broken ceramics industry put itself back together*. [Online]. The Conversation. Available at https://theconversation.com/how-englands-broken-ceramics-industry-put-itself-back-together-48196. Last accessed 21 June 2023.

Toohey, K. and Veal, A. (2000). *The Olympic Games: A Social Science Perspective*. Wallington: CABI.

Travison, T., Araujo, A., Hall, S., and McKinlay, J. (2009). 'Temporal trends in testosterone levels and treatment in older men'. *Current Opinion in Endocrinology, Diabetes, and Obesity*. 16 (3), pp 211–217.

Treadwell, J., Briggs, D., Winlow, S., and Hall, S. (2013). 'Shopocalypse Now: consumer culture and the English riots of 2011'. *British Journal of Criminology*. 53 (1), pp 1–17.

Tribe, K. (2015). 'Liberalism and Neoliberalism in Britain, 1930–1980'. In: P. Mirowski and D. Plehwe (eds) *The Road from Mont Pèlerin: The Making of the Neoliberal Thought Collective*. Cambridge, MA: Harvard University Press, pp 68–97.

Turnock, L. (2018). *'Gear is the next weed': a qualitative exploration of the beliefs, attitudes and behaviours of performance and image enhancing drug using subcultures in the south-west of England*. PhD Thesis. Winchester: University of Winchester.

Turnock, L. (2020). 'Inside a steroid "brewing" and supply operation in south-west England: an "ethnographic narrative case study"'. *Performance Enhancement & Health*. 7 (3–4), pp 1–8.

Turnock, L. (2021a). *Supplying Steroids Online: The cultural and market contexts of enhancement drug supply on one of the world's largest fitness & bodybuilding forums*. Plymouth: Plymouth Policy Research Press.

Turnock, L. (2021b). 'Polydrug use and drug market intersections within powerlifting cultures in remote south-west England'. *Performance Enhancement & Health*. 8 (4), pp 1–10.

Turnock, L.A. (2022). 'Exploring user narratives of self-medicated black market IPED use for therapeutic & wellbeing purposes'. *Performance Enhancement & Health*. 10 (2), p 100207. doi: 10.1016/j.peh.2021.100207.

Turnock, L. and Gibbs, N. (2023). 'Click, click, buy: the market for novel synthetic peptide hormones on mainstream e-commerce platforms in the UK'. *Performance Enhancement & Health* 11 (2), p 100251. doi: https://doi.org/10.1016/j.peh.2023.100251.

Tzanetakis, M., Kamphausen, G., Werse, B., and von Laufenberg, R. (2016). 'The transparency paradox: building trust, resolving disputes and optimising logistics on conventional and online drugs markets'. *International Journal of Drug Policy*. [Online]. 35, pp 58–68. doi: 10.1016/j.drugpo.2015.12.010.

Underwood, M. (2017). 'Exploring the social lives of image and performance enhancing drugs: an online ethnography of the Zyzz fandom of recreational bodybuilders'. *International Journal of Drug Policy*. 39 (1), pp 78–85.

Underwood, M. (2022). 'Taking "the God of all Steroids" and "Making a Pact With the Devil": Online bodybuilding communities and the negotiation of trenbolone risk'. In: A. Henning and J. Andreasson (eds) *Doping in Sport and Fitness*. Bingley: Emerald Publishing Limited, pp 111–136.

Underwood, M., van de Ven, K., and Dunn, M. (2020). 'Testing the boundaries: self-medicated testosterone replacement and why it is practised'. *International Journal of Drug Policy*, p 103087. doi: 10.1016/j.drugpo.2020.103087.

Vaaranen, H. (2004). 'Stories from the Streets: Fieldwork notes on the seduction of speed'. In: J. Ferrell, K. Hayward, W. Morrison, and M. Presdee (eds) *Cultural Criminology Unleashed*. New York: Sentry Press, pp 245–250.

van de Ven, K. and Koenraadt, R. (2017). 'Exploring the relationship between online buyers and sellers of image and performance enhancing drugs (IPEDs): quality issues, trust and self-regulation'. *International Journal of Drug Policy*. 50, pp 48–55.

van de Ven, K. and Mulrooney, K. (2017). 'Social suppliers: exploring the cultural contours of the performance and image enhancing drug (PIED) market among bodybuilders in the Netherlands and Belgium'. *International Journal of Drug Policy*. 40, pp 6–15.

van de Ven, K., Boardley, I., and Chandler, M. (2018). 'Health risk and health seeking behaviours among people who inject performance and image enhancing drugs who access needle syringe programs in Australia'. *Drug and Alcohol Review*. 37 (7), pp 837–846.

van de Ven, K., Dunn, M., and Mulrooney, K. (2020). 'Human enhancement drugs and new(?) research directions'. *Performance Enhancement & Health*. 7 (3), pp 1–4.

Van Hout, M.C. and Bingham, T. (2014). 'Responsible vendors, intelligent consumers: Silk Road, the online revolution in drug trading'. *International Journal of Drug Policy*. 25 (2), pp 183–189.

Van Hout, M. and Kean, J. (2015). 'An exploratory study of image and performance enhancement drug use in a male British South Asian community'. *International Journal of Drug Policy*. 26 (9), pp 860–867.

Veblen, T. (2005). *Conspicuous Consumption*. London: Penguin.

Wacquant, L. (2008). *Urban Outcasts: A Comparative Sociology of Advanced Marginality*. Cambridge: Polity Press.

Wacquant, L. (2015). 'For a sociology of flesh and blood'. *Qualitative Sociology*. 38, pp 1–11.

Waddington, I. and Smith, A. (2009). *An Introduction to Drugs in Sport*. London: Routledge.

Wagner, P. (2017). 'Bulking up (identities): a communication framework for male fitness identity'. *Communication Quarterly*. 65 (5), pp 580–602.

Wakeman, S. (2014). 'Fieldwork, biography and emotion: doing criminological autoethnography'. *British Journal of Criminology*. 54 (5), pp 705–721.

Walker Hanlon, W. (2015). *Pollution and Mortality in the 19th Century (NBER Working Paper No. 21647)*. Cambridge, MA: National Bureau of Economic Research.

Wernick, A. (1991). *Promotional Culture: Advertising, Ideology and Symbolic Expression*. London: SAGE Publications Ltd.

West, L. (2016). *Distress in the City: Racism, Fundamentalism and a Democratic Education*. London: UCL Institute of Education Press.

Wiens, B. and MacDonald, S. (2020). 'Feminist futures: #MeToo's possibilities as poiesis, techné, and pharmakon'. *Feminist Media Studies*. 21 (7), pp 1108–1124. doi: 10.1080/14680777.2020.1770312.

William, N. and Taylor, M.D. (2002). *Anabolic Steroids and the Athlete*. 2nd ed. Jefferson, NC: McFarland & Company Publishers.

Williams, P. (2006) *Pottery, Pride or Parochial Prejudice? The Impact of Media Indifference on Tourism Development in Stoke-on-Trent*. Christel DeHaan Tourism and Travel Research Institute. Nottingham University Business School. Presented 12 December 2006.

Willis, P. (1977). *Learning to Labour*. London: Saxon House.

Wilson, R., Gosling, S., and Graham, L. (2012). 'A review of Facebook research in the social sciences'. *Perspectives on Psychological Science*. 7 (3), pp 203–220.

Winlow, S. (2001). *Badfellas: Crime, Tradition and New Masculinities*. Oxford: Berg Publishers.

Winlow, S. (2019). 'What Lies Beneath? Some notes on ultra-realism, and the intellectual foundations of the "deviant leisure" perspective'. In: T. Raymen and O. Smith, *Deviant Leisure: Criminological Perspectives on Leisure and Harm*. London: Palgrave Macmillan UK, pp 45–66.

Winlow, S. and Hall, S. (2006). *Violent Night: Urban Leisure and Contemporary Culture*. Oxford: Berg Publishers.

Winlow, S. and Hall, S. (2012). 'What is an "ethics committee"? Academic governance in an epoch of belief and incredulity'. *British Journal of Criminology*. 52 (2), pp 400–416.

Winlow, S. and Hall, S. (2013). *Rethinking Social Exclusion*. London: SAGE Publications Ltd.

Yar, M. (2012). 'Crime, media and the will-to-representation: reconsidering relationships in the new media age'. *Crime Media Culture*. 8 (3), pp 245–260.

Zahnow, R., McVeigh, J., Bates, G., Hope, V., Kean, J., Campbell, J., and Smith, J. (2018). 'Identifying a typology of men who use anabolic androgenic steroids (AAS)'. *International Journal of Drug Policy*. 55, pp 105–112.

Žižek, S. (1997). *The Abyss of Freedom*. Ann Arbor: University of Michigan Press.

Žižek, S. (2000). *The Ticklish Subject: The Absent Centre of Political Ontology*. London: Verso.

Žižek, S. (2006). *How to Read Lacan*. London: Granta Publications.

Žižek, S. (2008). *For They Know Not What They Do: Enjoyment as a Political Factor*. London: Verso.

Žižek, S. (2009). *The Sublime Object of Ideology*. London: Verso.

Index